The Case Against Pornography

In this collection of essays, a wide range of distinguished thinkers – psychotherapists, social and moral philosophers, psychiatrists, economists, novelists, journalists and education-alists – raise important doubts about the present-day 'pornography explosion'.

Until recently pornography was suppressed in our society and was the preoccupation of a few disturbed individuals. Yet today not only is there permissiveness, but sick and sadistic fantasies are being thrust into people's lives on a massive scale. Because of the so-called 'sexual revolution', extremists who wield power over television, press and screen can censor and prevent open discussion of the problems of sexual explicitness and obscenity. Those who control the media have rigged the debate, so that many now feel it is all 'harmless'.

Pornography is a serious cultural issue. And while most progressives have aligned themselves with the exhibitionists and other exponents of depersonalized sexuality, many important liberal-minded thinkers remain doubtful. Some believe that pornography represents a nihilistic and fascist-like menace to democracy, civilized values and human creativity. Some believe that in promoting distorted attitudes to sex it threatens a new kind of repression, much worse than the old.

This anthology is essential reading for everyone who is worried about the self-brutalizing and destructive attitudes encouraged by pornography.

DAVID HOLBROOK, whose own books on sex in culture have already changed public opinion radically, offers this body of thought, in the name of human love and meaning, in defiance of the pseudo-revolutionaries of our time, who are, to use the telling old phrase from D. H. Lawrence, 'doing dirt on life'.

The Case Against Pornography

Edited by
David Holbrook

A Library Press Book
Open Court • La Salle • Illinois

First published in the United States in 1973 by
The Library Press

Copyright © This anthology David Holbrook 1972

ISBN 0-912050-28-4

Library of Congress Catalog Card No 72-5279

Printed in Great Britain

*Second Printing March 1974 in
the United States of America*

CONTENTS

THE CONTRIBUTORS

The Editor, David Holbrook, is author of the recent studies *Human Hope and the Death Instinct, Sex and Dehumanization, The Masks of Hate* and *The Pseudo-revolution*.

WALTER BERNS, Professor of Political Science at the University of Toronto.

DAVID BOADELLA, author of a new study of Wilhelm Reich. Editor of the Reichian *Energy and Character Journal.*

RONALD BUTT, Assistant Editor of *The Sunday Times.*

DR. LESLIE H. FARBER, consultant for The National Institute of Mental Health in America. Author of *The Ways of the Will.*

VIKTOR FRANKL, Professor of Psychiatry at the University of Vienna, and author of *The Doctor and The Soul.*

STORM JAMESON, novelist and critic.

PAMELA HANSFORD JOHNSON, novelist and Proustian critic.

MOIRA KEENAN, Woman's Page Editor of *The Times.*

MASUD R. KHAN, Editor of the International Psycho-Analytical Library.

IRVING KRISTOL, Henry Luce Professor of Urban Values at New York University.

ROLLO MAY, practising psychotherapist, author of *Love and Will.*

E. J. MISHAN, Reader in Economics at the London School of Economics.

DR. MARY MILES, psychotherapist and contributor to *The Observer.*

JOHN MACMURRAY, Professor Emeritus of Moral Philosophy in the University of Edinburgh, author of *Reason and Emotion.*

IAN ROBINSON, Editor of *The Human World.*

DR. BENJAMIN SPOCK, world-famous authority on child care.

DR. GEORGE STEINER, author of *Language and Silence.* Fellow of Churchill College, Cambridge.

TOM STACEY, author, journalist and book publisher.

DR. ROBERT J. STOLLER, Professor of Psychiatry at UCLA School of Medicine, Los Angeles.

DR. ERWIN STRAUS, Clinical Professor in Psychiatry at the University of Kentucky. Author of *Phenomenological Psychology* and *The Primary World of Senses*.

ERNEST VAN DER HAAG, Professor of Social Philosophy at New York University.

D. W. WINNICOTT, the late psychoanalyst and paediatrician. Author of *Playing and Reality* and many works on psychotherapy.

'Pornography always has in it somewhere a hatred of man, both of man as a human being able to respond to ideals, and of man as an animal. Pornography is not an affirmation but a denial of life, and commercial pornography is a denial of life for the sake of money.'

The Times, Editorial,
The Pollution of Culture
on the UNESCO Conference
on Culture, Autumn, 1970

'today's patients, as a whole, seem to be preoccupied with the head and genitals in their dreams, and to leave out the heart.'

Dreams and Symbols,
Leopold Caligor and Rollo May.

ACKNOWLEDGEMENTS

The author and publisher are grateful to the following for the use of copyright material: Mr Tom Stacey and the *Daily Telegraph* for *Letter to the Author's Children*; The Times Publishing Company and Mr Ronald Butt for *Politics and Morals*, *The Little Read Schoolbook*, *The Mistakes Liberals Make*, and *Television and Sex Education*; The Times Publishing Company for *Pornography and the Politics of Rage and Subversion* and Mr Masud Khan, which piece appeared first in *The Times Literary Supplement*; The Times Publishing Company for *Where do Babies Come From?* and *Stealers of Dreams* and Mrs Moira Keenan; *Is This What We Wanted?* originally appeared in the *New York Times*, under the title *Pornography, Obscenity, and the Case for Censorship*, Copyright © 1971 by Irving Kristol. Reprinted in *On the Democratic Idea in America* by Irving Kristol, Copyright © 1972 by Irving Kristol, by permission of Harper & Row, Publishers, Inc.; Ian Robinson and the Brynmill Publishing Company for the Editorial on Pornography from *The Human World*; Miss Pamela Hansford Johnson and *Encounter* for *Peddling the Pornography of Violence*; Professor Ernest Van Den Haag and *Encounter* for *Is Pornography a Cause of Crime?*; Dr Robert J. Stoller and the American Medical Association, for *Pornography and Perversion* from the *Archives of General Psychiatry*, Vol. 22, June 1970, obtainable from the Department of Psychiatry, UCLA School of Medicine, Los Angeles, 90024, USA; Walter Berns, 'Beyond the (garbage) pale, or democracy censorship and the arts', in Harry M. Clor, editor *Censorship, and Freedom of Expression* (Chicago, Rand, McNally and Company, 1971), Copyright © 1970 by the Public Affairs Center, Kenyon College, Gambier, Ohio, USA; Dr Mary Miles and *The Observer* and Curtis Brown Limited, for *Must We Show Children Sex?*; Mrs Clair Winnicott and Penguin Books Limited, for Sex Education in Schools from *The Child, The Family and the Outside World*; the Bodley Head for an extract from *A Young Person's Guide to Life and Love* by Dr Benjamin Spock; Penguin Books and Dr E. J.

Mishan for an extract from *The Costs of Economic Growth*; Dr Rollo May and the Souvenir Press for an extract from *Love and Will*; Dr Viktor Frankl and the Souvenir Press for an extract from *The Doctor and the Soul*; Dr Leslie H. Farber and Constable Limited for an extract from *The Ways of the Will*; The Tavistock Press and Dr Erwin Straus for an extract from *Phenomenological Psychology*; Mrs Storm Jameson and A. D. Peters and Collins-Harvill Limited for an extract from *Parthian Words*; Dr George Steiner and Faber and Faber Limited, and Georges Borchardt Inc. for Night Words from *Language and Silence*; Professor John MacMurray and Faber and Faber Limited for an extract from *Reason and Emotion*; Abbotsbury Publications for material from *Energy and character* Vol 3, No. 1, 1972, by David Boadella.

OTHER BOOKS BY THE EDITOR

POETRY

Imaginings Putnam 1961
Against the Cruel Frost Putnam 1963
Object Relations Methuen 1967
Old World, New World   Rapp and Whiting 1969

FICTION

Lights in the Sky Country Putnam 1962
Flesh Wounds Methuen 1966

ON EDUCATION

English for Maturity Cambridge 1961
English for the Rejected Cambridge 1964
The Secret Places Methuen 1964
The Exploring Word Cambridge 1967
Children's Writing Cambridge 1967
English in Australia Now Cambridge 1972

CRITICISM AND THE PSYCHOLOGY OF CULTURE

Llareggub Revisited Bowes and Bowes 1962
The Quest for Love   Methuen 1965
Human Hope and the Death Instinct Pergamon 1971
Sex and Dehumanization Pitman 1972
The Masks of Hate Pergamon 1972
Dylan Thomas and the Code of Night Athlone 1972
Sylvia Plath and the Problem of Existence Athlone 1972
The Pseudo-revolution Tom Stacey 1972
The Mass Media and the Mis-use of Symbolism Pitman 1972
T. F. Powys: Love Under Control Covent Garden 1972

PREFACE

In his analysis of the origins of Nazism, in *Knowing and Being*, Michael Polanyi uses a significant phrase. Discussing the way in which Nazi *realpolitik* and brutality emerged inevitably out of the naturalistic view of man predominant in the nineteenth century, he speaks of a moment at which the development of a consequent moral inversion grew 'beyond access of moral debate'.

Something of the same seems to be happening today, in the face of the increasing amount of brutalization of sex in our culture. At the moment of writing, The Advisory Centre for Education has declared 'the present heated debate on pornography is no service to education' while the *Assistant Librarian* speaks of 'the myth that explicit sexual material corrupts and depraves'.

If this is a 'myth', then so are all those forms of idealism which sustain education – and so is even the passionate belief in man and reason that sustains science.

The truth is that symbolism is the basis of the human identity and of our culture. Where symbolism is corrupted, civilization is threatened. The reduction of symbolism to forms of 'acting out' and to primitive sensationalism has its own meaning – and its inevitable *educational* effect. When pornography predominates in mass commercial culture, and directs itself especially to children, it is evidently an educational issue, and, at root, a deep philosophical and ethical one.

For when we examine the meaning of pornography, we encounter the problem of what, at root, we believe about man. We encounter problems of philosophical biology.

The essays and pieces gathered here are gathered in an attempt *to keep the debate open*. They are intended to show that this debate is urgent and respectable at all levels – the level of responsible journalism, of academic papers, and of serious philosophy and psychology. Moreover, it leads us into important questions – to do with the aims and purpose of life, and man's future. It involves the deepest

xv

questions of man's whole relationship to his world, and how we might bring about possible future forms of society that might dehumanize us less than the society we live in today.

To say, as Mr Jeremy Simmonds, the publisher, has declared, that the question needs no further debate is not only absurd – it is, fundamentally, anti-intellectual and irrational. The debate has been going on since Plato and Aristotle – and will (and must) continue.

Not all the articles and extracts gathered here express the view that pornography is so harmful that it needs suppression. They do, however, support the view that we urgently need a 'social psychology' capable of looking seriously at the problem and invoking appropriate ethical considerations. They certainly all convey the impression that in its implicit denial of love and tenderness, pornography threatens meaning, and has in it somewhere (as *The Times* has said) a 'hatred of man'. As Masud Khan has said, 'it is a stealer of dreams' – and so threatens the imaginative life, which is the basis of all perception and effective living.

In the face of such hatred what Khan calls the 'liberal idolization of perversion' – leading to a demand for 'total permissiveness' – is no answer. To *think* about the subject is, and, I believe, to persist in rational debate here is to sustain psychic health in the face of a subtle disease of spirit.

In the old days
The camera
Zoomed
In on
Moving wheels —

Look, something's going to happen!

These days
The camera
Zooms
In on
Sex Mechanisms —

Look, something's going to happen!

There are people who think
That art progresses.

D. J. Enright

INTRODUCTION

Pornography and Philosophical Anthropology

David Holbrook

I am an educationist, and I believe that by promoting creative activity in individuals, and by putting them in touch with their culture, they can find answers to such questions as 'What is it to be human?' and 'What is the point of life?' I believe that creative culture satisfies a primary need in man, and is the answer to his existential frustration.

From my point of view I can find no justification at all for the prevalent cult of pornography, and I cannot even believe that we gain anything by tolerating it. I am, however, prepared to accept that obscenity is sometimes necessary within the whole content of a serious work of art. Only I believe those works which really need obscenity are few and far between.

I suppose that there are few liberals, progressives, readers of this who would go along with me, and so I am in great difficulties, in trying to put my point of view forward. However, my main concern is to try to see this phenomenon in the light of the views of those who belong to the revolution in thought about man referred to by Marjorie Grene in her study *The Knower and the Known*. In this I would include the post-Kantian philosophers pursuing the question 'What is man?' – concerned with *sign* and *meaning*, i.e. Ernst Cassirer, and Suzanne Langer; the philosophical biologists Marjorie Grene discusses in *Approaches to a Philosophical Biology*, Helmuth Plessner, Adolf Portman, and Maurice Merleau-Ponty; and the psycho-analysts, especially the existentialist psychoanalysts in America (Rolla May, Leslie Farber) and Vienna (Viktor Frankl). This whole movement is against the reductionism of the whole Galilean-Newtonian-Cartesian approach to knowledge, not least knowledge of man, which, by objectifying, has tended to reduce nature and man to the status of dead objects. The key concept in their approach to knowledge is indicated by Polanyi's term 'Indwelling' – the capacity to 'attend from' the object of one's attention, rather than 'attend to' it. That is, one must throw oneself imaginatively into the thing one is seeking to know, and experience it from the inside. Thus, one knows sexual experience by imagining the inside life of the body and being, rather than by looking at the outside, as in sexology.

This new approach demands a considerable revision of our whole approach to experience. As Marjorie Grene says:

only when a deep-lying conceptual reform in our view of knowledge has been assimilated, when we have overcome within ourselves our Cartesian fear of the category of life, and our Newtonian simplemindedness about the nature of the nature we strive to know, only then will we be able to open our minds to a new ontology....

The Knower and the Known, p. 224

Our failure to discriminate against pornography, I believe, marks a deep failure in our intellectual life – which is so imprisoned in physicalism that we cannot find the 'category of life', and fear the deepest dimensions of being. Because of this we do not mind when these are insulted. And so we cannot find a new science of being – and so we cannot find man's essential creativity. Imprisonment in 'objectivity' and 'naturalism' is imprisonment in a very limited range of human possibilities – so that the 'sexual revolution', rather than representing a 'liberation' is actually placing new chains on our intentionality. If anyone doubts this, let him analyse the symbolic implications of nearly every novel, play and film that is running today in the major cities of the West. Where is there a vision of man that would make it worth surviving?

It is no surprise to me, as a consistent opponent of the exploitation of youth by 'pop', to find a savage undercurrent developing in pop festivals. It is no surprise to me, as an opponent of pornography, to find stage 'sex' shows and films becoming increasingly more sadistic, and primitive in their obsession with defacation, perversion and degradation. While the permissives still insist that in Denmark toleration has led to a reduction of sex crimes, it is no surprise to me to learn that in fact there has been no decline in serious sex crimes there – only in minor crimes such as exhibitionism, which are now committed instead, legally, in studios and clubs. It is no surprise to me to learn that in those cities in which shows like *Oh! Calcutta!* are staged, violent crimes have risen startlingly, even as pornography has been increasingly tolerated (New York, 30 per cent increase in murders; Sweden, 12 per cent increase in crimes of violence; London, a continual increase in crime). It is no surprise that actors and actresses in 'sex' shows are showing signs of illness.

2

The association between the excesses of dehumanization in our culture, here and there, and the increasing dehumanization in common life at large is hidden by the absurdities of the liberal approach to the increasing exploitation of voyeurism in culture, and the hideous debasement of the human image in such things as the 'underground' press, and the songs and images of 'pop' (It's a fuck of a song, man!' – advertisement in Oz).

As Rollo May's chapters indicate, the phenomena we are dealing with arise from schizoid tendencies in our civilization, which tends to dehumanize people. Nothing could be more dehumanizing than such technological devices as the TV pornographic cassette: it embodies a characteristic schizoid syndrome. As Frankl points out, discussing the psychology of schizophrenia, some schizoid patients have a belief that 'moving pictures were being taken of them'.

This 'film delusion' constitutes a genuine 'hallucination of knowledge' in Jasper's sense. . . .

The schizoid individual has trouble in 'finding' the world, and so has a feeling of unreality: the hallucinated experience of being filmed is the experience of that unreality, reversed.

the person experiences himself as an object – as the object of the lens of a movie camera or still camera, as the object of a recording apparatus, or the object of someone's eavesdropping or even seeking and thinking – in sum, then, the object of a variety of intentional acts of other people. All these patients experience themselves as the object of the psychic activity of other persons, for the various types of apparatus involved are simply symbols, the mechanical extensions of the intentional acts of seeing and hearing. . . .

This is the 'experience of pure objectiveness', which marks a central disturbance of the ego. This 'universal law of the psychology of schizophrenia', that in 'schizophrenia there takes place an experiential passivizing of the psychic functions' can, I believe, be extrapolated to the realm of culture.

As Rollo May points out, there are deep schizoid elements in much of our present-day sex, not least the way in which people have taught themselves to function sexually without letting their feelings be involved.

In the realm of pornography we have a human situation in which schizoid individuals come forward, to satisfy in a strange way their feeling of 'experiencing themselves as an object', bring it to be a reality, and make it socially acceptable. Their impulse is in fact a

3

perverted impulse, belonging to aim-inhibited sexuality, and they are exhibitionists, to whose willed body-activity the voyeur responds. The collusion between exhibitionist and voyeur helps both to feel a kind of 'confirmation' of each other's existence: each is made into 'a sort of thing in the other's dream'.

Yet, as Kahn points out in his analysis of perversion, there is a *huis clos* quality about the dynamic of sexual activity of this kind. It can never find the clue to meaning which it seeks – and its answers move towards schizoid dehumanization rather than towards love, and commitment. Yet the only answers to the problems pursued are in 'inwardness', and in what Buber called 'meeting'. There are also the schizoid elements for moral inversion, and '*abaissement mentale*'. The dangers to psychic hygiene lies in these schizoid elements, and in the educational effect of pornography in promoting what Frankl calls 'a thoroughly decadent sensuality' by dissociating sexuality from love and meaning.

Viktor Frankl, by contrast, makes it plain to us that from the point of view of philosophical anthropology, love belongs to 'meeting' (Martin Buber), 'encounter' (Helmuth Plessner), or 'confrontation' (Ernst Cassirer). This means through the face-to-face living togetherness of men, in which intuitive powers are dynamic – as by 'projective identification' or the capacity to put oneself in the shoes of others, and in going through experiences with them. The best example of this perhaps is the analytical situation between psychotherapist and patient: from this many significant modern insights into men's nature have emerged – and these emphasize, as the first truth of man's nature, his need for love and meaning.

From this kind of 'research' into the nature of man theories are developing which try to dislodge the theories based on physicalism and its basic reductionism – reducing men to 'nothing but' a product of impersonal drives, like the 'id'. As Viktor Frankl says,

in my opinion, man is neither dominated by the will-to-pleasure, nor by the will-to-power, but by what I should like to call man's will-to-meaning; that is to say, his deep-seated striving and struggling for a higher and ultimate meaning to his existence. . . . He is searching for a concrete – more than that, a unique – task, the uniqueness of which corresponds to the uniqueness of his personality and of each situation.

From Death Camp to Existentialism.

If we accept this view, and turn back to the problem of pornography, we can, I believe, see that it is inimical.

4

First, we may note its 'larger than life' aspect. When it comes to public performances, for pornography or sexology, most of us, as Farber says, could not hope to qualify, either as volunteers or scientists.

But this does not mean the differences are great between us and them. True, compared to ours, their lives have an oversized quality ... and ... they are in the vanguard. But in a sense our fleshly home is that laboratory. Whatever room we choose for our lovemaking, we shall make into our own poor laboratory, and nothing that is observed or undergone in the real laboratory of science is likely to escape us. . . . Whatever details the scientific will appropriates about sex rapidly becomes an injunction to be imposed on our bodies. . . .
The Ways of the Will, Leslie Farber.

The result is, says Farber, that we have to try to sustain a vision of an ideal sexual experience, that tends to 'be crudely derived from the failure of our bodies to meet these imperatives'. The effect of a 'sex education' film is thus to promote anxiety, and to cause sexual neurosis, because our own sex does not have that larger-than-life image of perfection, such as enacted on the circular bed, by actor and actress who have in fact made themselves perverts, capable of acting in a schizoid way, detached entirely from the 'messiness' of normal human encounters, and from love, meaning, and humanness.

What is taught, in fact, is something which is schizoid in itself – that is, a serious dissociation of act from meaning.

Progressives cling to two arguments, over pornography. One is that for any action to be taken against it, we must show that it has socially harmful results, by showing that some actual obscene work has an effect which is demonstrable in the behaviour of a certain person, and those acts which follow must actually be anti-social or debasing to that person. Even if he masturbates this is not enough to show that he is debased. The other argument is that no-one can define pornography.

Both these arguments can be disposed of easily by pointing out that one could not for a moment employ them in education – and yet we go on educating on assumptions which these demands implicitly deny. Since man is not a simple input-output machine, it is impossible ever to prove that a good cultural experience improves him, or a bad one harms him. Nor can anyone ever define any of the terms that we use in discussing such a problem, except by constant collocation and redefinition – yet there are terms which are adequate enough, and by which we can discriminate – as we demonstrate in the realm of racial discrimination. No-one would allow children to chant in class:

... keeping company with evil people can be just as harmful as eating a poisonous mushroom. One may even die. ...
And do you know who are these evil people these poisonous mushrooms of mankind?
Yes, Mummy, I know it – they are Jews. ... (Nazi textbook)

Many millions died, because such *cultural* persuasiveness was effective. As Polanyi reminds us, disasters of that kind begin in people's minds. The naturalistic scientific approach to man became immanent in the brute force of Nazism. The nihilism of German philosophers became immanent in the SS. The fanatical immoralism of German youth was the reservoir from which the SS and the SA were recruited. The same fanatical nihilism is abroad in the avant-garde and underground cult of pornography, while the whole pheno-menon of the 'sexual revolution' belongs to the same naturalism which led, according to Frankl, to Treblinka and Auschwitz. How did pornography ever become part of 'protest' and 'progressive' politics?

For pornography, and its toleration, belong to attitudes to man which cling to the emptiness of those 'objective' approaches to man which have already caused so much damage in our era by denying man's spirituality – even if we only speak of it in the purely human dimension. As Marjorie Grene says, in her approaches to a Philo-sophical Biology:

Galileo claims that in the bare mathematical bones of nature there is truth: all else is illusion. Yet that 'all else' includes the very roots of our being, and we forget them at our peril. ...

It will not do, therefore, to merely discuss pornography in terms of the statistics of sexual crime in Denmark: it requires examina-tion phenomenologically in terms of its meaning and symbolism.

The arguments coming from Denmark are in any case suspect. As Jean-Paul Lauret points out,[1] pornography is bringing in $6om a year to those who produce it, making it the third industry after agriculture and furniture-making. 50 per cent of this is exported. Germany takes 60 per cent of the export trade, and it is surely disturbing to learn that those who attended the Danish sex fairs were mostly German men born from 1940 to 1945 – and so brought up at the tail end of the society in which all values had been des-troyed by Nazism? There were, according to Lauret, 400 pornography shops in Copenhagen, and in the summer seventy establishments exhibiting sexual intercourse in public. As *Le Monde* said:

Impresarios . . . vie with one another to bring out the crudest shows have no trouble finding actors and actresses. . . .

The Danish Minister of Justice will not license brothels, because he says 'prostitutes are mental defectives' and must 'be protected from themselves and others'. If my theory is correct, those who come forward to perform sexually in public are also mentally ill and need protection. As Frankl points out, a woman does not become a prostitute for money – and it is quite hard to persuade a woman to take up prostitution even in the direst straits. Thus, those who come forward to make pornography are almost certainly doing so because they have a psychopathological need to do so. (I am led to conclude that the sole literary adviser to our National Theatre has a sick impulse to draw others into perverted acts on the stage, but in the light of psychoanalysis there is no other explanation.) Those who perform, those who exploit performers, and their audiences, need protection from themselves and others.

For one thing, there is no question of pornography being an aid to the 'release' from 'repression', as some liberators argue, on Freudian principles. This pessimistic view, based on instinct theory and a kind of steam-engine impulse psychology, has gradually become discredited. As Boadella says, Marcuse spoke of a 'repressive desublimation' – a new kind of inhibition resulting from too-explicit and sadistic sexuality. As Frankl argues, 'when existentialist frustration is most acute, sexual libido becomes rampant'. That is, desperate sensuality is a quest for a sense of meaning. But, as Frankl also argues, in the chapter on 'The Meaning of Love', mere sensuality does too little to overcome our sense of our own 'nothingness'. For once the moment of pleasure is over, one is left with one's mortality and existentialist emptiness. The only way in which these can be overcome is by the development of a love that has meaning, continuity, and can triumph over time and death. Mere 'release' through sensuality, which is what pornography encourages, could thus simply exacerbate the sense of meaninglessness in life. Moreover, as Stoller and Van der Haag argue, pornography, by its dynamic of hostility, reduces empathy.

The pseudo-revolution of those who have seized the opportunity provided by permissiveness to act out their sick and sadistic fantasies in public could thus place a limit on the potentialities of love in individuals, rather than provide them with 'release', or 'liberation'. As Viktor Frankl says, we are being persuaded from many directions that what is necessary is the relief of 'sexual frustration', as though sexual impulses threw up a head of steam which must, from time to time, be spent through a safety valve. As we shall see, Frankl declares this nonsense, and a 'shibboleth' (p. 63).

Pornography has the effect of urging individuals towards a 'mere sexuality', as Frankl and others argue. It includes a great deal of emphasis on sexual activity which is not bound up with individual uniqueness – group sex, and 'functions'. It fixes the mind on sensation, and rage. And certainly it does not have the effect of making sex 'consonant with human dignity'. As M. Lauret says, 'the basic motion is that of pleasure . . . After thousands of years, the individual discovers his own body . . .' But yet he does not discover the meanings of the body, such as are discussed by philosophers such as Merleau-Ponty. Philosophers of biology are now concentrating on the self-directed creative energy seen in living creatures, of which man's consciousness and creativity are manifestations. This is a new view of the dynamics of animal existence. The effect of pornography is to emphasize an animality that is implicitly reductive not only of human uniqueness and dignity, but that of animals, too. M. Lauret reports of a book marked 'special' at a Danish sex fair:

(there is a 'generously endowed' woman whose sexual partner tires). . . . For a moment she tries auto-satisfactions, without success, it seems. It is then that the man, forever considerate, leaves the room for a few minutes and comes back with a hog. The animal . . . starts sniffing at the woman, then pushes his snout against her genitalia . . . I can only feel a sick disgust . . . zooming lens on the animal's penis. . . .

For M. Lauret, the permissive society stops on the threshold of the pigsty. But it doesn't for pornography. Emlyn Williams recently reported pictures of a woman naked beneath a stallion, and *Le Monde* reports that a young woman has made a fortune and a name for herself performing with stallions and dogs. The Danish Society for the Prevention of Cruelty to Animals is petitioning the courts to stop the use of four-footed animals in sexual exhibitions.

This has its own symbolism, and may be seen as a direct consequence of scientific naturalism and Cartesian dualism. So, too, is sexology, with its assumptions that we can learn love from observing the outward realities of the sexual functions.

I believe that we could make a devastating study of the essential blindness of pornography, perhaps on the lines of the studies of perception being opened up in various directions by psychoanalysis and philosophy. As Santayana said, 'Without our contribution we see nothing'. That is, as Morag Coate points out in her book about madness, *Beyond All Reason*, one only sees by projecting over the world the interpretation one makes, in the subjective life, of the data that falls on one's retina. Unless one has been taught how to interpret one's world by one's mother, in love, one cannot see a meaningful world at all. In a study called *Recovery from Early Blindness* a psychologist called Gregory gives the history of a man who was cured of blindness that he had suffered from the age of six months. After the operation he could 'see' but he could not see. He received impressions, but he could not make them into meanings, or piece together a seen world that made sense to him. Previously, he had made sense of his world through the other senses. Now, with the vivid sense of sight at his disposal, he found the world insusceptible to his attempts to live meaningfully in it, and he died deeply unhappy and disturbed.

Something of the same seems to be happening to our sexual experience. We experience 'sex' from the inside of our bodies, mostly in the dark, with our eyes shut, and we piece the meaning of love together from the whole life realm of this body-life, indivisible as it is from consciousness, imagination, and the visionary qualities of love. The discovery of the 'significant other', is a complex process of imaginative projection – of throwing oneself into the 'inwardness' of the other person, of 'attending from' them. The degree to which one can achieve this successfully depends upon how successfully one was enabled, by the 'creative reflection' of one's mother and family, to develop the capacity for human empathy, and to find meaning in relationship. As Freud said, there are four antecedents to any sexual act – i.e. the four parents of the couple. Most important is the degree to which each has developed the 'female element' capacity for the mother to imagine, and to create.

For me to make love joyfully to the woman with whom I am in love demands of me the capacity to imagine what she is experiencing of me. I can to some extent hear and feel from her body whether what I believe is true, and I can also feel and hear that she, in her part, is attentive to my experience, as she imagines it, and goes with it. These capacities, which generate ecstasy, are enlarged more by the sharing of a whole range of common interests, and by the enlargement of imaginative experience by reading, say Jane Austen or Donne, than they are by reading 'sex technique' books. That is, the capacity to love depends upon culture and the capacity to 'find

9

the other', rather than on any external knowledge of 'what should happen' in physical love. The knowledge of mechanics, indeed, derived from films with their record of movements and sound which are meaningless outside the complex I have described, may simply offer, as life did to the man cured of blindness, nothing meaningful – and so deeply undermine our existential security. As Khan says in an interview below, the 'whole human dialogue is reduced to a sort of expertise of organs', while in his chapter he suggests that pornography, in its negating effects, cuts us off both from ourselves and the 'significant other'.

We could also, I believe, compare the tone of various forms of writing today with profit. There is no doubt in my mind that the true vision of man's creativity today is held by the scientist. The world of culture has lost its vision. Compare with the visions above, of a woman with a pig, or the disembodied penis crushed and abused in any Danish sex film, the attitude to man in such writing as that of Adolf Portmann (discussing the Arctic tern):

All necessity is transcended in these great formative processes, into which tellurian events are integrated as wonderful alarm signals for the awakening and enriching of organic life in time. The passage of clock time, meaningless in itself, is employed for the enrichment of life. It needs hardly be added that human life is a magnificent configuration of time in this same dimension, offering in its successive ages ever new possibilities of development in time and hence of living riches.

Animals as Social Beings, quoted in
Approaches to A Philosophical Biology, p. 42.

Though pornography is sometimes spoken of as reducing man to the level of the animal, it would seem, in the light of this, to be unfair to the animals to say so, while from the biologist's point of view, man's link with the animals only reveals his even greater creativity. As Marjorie Grene says:

We *are* the upsurge of time, and creative imagination, which moulds the present and even the vision of the past out of futurity out of its projection of what we long to be, of what we believe we ought to be – creative imagination through which we shape the time which we are: this is our most essential gift.

This 'essential gift' is being undermined by the predominance in our culture of pornography, which is shaping in people's minds what we believe we ought to be – not least, by its 'ripple' effect, through newspapers and magazines, on children, who are very quickly picking up the implications in our 'amorality' over this issue, that we have no values, and do not care what image of man is put abroad.

Frankl warns us of the 'homunculism' in our thinking about man; the view that man was 'nothing but' the product of impersonal forces has caused disasters before. The danger is always that 'The Idolizers become like the Idols they were worshipping'. What happens if we do become like the Idols of larger-than-life, perverted, depersonalized, and meaningless sexuality of the present-day play and novel? If we became like the 'characters' in *Oh! Calcutta!*? Or if we move over from symbolism, into the 'acting out' of perverted phantasies, such as this kind of 'entertainment' encourages, by reducing the theatre to the level of the brothel and lunatic asylum? What new disaster is the 'sexual revolution' preparing for us, in the name of 'freedom'?

Moreover, there is only blindness in our way of looking at sex from the 'outside', and separated from 'whole being'. As Marjorie Grene says, because of the whole intellectual system in which we dwell

we acquire ... the intellectual framework of modern objective thought ... we assimilate it to our persons and identify with it on the one hand with our primary world and on the other with reality itself. So nature comes to *mean* to us Galilean nature, and the existence of the primary life world is ignored. ...

Approaches, p. 12.

The result is that

there is no alternative for any form of life (within the Cartesian heritage) except either to be a body spread out in space, completely and secretly 'within' ... it is inconceivable that there should be real entities which do not fall into one or the other of these categories. ...

ibid, p. 72.

So, the seeming unity of mind and body must be only a seeming: either everything is really matter or really mind. Pornography belongs to the imprisonment of physicalism: to 'free' it is to free a disease that paralyzes the soul's vision.

To 'scientific sexology' and the sex emancipationists it is only 'reasonable' to treat love and idealism as belonging to 'only mind' and sex as belonging to 'only matter', and thus purely to be approached mechanically, and seen as completely external. Yet, as Marjorie Grene

11

points out, it is just this dualism that has 'made a rational foundation for the biological and social sciences impossible'. The 'social science' of a Kinsey is, thus, from the point of view of philosophical anthropology irrational, since it employs a methodology belonging to a science 'imprisoned in physicalism' in a sphere where the realities belong to entities in which body and mind are, from the rational point of view, inseparable. Pornography menaces the life-sciences, by its symbolic effects on thinking.

As Merleau-Ponty has pointed out, there are meanings which belong to the body which arise from its creative dynamics as an animal organism, which are bound up with that special manifestation of the human animal which is consciousness. (See him on nakedness in 'The Body In Its Sexual Being' in *The Phenomenology of Perception*. See also the anti-Cartesian essays in *The Philosophy of the Body*, ed. S. F. Spicker, Quadrangle Books).[2] The philosophy of biology is only just beginning to forge intellectual tools to *begin* to understand the philosophy of the body. Nothing, therefore, could be more absurd than the air of the world of Western culture, the avant-garde and the 'progressive' realm of opinion, that, after various forms of 'breakthrough', from *Lady Chatterley* to Andy Warhol, and now to the maliciousness of *The Clockwork Orange*, that we are approaching the final and basic realities of 'sex'. It is, rather, as if we have looked at everything in the wrong way, and found nothing. Pornography is the final irrationality and blindness to the problems of meaning that centre in our most creative area of being; the ultimate absurdity. And what is involved, in dealing with it, is nothing less than our concept of *what man is*.

1 *The Danish Sex Fairs.*
2 Unfortunately I was refused permission to quote from *An Existentialist Aesthetic* by Professor Eugene Kaelin, University of Wisconsin Press, a work which gives a useful summary of the conflicting views of Sartre and Merleau-Ponty, and their relevance to the issue of pornography.

SEX AND LOVE

Before we can tackle the problem of pornography, we must try to distinguish between the different levels of sexual and emotional experience – and examine aspects of sex in society. From their long-term contact with patients, and their deep concern with human values, psychotherapists would seem to be throwing up 'ethical statements' which we need to take seriously. The 'existentialist' psychotherapists represented here believe that man's quest for meaning through love is his primary drive.

PARADOXES OF SEX AND LOVE IN MODERN SOCIETY

Rollo May

Sexual intercourse is the human counterpart of the cosmic process

– Proverb of Ancient China

A patient brought in the following dream : 'I am in bed with my wife, and between us is my accountant. He is going to have intercourse with her. My feeling about this is odd – only that somehow it seemed appropriate.'

– Reported by Dr John Schimel

THERE are four kinds of love in Western tradition. One is *sex*, or what we call lust, libido. The second is *eros*, the drive of love to procreate or create – the urge, as the Greeks put it, toward higher forms of being and relationship. A third is *philia*, or friendship, brotherly love. The fourth is *agape* or *caritas* as the Latins called it, the love which is devoted to the welfare of the other, the prototype of which is the love of God for man. Every human experience of authentic love is a blending, in varying proportions, of these four.

We begin with sex not only because that is where our society begins but also because that is where every man's biological existence begins as well. Each of us owes his being to the fact that at some moment in history a man and a woman leapt the gap, in T. S. Eliot's words, 'between the desire and the spasm'. Regardless of how much sex may be banalized in our society, it still remains the power of procreation, the drive which perpetuates the race, the source at once of the human being's most intense pleasure and his most pervasive anxiety. It can, in its daimonic form, hurl the individual into sloughs of despond, and, when allied with eros, it can lift him out of his despondency into orbits of ecstasy.

The ancients took sex, or lust, for granted just as they took death for granted. It is only in the contemporary age that we have succeeded, on a fairly broad scale, in singling out sex for our chief concern and have required it to carry the weight of all four forms of love. Regardless of Freud's overextension of sexual phenomena as such – in which he is but the voice of the struggle of thesis and antithesis of modern history – it remains true that sexuality is basic to the ongoing power of the race and surely has the *importance* Freud gave it, if not the *extension*. Trivialize sex in our novels and dramas as we will, or defend ourselves from its power by cynicism and playing it cool as we wish, sexual passion remains ready at any moment to catch us off guard and prove that it is still the *mysterium tremendum*.

But as soon as we look at the relation of sex and love in our time, we find ourselves immediately caught up in a whirlpool of contradictions. Let us, therefore, get our bearings by beginning with a brief phenomenological sketch of the strange paradoxes which surround sex in our society.

Sexual Wilderness
In Victorian times, when the denial of sexual impulses, feelings, and drives was the mode and one would not talk about sex in polite company, an aura of sanctifying repulsiveness surrounded the whole topic. Males and females dealt with each other as though neither possessed sexual organs. William James, that redoubtable crusader who was far ahead of his time on every other topic, treated sex with the polite aversion characteristic of the turn of the century. In the whole two volumes of his epoch-making *Principles of Psychology*, only one page is devoted to sex, at the end of which he adds, 'These details are a little unpleasant to discuss. . . .' But William Blake's warning a century before Victorianism, that 'He who desires but acts not, breeds pestilence,' was amply demonstrated by the later psychotherapists. Freud, a Victorian who did look at sex, was right in his description of the morass of neurotic symptoms which resulted from cutting off so vital a part of the human body and the self.

Then, in the 1920's, a radical change occurred almost overnight. The belief became a militant dogma in liberal circles that the opposite

14

of repression – namely, sex education, freedom of talking, feeling, and expression – would have healthy effects, and obviously constituted the only stand for the enlightened person. In an amazingly short period following World War I, we shifted from acting as though sex did not exist at all to being obsessed with it. We now placed more emphasis on sex than any society since that of ancient Rome, and some scholars believe we are more preoccupied with sex than any other people in all of history. Today, far from not talking about sex, we might well seem, to a visitor from Mars, dropping into Times Square, to have no other topic of communication.

And this is not solely an American obsession. Across the ocean in England, for example, 'from bishops to biologists, everyone is in on the act.' A perceptive front page article in *The Times Literary Supplement*, London, goes on to point to the 'whole turgid flood of post-Kinsey utilitarianism and post-Chatterley moral uplift. Open any newspaper, any day (Sunday in particular), and the odds are you will find some pundit treating the public to his views on contraception, abortion, adultery, obscene publications, homosexuality between consulting adults or (if all else fails) contemporary moral patterns among our adolescents.'[1]

Partly as a result of this radical shift, many therapists today rarely see patients who exhibit repression of sex in the manner of Freud's pre-World War I hysterical patients. In fact, we find in the people who come for help just the opposite: a great deal of talk about sex, a great deal of sexual activity, practically no one complaining of cultural prohibitions over going to bed as often or with as many partners as one wishes. But what our patients do complain of is lack of feeling and passion. 'The curious thing about this ferment of discussion is how little anyone seems to be *enjoying* emancipation.'[2] So much sex and so little meaning or even fun in it!

Where the Victorian didn't want anyone to know that he or she had sexual feelings, we are ashamed if we do not. Before 1910, if you called a lady 'sexy' she would be insulted; nowadays, she prizes the compliment and rewards you by turning her charms in your direction. Our patients often have the problems of frigidity and impotence, but the strange and poignant thing we observe is how desperately they struggle not to let anyone find out they don't feel sexually. The Victorian nice man or woman was guilty if he or she did experience sex; now we are guilty if we *don't*.

One paradox, therefore, is that enlightenment has not solved the sexual problems in our culture. To be sure, there are important positive results of the new enlightenment, chiefly in increased free-

B

dom for the individual. Most external problems are eased: sexual knowledge can be bought in any bookstore, contraception is available everywhere except in Boston where it is still believed, as the English countess averred on her wedding night, that sex is 'too good for the common people.' Couples can, without guilt and generally without squeamishness, discuss their sexual relationship and undertake to make it more mutually gratifying and meaningful. Let these gains not be underestimated. External social anxiety and guilt have lessened; dull would be the man who did not rejoice in this.

But *internal* anxiety and guilt have increased. And in some ways these are more morbid, harder to handle, and impose a heavier burden upon the individual than external anxiety and guilt.

The challenge a woman used to face from men was simple and direct – would she or would she not go to bed? – a direct issue of how she stood vis-à-vis cultural mores. But the question men ask now is no longer, 'Will she or won't she?' but 'Can she or can't she?' The challenge is shifted to the woman's personal adequacy, namely, her own capacity to have the vaunted orgasm – which should resemble a *grand mal* seizure. Though we might agree that the second question places the problem of sexual decision more where it should be, we cannot overlook the fact that the first question is much easier for the person to handle. In my practice, one woman was afraid to go to bed for fear that the man 'won't find me very good at making love.' Another was afraid because 'I don't even know how to do it,' assuming that her lover would hold this against her. Another was scared to death of the second marriage for fear that she wouldn't be able to have the orgasm as she had not in her first. Often the woman's hesitation is formulated as, 'He won't like me well enough to come back again.'

In past decades you could blame society's strict mores and preserve your own self-esteem by telling yourself what you did or didn't do was society's fault and not yours. And this would give you some time in which to decide what you do want to do, or to let yourself grow into a decision. But when the question is simply how you can perform, your own sense of adequacy and self-esteem is called immediately into question, and the whole weight of the encounter is shifted inward to how you can meet the test.

College students, in their fights with college authorities about hours girls are to be permitted in the men's rooms, are curiously blind to the fact that rules are often a boon. Rules give the student time to find himself. He has the leeway to consider a way of behaving without being committed before he is ready, to try on for size, to venture into relationships tentatively – which is part of any grow-ing up. Better to have the lack of commitment direct and open rather than to go into sexual relations under pressure – doing vio-lence to his feelings by having physical commitment without psychological. He may flaunt the rules; but at least they give some structure to be flaunted. My point is true whether he obeys the rule or not. Many contemporary students, understandably anxious be-cause of their new sexual freedom, repress this anxiety, ('one should *like* freedom') and then compensate for the additional anxiety the repression gives them by attacking the parietal authorities for not giving them more freedom!

What we did not see in our short-sighted liberalism in sex was that throwing the individual into an unbounded and empty sea of free choice does not in itself give freedom, but is more apt to increase inner conflict. The sexual freedom to which we were de-voted fell short of being fully human.

In the arts, we have also been discovering what an illusion it was to believe that mere freedom would solve our problem. Consider, for example, the drama. In an article entitled 'Is Sex Kaput?', Howard Taubman, former drama critic of *The New York Times*, sum-marized what we have all observed in drama after drama: 'Engag-ing in sex was like setting out to shop on a dull afternoon; desire had nothing to do with it and even curiosity was faint.'³ Consider also the novel. In the 'revolt against the Victorians,' writes Leon Edel, 'the extremists have had their day. Thus far they have impover-ished the novel rather than enriched it.' Edel perceptively brings out the crucial point that in sheer realistic 'enlightenment' there has occurred a *dehumanization* of sex in fiction. There are 'sexual en-counters in Zola,' he insists, 'which have more truth in them than any D. H. Lawrence described – and also more humanity.'⁴

The battle against censorship and for freedom of expression surely was a great battle to win, but has it not become a new strait jacket? The writers, both novelists and dramatists, 'would rather hock their typewriters than turn in a manuscript without the obligatory scenes of unsparing anatomical documentation of their characters' sexual behavior. . . .' Our 'dogmatic enlightenment' is self-defeating; it ends up destroying the very sexual passion it set out to protect. In the great tide of realistic chronicling, we forgot, on the stage and in the novel and even in psychotherapy, that imagination is the life-blood of eros, and that realism is neither sexual nor erotic. Indeed, there is nothing *less* sexy than sheer nakedness, as a random hour at any nudist camp will prove. It requires the infusion of the imagination

17

(which I shall later call intentionality) to transmute physiology and anatomy into *interpersonal* experience – into art, into passion, into eros in a million forms which has the power to shake or charm us.

Could it not be that an 'enlightenment' which reduces itself to sheer realistic detail is itself an escape from the anxiety involved in the relation of human imagination to erotic passion?

Salvation Through Technique

A second paradox is that *the new emphasis on technique in sex and love-making backfires*. It often occurs to me that there is an inverse relationship between the number of how-to-do-it books perused by a person or rolling off the presses in a society and the amount of sexual passion or even pleasure experienced by the persons involved. Certainly nothing is wrong with technique as such, in playing golf or acting or making love. But the emphasis beyond a certain point on technique in sex makes for a mechanistic attitude toward love-making, and goes along with alienation, feelings of loneliness, and depersonalization.

One aspect of the alienation is that the lover, with his age-old art, tends to be superseded by the computer operator with his modern efficiency. Couples place great emphasis on bookkeeping and time-tables in their love-making – a practice confirmed and standardized by Kinsey. If they fall behind schedule they become anxious and feel impelled to go to bed whether they want to or not. My colleague, Dr John Schimel, observes, 'My patients have endured stoically, or without noticing, remarkably destructive treatment at the hands of their spouses, but they have experienced falling behind in the sexual time-table as a loss of love.'[5] The man feels he is somehow losing his masculine status if he does not perform up to schedule, and the woman that she has lost her feminine attractiveness if too long a period goes by without the man at least making a pass at her. The phrase 'between men', which women use about their affairs, similarly suggests a gap in time like the *entr'acte*. Elaborate accounting- and ledger-book lists – how often this week have we made love? did he (or she) pay the right amount of attention to me during the evening? was the foreplay long enough? – make one wonder how the spontaneity of this most spontaneous act can possibly survive. The computer hovers in the stage wings of the drama of love-making the way Freud said one's parents used to.

It is not surprising then, in this preoccupation with techniques, that the questions typically asked about an act of love-making are not, Was there passion or meaning or pleasure in the act? but, How well did I perform? Take, for example, what Cyril Connolly calls 'the tyranny of the orgasm', and the preoccupation with achieving a simultaneous orgasm, which is another aspect of the alienation. I confess that when people talk about the 'apocalyptic orgasm', I find myself wondering, Why do they have to try so hard? What abyss of self-doubt, what inner void of loneliness, are they trying to cover up by this great concern with grandiose effects?

Even the sexologists, whose attitude is generally the more sex the merrier, are raising their eyebrows these days about the anxious overemphasis on achieving the orgasm and the great importance attached to 'satisfying' the partner. A man makes a point of asking the woman if she 'made it', or if she is 'all right', or uses some other euphemism for an experience for which obviously no euphemism is possible. We men are reminded by Simone de Beauvoir and other women who try to interpret the love act that this is the last thing in the world a woman wants to be asked at that moment. Furthermore, the technical preoccupation robs the woman of exactly what she wants most of all, physically and emotionally, namely the man's spontaneous abandon at the moment of climax. This abandon gives her whatever thrill or ecstasy she and the experience are capable of. When we cut through all the rigmarole about roles and performance, what still remains is how amazingly important the sheer fact of intimacy of relationship is – the meeting, the growing closeness with the excitement of not knowing where it will lead, the assertion of the self, and the giving of the self – in making a sexual encounter memorable. Is it not this intimacy that makes us return to the event in memory again and again when we need to be warmed by whatever hearths life makes available?

It is a strange thing in our society that what goes into building a relationship – the sharing of tastes, fantasies, dreams, hopes for the future, and fears from the past – seems to make people more shy and vulnerable than going to bed with each other. They are more wary of the tenderness that goes with psychological and spiritual nakedness than they are of the physical nakedness in sexual intimacy.

The New Puritanism

The third paradox is that our highly-vaunted sexual freedom has turned out to be a new form of puritanism. I spell it with a small 'p' because I do not wish to confuse this with the original Puritanism. That, as in the passion of Hester and Dimmesdale in Hawthorne's *The Scarlet Letter*, was a very different thing. I refer to puritanism as it came down via our Victorian grandparents and became allied with industrialism and emotional and moral compartmentalization.

I define this puritanism as consisting of three elements. First, *a state of alienation from the body.* Second, *the separation of emotion from reason.* And third, *the use of the body as a machine.*

In our new puritanism, bad health is equated with sin.[6] Sin used to mean giving in to one's sexual desires; it now means not having full sexual expression. Our contemporary puritan holds that it is immoral *not* to express your libido. Apparently this is true on both sides of the ocean: 'There are few more depressing sights,' the London *Times Literary Supplement* writes, 'than a progressive intellectual determined to end up in bed with someone from a sense of moral duty. . . . There is no more high-minded puritan in the world than your modern advocate of salvation through properly directed passion. . . .' A woman used to be guilty if she went to bed with a man; now she feels vaguely guilty if after a certain number of dates she still refrains; her sin is 'morbid repression', refusing to 'give'. And the partner, who is always completely enlightened (or at least pretends to be) refuses to allay her guilt by getting overtly angry at her (if she could fight him on the issue, the conflict would be a lot easier for her). But he stands broadmindedly by, ready at the end of every date to undertake a crusade to assist her out of her fallen state. And this, of course, makes her 'no' all the more guilt-producing for her.

This all means, of course, that people not only have to learn to perform sexually but have to make sure, at the same time, that they can do so without letting themselves go in passion or unseemly commitment – the latter of which may be interpreted as exerting an unhealthy demand upon the partner. *The Victorian person sought to have love without falling into sex; the modern person seeks to have sex without falling into love.*

I once diverted myself by drawing an impressionistic sketch of the attitude of the contemporary enlightened person towards sex and love. I would like to share this picture of what I call the new sophisticate:

The new sophisticate is not castrated by society, but like Origen is self-castrated. Sex and the body are for him not something to be and live out, but tools to be cultivated like a TV announcer's voice. The new sophisticate expresses his passion by devoting himself passionately to the moral principle of dispersing all passion, loving everybody until love has no power left to scare anyone. He is deathly afraid of his passions unless they are kept under leash, and the theory of total expression is precisely his leash. His dogma of liberty is his repression; and his principle of full libidinal health, full sexual satisfaction, is his denial of eros. The old Puritans repressed sex and were passionate; our new puritan represses passion and is sexual. His purpose is to hold back the body, to try to make nature a slave. The new sophisticate's rigid principle of full freedom is not freedom but a new straitjacket. He does all this because he is afraid of his body and his compassionate roots in nature, afraid of the soil and his procreative power. He is our latter-day Baconian devoted to gaining power *over* nature, gaining knowledge in order to get more power. And you gain power over sexuality (like working the slave until all zest for revolt is squeezed out of him) precisely by the role of full expression. Sex becomes our tool like the caveman's bow and arrows, crowbar, or adz. Sex, the new machine, the *Machina Ultima.*

This new puritanism has crept into contemporary psychiatry and psychology. It is argued in some books on the counseling of married couples that the therapist ought to use only the term 'fuck' when discussing sexual intercourse, and to insist the patients use it; for any other word plays into the patients' dissimulation. What is significant here is not the use of the term itself: surely the sheer lust, animal but self-conscious, and bodily abandon which is rightly called fucking is not to be left out of the spectrum of human experience. But the interesting thing is that the use of the once-forbidden word is now made into an *ought* – a duty for the moral reason of honesty. To be sure, it *is* dissimulation to deny the biological side of copulation. But it is also dissimulation to use the term fuck for the sexual experience when what we seek is a relationship of personal intimacy which is more than a release of sexual tension, a personal intimacy which will be remembered tomorrow and many weeks after tomorrow. The former is dissimulation in the service of inhibition; the latter is dissimulation in the service of alienation of the self, a defense of the self against the anxiety of intimate relationship. As the former was the particular problem of Freud's day, the latter is the particular problem of ours.

The new puritanism brings with it a depersonalization of our whole language. Instead of making love, we 'have sex'; in contrast to intercourse, we 'screw'; instead of going to bed, we 'lay' someone or (heaven help the English language as well as ourselves!) we 'are laid'. This alienation has become so much the order of the day that in some psychotherapeutic training schools, young psychiatrists and psychologists are taught that it is 'therapeutic' to use solely the four-letter words in sessions; the patient is probably masking some repression if he talks about making love; so it becomes our righteous duty – the new puritanism incarnate! – to let him know he only fucks. Everyone seems so intent on sweeping away the last vestiges of Victorian prudishness that we entirely forget that these different words refer to different kinds of human experience. Probably most people have experienced the different forms of sexual relationship described by the different terms and don't have much difficulty distinguishing among them. I am not making a value judgment among these different experiences; they are all appropriate to their own kinds of relationship. Every woman wants at some time to be 'laid' – transported, carried away, 'made' to have passion when at first she has none, as in the famous scene between Rhett Butler and Scarlett O'Hara in *Gone with the Wind*. But if being 'laid' is all that ever happens in her sexual life, then her experience of personal alienation and rejection of sex are just around the corner. If the therapist does not appreciate these diverse kinds of experience, he will be presiding at the shrinking and truncating of the patient's consciousness, and will be confirming the narrowing of the patient's bodily awareness as well as his or her capacity for relationship. This is the chief criticism of the new puritanism: it grossly limits feelings, it blocks the infinite variety and richness of the act, and it makes for emotional impoverishment.

It is not surprising that the new puritanism develops smoldering hostility among the members of our society. And that hostility, in turn, comes out frequently in references to the sexual act itself. We say 'go fuck yourself' or 'fuck you' as a term of contempt to show that the other is of no value whatever beyond being used and tossed aside. The biological lust is here in its *reductio ad absurdum*. Indeed, the word fuck is the most common expletive in our contemporary language to express violent hostility. I do not think this is by accident.

Freud and Puritanism

How Freudian psychoanalysis was intertwined with both the new sexual libertarianism and puritanism is a fascinating story. Social critics at cocktail parties tend to credit Freud with being the prime mover of, or at least the prime spokesman for, the new sexual freedom. But what they do not see is that Freud and psychoanalysis

22

reflected and expressed the new puritanism in both its positive and negative forms.

The psychoanalytic puritanism is positive in its emphasis on rigorous honesty and cerebral rectitude, as exemplified in Freud himself. It is negative in its providing a new system by which the body and self can be viewed, rightly or wrongly, as a mechanism for gratification by way of 'sexual objects'. The tendency in psychoanalysis to speak of sex as a 'need' in the sense of a tension to be reduced plays into this puritanism.

We thus have to explore this problem to see how the new sexual values in our society were given a curious twist as they were rationalized psychoanalytically. 'Psychonalysis is Calvinism in Bermuda shorts,' pungently stated Dr C. Macfie Campbell, president of the American Psychiatric Association in 1936–37, discussing the philosophical aspects of psychoanalysis. The aphorism is only half true, but that half is significant. Freud himself was an excellent example of a puritan in the positive sense in his strength of character, control of his passions, and compulsive work. Freud greatly admired Oliver Cromwell, the Puritan commander, and named a son after him. Philip Rieff, in his study *Freud: The Mind of the Moralist*, points out that this 'affinity for militant puritanism was not uncommon among secular Jewish intellectuals, and indicates a certain preferred character type, starched with independence and cerebral rectitude rather than a particular belief or doctrine.'[7] In his ascetic work habits, Freud shows one of the most significant aspects of puritanism, namely the use of *science as a monastery*. His compulsive industry was rigorously devoted to achieving his scientific goals, which transcended everything else in life (and, one might add, life itself) and for which he sublimated his passion in a quite real rather than figurative sense.

Freud himself had a very limited sexual life. His own sexual expression began late, around thirty, and subsided early, around forty, so his biographer Ernest Jones tells us. At forty-one, Freud wrote to his friend Wilhelm Fliess complaining of his depressed moods, and added, 'Also sexual excitation is of no more use to a person like me.' Another incident points to the fact that around this age his sexual life had more or less ended. Freud reports in *The Interpretation of Dreams* that at one time, in his forties, he felt physically attracted to a young woman and reached out half-voluntarily and touched her. He comments on how surprised he was that he was 'still' able to find the possibility for such attraction in him.

Freud believed in the control and channeling of sexuality, and was

23

convinced that this had specific value both for cultural development and for one's own character. In 1883, during his prolonged engagement to Martha Bernays, the young Freud wrote to his future wife:

... it is neither pleasant nor edifying to watch the masses amusing themselves; we at least don't have much taste for it. ... I remember something that occurred to me while watching a performance of *Carmen*: the mob gives vent to its appetites, and we deprive ourselves. We deprive ourselves in order to maintain our integrity, we economize in our health, our capacity for enjoyment, our emotions; we save ourselves for something, not knowing for what. And this constant suppression of natural instincts gives us the quality of refinement. ... And the extreme case of people like ourselves who chain themselves together for life and death, who deprive themselves and pine for years so as to remain faithful, who probably wouldn't survive a catastrophe that robbed them of their beloved. ...[8]

The basis of Freud's doctrine of sublimation lies in this belief that libido exists in a certain quantity in the individual, that you can deprive yourself, 'economize' emotionally in one way to increase your enjoyment in another, and that if you spend your libido in direct sexuality you will not have it for utilization, for example, in artistic creation. In a positive statement of appreciation of Freud's work, Paul Tillich nevertheless remarks that the 'concept of sublimation is Freud's most puritanical belief'.

I am not making a simple derogatory value judgment about psychoanalysis when I point out the association between it and puritanism. The *original* Puritan movement, in its best representatives and before its general deterioration into the moralistic compartments of Victorianism at the end of the nineteenth century, was characterized by admirable qualities of dedication to integrity and truth. The progress of modern science owes a great deal to it and, indeed, would probably not have been possible without these virtues of the secular monks in their scientific laboratories. Furthermore, a cultural development like psychoanalysis is always effect as well as cause: it *reflects* and *expresses* the emerging trends in the culture, as well as molds and influences these trends. If we are conscious of what is going on, we can, in however slight a way, influence the direction of the trends. We can then hopefully develop new values which will be relevant to our new cultural predicament.

But if we try to take the content of our values from psychoanalysis, we are thrown into a confusing contradiction not only of the values themselves but of our own self-image. It is an error to expect psychoanalysis to carry the burden of providing our values. Psychoanalysis can, by its unfolding and revealing of previously denied motives and desires and by enlarging consciousness, prepare the way for the patient's working out values by means of which he can change. But it can never, in itself, carry the burden for the value decisions which do change a person's life. The great contribution of Freud was his carrying of the Socratic injunction 'Know thyself' into new depths that comprise, in effect, a new continent, the continent of repressed, unconscious motives. He also developed techniques in the personal relationships in therapy, based on the concepts of transference and resistance, for bringing these levels into conscious awareness. Whatever the ebb and flow of the popularity of psychoanalysis, it will remain true that Freud's discoveries and those of the others in this field are an invaluable contribution not only to the area of psychological healing but also to morality in clearing away hypocritical debris and self-deceit.

What I wish to make clear is that many people in our society, yearning for the nirvana of automatic change in their characters and relief from responsibility that comes from handling over one's psyche to a technical process, have actually in their values of 'free expression' and hedonism simply *bootlegged in from psychoanalysis new contents to their old puritanism*. The fact that the change in sexual attitudes and mores occurred so quickly – virtually in the one decade of the 1920's – also argues for the assumption that we changed our clothes and our roles more than our characters. What was omitted was the opening of our senses and imaginations to the enrichment of pleasure and passion and the meaning of love; we relegated these to technical processes. In this kind of 'free' love, one does not learn to love; and freedom becomes not a liberation but a new straitjacket. The upshot was that our sexual values were thrown into confusion and contradiction, and sexual love presented the almost insoluble paradoxes we are now observing.

I do not wish to overstate the case, nor to lose sight at any point of the positive benefits of the modern fluidity in sexual mores. The confusions we are describing go hand in hand with the real possibilities of freedom for the individual. Couples are able to affirm sex as a source of pleasure and delight; no longer hounded by the misconception that sex as a natural act is evil, they can become more sensitive to the actual evils in their relationships such as manipulation of each other. Free to a degree Victorians never were, they can explore ways of making their relationship more enriching. Even the growing frequency of divorce, no matter how sobering the problems it raises, has the positive psychological effect of making it harder for couples to rationalize a bad marriage by the dogma that they are 'stuck' with each other. The possibility of finding a new lover makes it more necessary for us to accept the responsibility of choosing the one we *do* have if we stay with him or her. There is the possibility of developing a courage that is midway between – and includes both – biological lust on one hand and on the other the desire for meaningful relationship, a deepening awareness of each other, and the other aspects of what we call human understanding. Courage can be shifted from simply fighting society's mores to the inward capacity to commit one's self to another human being.

But these positive benefits, it is now abundantly clear, do not occur automatically. They become possible only as the contradictions which we have been describing are understood and worked through.

Motives of the Problem

In my function as a supervisory analyst at two analytic institutes, I supervise one case of each of six psychiatrists or psychologists who are in training to become analysts. I cite the six patients of these young analysts both because I know a good deal about them by now and also because, since they are not my patients, I can see them with a more objective perspective. Each one of these patients goes to bed without ostensible shame or guilt – and generally with different partners. The women – four of the six patients – all state they don't feel much in the sex act. The motives of two of the women for going to bed seem to be to hang on to the man and to live up to the standard that sexual intercourse is 'what you do' at a certain stage. The third woman has the particular motive of generosity : she sees going to bed as something nice you give a man – and she makes tremendous demands upon him to take care of her in return. The fourth woman seems the only one who does experience some real sexual lust, beyond which her motives are a combination of generosity to and anger at the man ('I'll *force* him to give me pleasure !'). The two male patients were originally impotent, and now, though able to have intercourse, have intermittent trouble with potency. But the outstanding fact is they never report getting much of a 'bang' out of their sexual intercourse. Their chief motive for engaging in sex seems to be to demonstrate their masculinity. The specific purpose of one of the men, indeed, seems more to tell his analyst about his previous night's adventure, fair or poor as it may have been, in a kind of backstage interchange of confidence between men, than to enjoy the love-making itself.

Let us now pursue our inquiry on a deeper level by asking, What are the underlying motives in these patterns? What drives people towards the contemporary compulsive preoccupation with sex in place of their previous compulsive denial of it?

The struggle to prove one's identity is obviously a central motive — an aim present in women as well as men, as Betty Friedan in *The Feminine Mystique* made clear. This has helped spawn the idea of *egalitarianism* of the sexes and the *interchangeability* of the sexual roles. Egalitarianism is clung to at the price of denying not only biological differences — which are basic, to say the least — between men and women, but emotional differences from which come much of the delight of the sexual act. The self-contradiction here is that the compulsive need to prove you are identical with your partner means that you repress your own unique sensibilities — and this is exactly what undermines your own sense of identity. This contradiction contributes to the tendency in our society for us to become machines even in bed.

Another motive is the individual's hope to overcome his own solitariness. Allied with this is the desperate endeavor to escape feelings of emptiness and the threat of apathy: partners pant and quiver hoping to find an answering quiver in someone else's body just to prove that their own is not dead; they seek a responding, a longing in the other to prove their own feelings are alive. Out of an ancient conceit, this is called love.

One often gets the impression, amid the male's flexing of sexual prowess, that men are in training to become sexual athletes. But what is the great prize of the game? Not only men, but women struggle to prove their sexual power — they too must keep up to the timetable, must show passion, and have the vaunted orgasm. Now it is well accepted in psychotherapeutic circles that, dynamically, the overconcern with potency is generally a compensation for feelings of impotence.

The use of sex to prove potency in all these different realms has led to the increasing emphasis on technical performance. And here we observe another curiously self-defeating pattern. It is that the excessive concern with technical performance in sex is actually correlated with the reduction of sexual feeling. The techniques of achieving this approach the ludicrous: one is that an anesthetic ointment is applied to the penis before intercourse. Thus feeling

27

less, the man is able to postpone his orgasm longer. I have learned from colleagues that the prescribing of this anesthetic 'remedy' for premature ejaculation is not unusual. 'One male patient,' records Dr Schimel, 'was desperate about his "premature ejaculations", even though these ejaculations took place after periods of penetration of ten minutes or more. A neighbor who was an urologist recommended an anesthetic ointment to be used prior to intercourse. This patient expressed complete satisfaction with the solution and was very grateful to the urologist.' Entirely willing to give up any pleasure of his own, he sought only to prove himself a competent male.

A patient of mine reported that he had gone to a physician with the problem of premature ejaculation, and that such an anesthetic ointment had been prescribed. My surprise, like Dr Schimel's, was particularly over the fact that the patient had accepted this solution with no questions and no conflicts. Didn't the remedy fit the necessary bill, didn't it help him turn in a better performance? But by the time that young man got to me, he was impotent in every way imaginable, even to the point of being unable to handle such lady-like behavior on the part of his wife as her taking off her shoe while they were driving and beating him over the head with it. By all means the man was impotent in this hideous caricature of a marriage. And his penis, before it was drugged senseless, seemed to be the only character with enough 'sense' to have the appropriate intention, namely to get out as quickly as possible.

Making one's self *feel less* in order to *perform better*! This is a symbol, as macabre as it is vivid, of the vicious circle in which so much of our culture is caught. The more one must demonstrate his potency, the more he treats sexual intercourse – this most intimate and personal of all acts – as a performance to be judged by exterior requirements, the more he then views himself as a machine to be turned on, adjusted, and steered, and the less feeling he has for either himself or his partner; and the less feeling, the more he loses genuine sexual appetite and ability. The upshot of this self-defeating pattern is that, in the long run, *the lover who is most efficient will also be the one who is impotent*.

A poignant note comes into our discussion when we remind ourselves that this excessive concern for 'satisfying' the partner is an expression, however perverted, of a sound and basic element in the sexual act: the pleasure and experience of self-admiration in being able to *give* to the partner. The man is often deeply grateful toward the woman who lets herself be gratified by him – lets him give her

28

an orgasm, to use the phrase that is often the symbol for this experience. This is a point midway between lust and tenderness, between sex and agapé – and it partakes of both. Many a male cannot feel his own identity either as a man or as person in our culture until he is able to gratify a woman. The very structure of human interpersonal relations is such that the sexual act does not achieve its full pleasure or meaning if the man and woman cannot feel they are able to gratify the other. And it is the inability to experience this pleasure at the gratification of the other which often underlies the exploitative sexuality of the rape type and the compulsive sexuality of the Don Juan seduction type. Don Juan has to perform the act over and over again because he remains forever unsatisfied, quite despite the fact that he is entirely potent and has a technically good orgasm.

Now the problem is not the desire and need to satisfy the partner as such, but the fact that this need is interpreted by the persons in the sexual act in only a technical sense – giving physical sensation. What is omitted even from our very vocabulary (and thus the words sound 'square' as I say them here) is the experience of giving feelings, sharing fantasies, offering the inner psychic richness that normally takes a little time and enables sensation to transcend itself in emotion and emotion to transcend itself in tenderness and sometimes love.

It is not surprising that contemporary trends toward the mechanization of sex have much to do with the problem of impotence. The distinguishing characteristic of the machine is that it can go through all the *motions* but it never *feels*. A knowledgeable medical student, one of whose reasons for coming into analysis was his sexual impotence, had a revealing dream. He was asking me in the dream to put a pipe in his head that would go down through his body and come out at the other end as his penis. He was confident in the dream that the pipe would constitute an admirably strong erection. What was entirely missing in this intelligent scion of our sophisticated times was any understanding at all that *what he conceived of as his solution was exactly the cause of his problem*, namely the image of himself as a 'screwing machine'. His symbol is remarkably graphic : the brain, the intellect, is included, but a true symbol of our alienated age, his shrewd system bypasses entirely the seats of emotion, the thalamus, the heart and lungs, even the stomach. Direct route from head to penis – but what is lost is the heart![9]

I do not have statistics on hand concerning the present incidence of impotence in comparison with past periods, nor does anyone else so far as I have been able to discover. But my impression is that impotence is increasing these days despite (or is it because of) the unrestrained freedom on all sides. All therapists seem to agree that more men are coming to them with that problem – though whether this represents a real increase in the prevalence of sexual impotence or merely a greater awareness and ability to talk about it cannot be definitely answered. Obviously, it is one of those topics on which meaningful statistics are almost impossible to get. The fact that the book dealing with impotence and frigidity, *Human Sexual Response*, clung near the top of the best-seller lists for so many months, expensive and turgidly-written as it was, would seem to be plenty of evidence of the urge of men to get help on impotence. Whatever the reason, it is becoming harder for the young man as well as the old to take 'yes' for an answer.

To see the curious ways the new puritanism shows itself, you have only to open an issue of *Playboy*, that redoubtable journal reputedly sold mainly to college students and clergymen. You discover the naked girls with silicated breasts side by side with the articles by reputable authors, and you conclude on first blush that the magazine is certainly on the side of the new enlightenment. But as you look more closely you see a strange expression in these photographed girls: detached, mechanical, uninviting, vacuous – the typical schizoid personality in the negative sense of that term. You discover that they are not 'sexy' at all but that *Playboy* has only shifted the fig leaf from the genitals to the face. You read the letters to the editor and find the first, entitled 'Playboy Priest', telling of a priest who 'lectures on Hefner's philosophy to audiences of young people and numerous members of the clergy,' that 'true Christian ethics and morality are not incompatible with Hefner's philosophy,' and – written with enthusiastic approbation – that 'most clergymen in their fashionable parsonages live more like playboys than ascetics.'[10] You find another letter entitled 'Jesus was a playboy,' since he loved Mary Magdalene, good food, and good grooming, and castigated the Pharisees. And you wonder why all this religious justification and why people, if they are going to be 'liberated', can't just enjoy their liberation?

Whether one takes the cynical view that letters to the editor are 'planted', or the more generous one that these examples are selected from hundreds of letters, it amounts to the same thing. An image of a type of American male is being presented – a suave, detached, self-assured bachelor, who regards the girl as a 'Playboy accessory' like items in his fashionable dress. You note also that *Playboy* carries no advertising for trusses, bald heads, or anything that would detract from this image. You discover that the good articles (which, frankly, can be bought by an editor who wants to hire an assistant with taste and pay the requisite amount of money) give authority to this male image. Harvey Cox concludes that *Playboy* is basically antisexual, and that it is the 'latest and slickest episode in man's continuing refusal to be human.' He believes 'the whole phenomenon of which *Playboy* is only a part vividly illustrates the awful fact of the new kind of tyranny.'[11] The poet-sociologist Calvin Herton, discussing *Playboy* in connection with the fashion and entertainment world, calls it the new sexual fascism.

Playboy has indeed caught on to something significant in American society: Cox believes it to be 'the repressed fear of involvement with women.' I go farther and hold that it, as an example of the new puritanism, gets its dynamic from a repressed anxiety in American men that underlies even the fear of involvement. This is the repressed anxiety about impotence. Everything in the magazine is beautifully concocted to bolster the *illusion of potency* without ever putting it to the test or challenge at all. Non-involvement (like playing it cool) is elevated into the ideal model for the Playboy. This is possible because the illusion is air-tight, ministering as it does to men fearful for their potency, and capitalizing on this anxiety. The character of the illusion is shown further in the fact that the leadership of *Playboy* drops off significantly after the age of thirty, when men cannot escape dealing with real women. This illusion is illustrated by the fact that Hefner himself, a former Sunday-school teacher and son of devout Methodists, practically never goes outside his large establishment in North Chicago. Ensconced there, he carries on his work surrounded by his bunnies and amidst his nonalcoholic bacchanals on Pepsi-Cola.

The Revolt Against Sex
With the confusion of motives in sex that we have noted above – almost every motive being present in the act except the desire to make love – it is no wonder that there is a diminution of feeling and that passion has lessened almost to the vanishing point. This diminution of feeling often takes the form of a kind of anesthesia (now with no need of ointment) in people who can perform the mechanical aspects of the sexual act very well. We are becoming used to the plaint from the couch or patient's chair that 'We made love, but I didn't feel anything.' Again, the poets tell us the same things as our patients. T. S. Eliot writes in *The Waste Land* that after

'lovely woman stoops to folly,' and the carbuncular clerk who seduced her at tea leaves,

> She turns and looks a moment in the glass,
> Hardly aware of her departed lover;
> Her brain allows one half-formed thought to pass;
> 'Well now that's done: and I'm glad it's over.'
> When lovely woman stoops to folly and
> Paces about her room again, alone,
> She smoothes her hair with automatic hand,
> And puts a record on the gramophone.
>
> (III : 249–256)

Sex is the 'last frontier', David Riesman meaningfully phrases it in *The Lonely Crowd*. Gerald Sykes, in the same vein, remarks, 'In a world gone grey with market reports, time studies, tax regulations and path lab analyses, the rebel finds sex to be the one green thing.' It is surely true that the zest, adventure, and trying out of one's strength, the discovering of vast and exciting new areas of feeling and experience in one's self and in one's relations to others, and the validation of the self that goes with these are indeed 'frontier experiences'. They are rightly and normally present in sexuality as part of the psychosocial development of every person. Sex in our society did, in fact, have this power for several decades after the 1920's, when almost every other activity was becoming 'other-directed', jaded, emptied of zest and adventure. But for various reasons – one of them being that sex by itself had to carry the weight for the validation of the personality in practically all other realms as well – the frontier freshness, newness, and challenge become more and more lost.

For we are now living in the post-Riesman age, and are experiencing the long-run implications of Riesman's 'other-directed' behavior, the radar-reflected way of life. The last frontier has become a teeming Las Vegas and no frontier at all. Young people can no longer get a bootlegged feeling of personal identity out of revolting in sexuality since there is nothing to revolt against. Studies of drug addiction among young people report them as saying that the revolt against parents, the social 'kick of feeling their own oats' which they used to get from sex, they now have to get from drugs. One such study indicates that students express a 'certain boredom with sex, while drugs are synonymous with excitement, curiosity, forbidden adventure, and society's abounding permissiveness.'[12]

It no longer sounds new when we discover that for many young people what used to be called love-making is now experienced as a futile 'panting palm to palm', in Aldous Huxley's predictive phrase; that they tell us that it is hard for them to understand what the poets were talking about, and that we should so ofen hear the disappointed refrain, 'We went to bed but it wasn't any good.'

Nothing to revolt against, did I say? Well, there is obviously one thing left to revolt against, and that is sex itself. The frontier, the establishing of identity, the validation of the self can be, and not infrequently does become for some people, a revolt against sexuality entirely. I am certainly not advocating this. What I wish to indicate is that the very revolt against sex – this modern Lysistrata in robot's dress – is rumbling at the gates of our cities or, if not rumbling, at least hovering. The sexual revolution comes finally back on itself not with a bang but a whimper.

Thus it is not surprising that, as sex becomes more machinelike, with passion irrelevant and then even pleasure diminishing, the problem has come full circle. And we find, *mirabile dictu,* a progression from an *anesthetic* attitude to an *antiseptic* one. Sexual contact itself then tends to get put on the shelf and to be avoided. This is another and surely least constructive aspect of the new puritanism: it returns, finally, to a new asceticism. This is said graphically in a charming limerick that seems to have sprung up on some sophisticated campus:

> The word has come down from the Dean
> That with the aid of the teaching machine,
> > King Oedipus Rex
> > Could have learned about sex
> Without ever touching the Queen.

Marshall McLuhan, among others, welcomes this revolt against sex. 'Sex as we now think of it may soon be dead,' write McLuhan and Leonard. 'Sexual concepts, ideals and practices already are being altered almost beyond recognition. . . . The foldout playmate in *Playboy* magazine – she of outside breast and buttocks, pictured in sharp detail – signals the death throes of a departing age.'[13] McLuhan and Leonard then go on to predict that eros will not be lost in the new sexless age but diffused, and that all life will be more erotic than now seems possible.

This last reassurance would be comforting indeed to believe. But as usual, McLuhan's penetrating insights into *present* phenomena are unfortunately placed in a framework of history – 'pretribalism' with its so-called lessened distinction between male and female – which

33

has no factual basis at all. And he gives us no evidence whatever for his optimistic prediction that new eros, rather than apathy, will succeed the demise of *vive la difference*. Indeed, there are amazing confusions in this article arising from McLuhan's and Leonard's worship of the new electric age. In likening Twiggy to an X-ray as against Sophia Loren to a Rubens, they ask, 'And what does an X-ray of a woman reveal? Not a realistic picture, but a deep, involving image. Not a specialized female, but a *human being*.' Well! An X-ray actually reveals not a human being at all but a depersonalized, fragmentized segment of bone or tissue which can be read only by a highly specialized technician and from which we could never in a thousand years recognize a human being or any man or woman we know, let alone one we love. Such a 'reassuring' view of the future is frightening and depressing in the extreme.

And may I not be permitted to prefer Sophia Loren over Twiggy for an idle erotic daydream without being read out of the New Society?

Our future is taken more seriously by the participants in the discussion on this topic at the Center for the Study of Democratic Institutions at Santa Barbara. Their report, called 'The A-Sexual Society,' frankly faces the fact that we are hurtling into, not a bisexual or a multi-sexual, but an a-sexual society: the boys grow long hair and the girls wear pants. . . . Romance will disappear; in fact, it has almost disappeared now. . . . Given the guaranteed Annual Income and The Pill, will women choose to marry? Why should they?' Mrs Eleanor Garth, a participant in the discussion and writer of the report, goes on to point out the radical change that may well occur in having and rearing children. 'What of the time when the fertilized ovum can be implanted in the womb of a mercenary, and one's progeny selected from a sperm-bank? Will the lady choose to reproduce her husband, if there still are such things? . . . No problems, no jealousy, no love-transference. . . . And what of the children, incubated under glass? . . . Will communal love develop the human qualities that we assume emerge from the present rearing of children? Will women under these conditions lose the survival drive and become as death-oriented as the present generation of American men? . . . I don't raise the question in advocacy,' she adds, 'I consider some of the possibilities horrifying.'

Mrs Garth and her colleagues at the Center recognize that the real issue underlying this revolution is not what one does with sexual organs and sexual functions per se, but what happens to man's humanity. 'What disturbs me is the real possibility of the disappear-

34

ance of our humane, life-giving qualities with the speed of the developments in the life sciences, and the fact that no one seems to be discussing the alternative possibilities for good and evil in these developments.'

The purpose of our discussion in this book is precisely to raise the questions of the alternative possibilities for good and evil – that is, the destruction of the enhancement of the qualities which constitute man's 'humane, life-giving qualities.'

From *Love and Will*

1 *The Times Literary Supplement*, 1965.
2 Ibid.
3 Howard Taubman, 'Is Sex Caput?' *New York Times*, January 17, 1965.
4 Leon Edel, 'Sex and the Novel', *New York Times*, November 1, 1964.
5 'Ideology and Sexual Practices', John L. Schimel, *Sexual Behaviour and the Law*, ed. Slovenko, Springfield, Ill., Charles Thomas, 165, p. 195.
6 I have omitted here a fascinating note on Puritanism. See *Love and Will*, p. 328.
7 Philip Rieff, *Freud: The Mind of the Moralist*, Viking Press, 1959.
8 Marcus, *The Other Victorians*, pp. 146–147.
9 *Dreams and Symbols*, Leopold Caliger and Rollo May, reveals that people today are preoccupied with the head and genitals in their dreams, and leave out the heart.
10 *Playboy*, April, 1957.
11 'Playboy's Doctrine of the Male', *Christianity and Crisis*, April 17, 1961, Harvey Cox.
12 *New York Times*, November 26, 1967.
13 *Look* magazine, July 25, 1967.

THE MEANING OF LOVE

Viktor Frankl

THE meaningfulness of human existence is based upon the uniqueness and singularity of the human person. Creative values are actualized in the form of accomplishments that bear on community. Community in its turn confers existential meaning upon personal uniqueness and singularity. But community can also be a rich field of human experience. This is especially so with 'twoness', the intimate community of one self with another. Let us put aside all the more or less vague ideas about love and consider it in the light of existential meaning. Seen so, it proves to be the area in which experiential values are especially realizable. Love is living the experience of another person in all his uniqueness and singularity.

It thus appears that there are two ways to validate the uniqueness and singularity of the self. One way is active, by the realization of creative values. The other is, as it were, passive, in which everything that a person otherwise has to win by action falls into his lap. This way is the way of love – or rather, the way of being loved. Without any contribution of his own, without effort or labor – by grace, so to speak – a person obtains that fulfillment which is found in the realization of his uniqueness and singularity. In love the beloved person is comprehended in his very essence, as the unique and singular being that he is; he is comprehended as a Thou, and as such is taken into the self. As a human person he becomes for the one who loves him indispensable and irreplaceable without having done anything to bring this about. The person who is loved 'can't help' having the uniqueness and singularity of his self – that is, the value of his personality – realized. Love is not deserved, is unmerited – it is simply grace.

But love is not only grace; it is also enchantment. For the lover, it casts a spell upon the world, envelops the world in added worth. Love enormously increases receptivity to the fullness of values. The gates to the whole universe of values are, as it were, thrown open. Thus, in his surrender to the Thou the lover experiences an inner enrichment which goes beyond that Thou; for him the whole cosmos broadens and deepens in worth, glows in the radiance of those values which only the lover sees. For it is well known that love does not make one blind but seeing – able to see values.

In addition to the grace of being loved and the enchantment of loving, a third factor enters into love: the miracle of love. For through love the incomprehensible is accomplished – there enters (via a detour through the realm of biology) into life a new person, itself complete with the mystery of the uniqueness and singularity of its existence: a child!

We have already spoken of the phased and layered structure of the human being. And we have also emphasized that we see man as a physical-psychic-spiritual totality. We have called upon psycho-therapy to recognize this totality as such, so that not only the psyche, but the spiritual aspects of man will be taken into account.

Now, however, we wish to show how man as lover, as experiencer of love, and as experiencer, in love, of another person's self, can react differently to the many-layered structure of the human person. For just as there are the three layers of the human person, so are there three possible attitudes toward it. The most primitive attitude concerns itself with the outermost layer: this is the sexual attitude. The bodily appearance of the other person happens to be sexually arousing, and this arousal sets off the sex drive in the sexually dis-posed person, directly affecting that person's physical being. Stand-ing one step higher in the ranking of attitudes toward the partner is the erotic – for the sake of our analysis here we are making a sharp distinction between eroticism and sexuality. The erotically disposed person, in this special sense of the word 'erotic', is not just sexually excited, not just sexually desirous. His attitude does not stem only from a sex drive and is not provoked by the other as a mere sexual partner. If we think of the partner's physical being as his or her outermost layer, it can be said that the erotically disposed person penetrates deeper than the one who is only sexually disposed. Eroticism penetrates into the next deeper layer, enters into the psychic structure of the other person. This attitude toward the part-ner, considered as one phase of the relationship, is identical with what is commonly called 'infatuation'. The physical traits of the partner stir us sexually, but we are also 'infatuated' with the other's psychic characteristics. The infatuated person, then, is no longer in a state of mere physical excitation; rather, his psychic emotionality is stirred – stirred by the peculiar (but not unique) psyche of the

37

partner; let us say, by particular character traits of the partner. The merely sexual attitude, then, is directed toward the partner's physical being and does not wish to go beyond this layer. The erotic attitude, the attitude of infatuation, is directed toward the psychic being; but it too does not penetrate to the core of the other person. This is done only by the third possible attitude: love itself. Loving (in the narrowest sense of the word) represents the end stage of eroticism (in the broadest sense of the word), since it alone penetrates as deeply as possible into the personal structure of the partner. Loving represents a coming to relationship with another as a spiritual being. The close connection with spiritual aspects of the partner is the ultimate attainable form of partnership. The lover is no longer aroused in his own physical being, nor stirred in his own emotionality, but moved to the depths of his spiritual core, moved by the partner's spiritual core. Love, then, is an entering into direct relationship with the personality of the beloved, with the beloved's uniqueness and singularity. The spiritual core is the carrier of those psychic and bodily characteristics toward which the erotic or sexually disposed person is attracted; the spiritual core is what lies back of those physical or psychic appearances; it is what 'appears' in those appearances. The bodily and psychic lineaments of the personality are, so to speak, the outer 'dress' which the spiritual core 'wears'. While the sexually disposed person or the infatuated person feels attracted by the physical characteristics or psychic traits 'of' the partner – that is, something this other person 'has' – the lover loves the beloved's self – not something the beloved 'has', but what he 'is'. The lover's gaze looks through the physical and the psychic 'dress' of the spiritual core, looks to the core of the other's being. He is no longer interested in an alluring physical 'type' or attractive temperament; he is concerned with the person, with the partner as unique, irreplaceable, and incomparable.

The tendencies we encounter in 'infatuation' – which, as we have indicated, are not strictly of a sexual nature – have been termed by psychoanalysis 'aim-inhibited' tendencies. The term is quite apt – though in an opposite sense from that intended by psychoanalysis. The psychoanalysts consider these tendencies aim-inhibited because according to their theory the instinctual aim is genito-sexual. To our mind these tendencies are aim-inhibited in a different sense – inhibited from passing on to the next higher attitudinal form, genuine love; inhibited from penetrating to the next deeper layer of the partner's personality, the spiritual core.

That the true lover really seeks the uniqueness and singularity of his partner's spiritual core can be made plain even to the person whose ideas are based on simple empiricism. Let us ask the skeptic to imagine that the one he loves is lost to him forever, either through death or departure and permanent separation. He is then offered a double of the beloved person – someone who in body and temperament perfectly resembles her. We then ask whether the lover can transfer his love to this other person – and he will have to admit that he would be unable to do so. Such a 'transfer' of true love is inconceivable. For the true lover does not 'care about' particular psychic or physical characteristics 'of' the beloved person, he does not care about some trait that she 'has', but about what she 'is' in her uniqueness. As a unique person, she can never be replaced by any double, no matter how perfect a duplicate. But someone who is merely infatuated could probably find a double satisfactory for his purposes. His affections could be transferred without difficulty to the double. For his feelings are concerned only with the temperament the partner 'has', not with the spiritual person that the partner 'is'.

The spiritual core as the object of the true attitude of love is, then, irreplaceable and inexchangeable for the true lover, because it is unique and singular. It follows from this that true love is its own warrant of permanence. For a physical state passes, and a psychological state is also impermanent. Sexual excitement is only temporary; the sex drive vanishes promptly after gratification. And infatuation, too, is seldom of long duration. But the spiritual act by which the person comprehends the spiritual core of another outlasts itself; to the degree that the content of that act is valid, it is valid once and for all. Thus true love as a spiritual relationship to the other person's being, as the beholding of another peculiar essence, is exempt from the transistoriness which marks the merely temporary states of physical sexuality or psychological eroticism. Love is more than an emotional condition; love is an intentional act. What it intends is the essence of the other person. This essence is ultimately independent of existence; *essentia* is not contingent upon *existentia*, and insofar as it has this freedom, it is superior to *existentia*. That is why love can outlast the death of the beloved; in that sense we can understand why love is 'stronger' than death. The existence of the beloved may be annihilated by death, but his essence cannot be touched by death. His unique being is, like all true essences, something timeless and thus imperishable. The 'idea' of a person – which is what the lover sees – belongs to a realm beyond time. These considerations, it is true, go back to scholastic or Platonic philosophy.

But let us not imagine that they are therefore too far removed from the simple empiricism which, we must also recognize, has its intellectual validity and dignity. For example, we have the following narrative by a former concentration-camp inmate:

'All of us in camp, my comrades and myself as well, were certain that no happiness on earth could ever in the future make up for what we were compelled to endure during our imprisonment. If we had drawn up a balance sheet of happiness, the only choice left to us would have been to 'run into the wire' – that is, to kill ourselves. Those who did not do so were acting out of a deep sense of some obligation. As far as I was concerned, I felt duty-bound toward my mother to stay alive. We two loved one another beyond all else. Therefore my life had a meaning – in spite of everything. But I had to count upon death any minute of every day. And therefore my death also should somehow have meaning – as well as all the suffering that I would have yet to go through before it came. And so I made a pact with Heaven: if I should have to die, then let my death preserve my mother's life; and whatever I should have to suffer up until the time of my death was to purchase for her a sweet and easy death when her time came. Only by imagining it in terms of such a sacrifice was my tormented existence endurable. I could live my life only if it had a meaning; but I also wanted to suffer my suffering and die my death only if suffering and death also had a meaning.'

The prisoner then goes on to recount that whenever time and conditions in the camp permitted, he dwelt upon the inner personality of his mother. We might put it this way: while in his actual situation it was impossible for him to realize creative values, he was learning the inner enrichment and fulfillment of devoted love; in loving contemplation and loving memory he was realizing experiential values. The continuation of his account strikes us as wholly remarkable: 'But I did not know whether my mother herself was still alive. All the time I was in the camp we were without news of one another. Then it struck me that when, as I so frequently did, I was holding imaginary dialogues with my mother, the fact that I did not even know whether she was alive hardly disturbed me!'

That is, at no time did this man know whether the person he loved still had physical existence, and nevertheless this so little affected his feeling for her that he stumbled upon the question of her 'existence' only incidentally – without its being a stumbling-block. Love is so little directed toward the body of the beloved that it can easily outlast the other's death, can exist in the lover's heart until his own death. The true lover can never really grasp the death of the loved one, any more than he can 'grasp' his own death. For it is well known that no one can ever fully realize the fact of his own death, which is fundamentally as inconceivable as the fact of not having been before one's own birth. Anyone who really believes or claims that he can grasp the death of a person is deceiving himself. For what he would have us believe is ultimately incomprehensible: that a personal entity is removed from the world simply because the organism which is its vehicle has become a cadaver, and that thereafter no form of being pertains to it. Scheler in a posthumously published essay on the survival of personality after the death of the body has pointed out that even in a person's lifetime we apprehend far more of the person – as soon as we really 'intend' him – than 'the few scraps of sensuous data' his physical appearance gives us. The latter is all we miss after death! When that is gone, it is far from the same as saying that the person himself no longer exists. The most we can say is that he can no longer manifest himself, for manifestation requires physical forms of expression (speech, etc.). Once more, then, we see why and in what sense the true intending of love, the intending of another personality as such, is independent of the person's physical presence – independent, in fact, of the person's bodily existence altogether.

All this, of course, is not to say that love has no desire to 'embody' itself. But it is independent of the body to the extent that it does not need the body. Even in love between the sexes the body, the sexual element, is not primary; it is not an end in itself, but a means of expression. Love as such can exist without it. Where sexuality is possible, love will desire and seek it; but where renunciation is called for, love will not necessarily cool or die. The spiritual self takes form in giving shape to its psychic and physical modes of appearance and expression. That is, in the totality which is centered around the personal core the outer layers serve as means by which the inner layers are expressed. A person's body expresses his character and his character expresses the person as spiritual being. The spirit attains to expression – and demands expression – in the body and the psyche. Thus the bodily appearance of the beloved person becomes for a lover a symbol, a mere token for something behind it which manifests itself in the external appearance but is not fully contained in that. True love in and for itself needs the body neither for arousal nor for fulfillment, though it makes use of the body for both. Arousal in a man of healthy instincts is stimulated by the partner's body – although his love is not directed toward the partner's body. But in given circumstances the partner's body as expression of the spirit will guide the lover's choice in that, with the sureness of instinct, he prefers one person to another. Certain physical characteristics or traits of character would then lead the lover to a particular partner – to the one particularly meant for him. While the 'shallow' person sees only the partner's surface and cannot grasp the depth, the 'deeper' person sees the surface itself as an expression of the depths, not as an essential and decisive expression, but as a significant one. In this sense love uses the body for arousal. We have said that it also uses the body for fulfillment. For in fact physically mature lovers will in general be impelled toward a physical relationship. But for the real lover the physical, sexual relationship remains a mode of expression for the spiritual relationship which his love really is, and as a mode of expression it is love, the spiritual act, which gives it human dignity. We can therefore say : as the body is for the lover the expression of the partner's spiritual being, the sexual act is for the lover the expression of a spiritual intention.

A person's physical appearance, then, has comparatively little to do with his being loved. His actual physical traits and temperamental features acquire their erotic significance from love itself; it is love which makes these characteristics 'lovable'. For this reason we must take a reserved and critical view of the use of cosmetics. For even blemishes are an essential part of the personality. Insofar as externals affect the lover, they do not affect him in themselves, but as part of the beloved person. A patient, for example, was considering plastic surgery to beautify ugly breasts, hoping thereby to assure her husband's love. She asked the doctor for advice. The doctor warned against the projected operation; he remarked that since her husband really loved her, he loved her body just as it was. An evening dress, he pointed out, does not affect a man 'in itself'; he thinks it beautiful only when the woman he loves is wearing it. Finally the patient asked her husband his opinion. And he did indicate that the result of the operation would only be troubling to him; he would be forced to think : 'Somehow this is no longer my wife.'

Psychologically, of course, it is understandable that an unattractive person will painfully and artificially seek what seems to come so easily to the attractive. The ugly person will overestimate the love life – and the less joy he has in his own love life, the more he will exaggerate its importance. In fact love is only one of the possible ways to fill life with meaning, and is not even the best way. Our existences would have come to a sad pass and our lives would

42

be poor indeed if their meaning depended upon whether or not we experienced happiness in love. Life is infinitely rich in chances to realize values. We need only remember the primacy of creative realization of values. But the individual who neither loves nor is loved can still shape his life in a highly meaningful manner. The only question is whether the failure to achieve love is really imposed by destiny and is not a neurotic failure, one for which the person has himself to blame. We have already discussed those cases where the actualization of creative values must be put aside, and attitudinal values cultivated in their stead. We have emphasized that the renunciation must not be arbitrary or premature. The same point may be made in regard to renouncing the experiential values of love. The danger of premature resignation is on the whole considerable. For people tend to forget how relatively unimportant outward attractiveness is, how much more important personality is to the love life. We all know shining (and consoling) examples of unattractive or unprepossessing persons who by virtue of their charm and temperament had successful love lives. We may recall our case of the cripple who under the most unfavorable circumstances was remarkably successful not only intellectually, but erotically also. To be unattractive is not a sufficient reason for being resigned. And resignation has a bad side-effect: resentment. For a neurotic person who fails to gain fulfillment in a particular realm of values ends either by overvaluing or devaluing that particular aspect of life. Neurotic straining after 'happiness' in love leads, precisely because of the strain involved, to 'unhappiness'. The person who has a fixation on overvalued eroticism tries to force open that 'door to happiness' of which we have remarked, with Kierkegaard, that it 'opens outward' and does not yield to violent assault. On the other hand, the person who is negatively fixated on the love life, who devalues it in an effort to make himself feel better about what he has not attained and considers unattainable – such a person also blocks his own way to erotic happiness. Inner resentment coupled with renunciation brings about the same result as revolt and protest against fate: both reaction patterns rob the individuals of their own chance. On the other hand, the easy, unresenting attitude of someone who is sincerely but not irrevocably resigned permits the color of his personality to shine through and so offers a last chance for love to come his way. There is much truth to the old maxim: 'By abstaining we obtain.'

Stress on appearance leads to general overestimation of the value of 'beauty' in erotic life. At the same time the person as such is devalued. There is something insulting in identifying a woman as 'beautiful'. Does not the use of this adjective ultimately mean that we are deliberately refraining from using any others, from judging the qualities of her mind, say? A high rating in a category of relatively low valuation arouses the suspicion of tacit unwillingness to give any rating in a category of higher valuation. Stressing externals, moreover, implies not only a devaluation of the person being judged, but also of the one who delivers the judgment. For if I talk about a woman's beauty, that suggests not only that I have nothing favorable to say about her personality, but that I am not interested in her personality – because I do not value qualities of the personality.

All flirtation, all the common, ordinary gallantries of the past and present, disregard the partner's inner personality with unconscious intent. The uniqueness and singularity of the other person is deliberately left out of such encounters. People who go in for such superficial eroticism flee from the obligations of real love, from any sense of having true ties with the partner – because such ties involve responsibility. They take refuge in a collective concept, preferring a 'type'; their partner at any given time is a more or less chance representative of that type. They choose the type rather than any particular person. Their love is directed toward typical but impersonal 'looks'. A feminine type very commonly preferred is that of the chorus girl. This can easily be understood when we consider how thoroughly depersonalized a type she is. The chorus girl is, so to speak, a symbol of girls 'wholesale'. She is a component part of a precision mechanism: the chorus line. She is a member of a dance troupe, therefore part of a collective group. As such she cannot step out of her framework, cannot drop out of her role among the others who are tripping in step across the stage. In life as well she must keep in step. Today's average man takes this type of woman for his erotic ideal because she cannot, in her impersonality, burden him with responsibility. The type is ubiquitous. Just as one chorus girl in the revue can be replaced by any other, so in life this type of woman is easily replaceable. The chorus-girl type is impersonal woman with whom a man need have no personal relationship, no obligations; a woman he can 'have' and therefore need not love. She is property, without personal traits, without personal value. Only the human person can be loved; the impersonality of the chorus-girl type cannot be loved. With her, no question of faithfulness is involved; infidelity follows from impersonality. Not only is infidelity in such erotic relationships feasible; it is necessary. For where the quality of happiness in love is lacking, the lack must be compensated by quantity of sexual pleasure.

44

This kind of eroticism represents a crippled form of love. The use of such a phrase as 'I have "had" this woman' fully exposes the nature of such eroticism. What you 'have' you can swap; what you possess you can change. If a man has 'possessed' a woman, he can easily exchange her, can even 'buy' himself another. This relationship of 'having' has its counterpart in the woman's attitude. For such superficial eroticism which regards only the partner's surface, the outward appearance, is equally a surface matter for the woman. What a person 'is' as such does not count, only how much sex appeal the person has as a possible sexual partner. What you have can be altered, and a woman's 'surface' can likewise be changed – by make-up. Thus the woman's attitude corresponds to the man's. The woman will do her best to conceal all personal qualities, in order not to bother the man with them, and in order to give the man what he is looking for: his preferred type. The woman – or, rather, the contemporary urban 'doll' is completely engrossed in her appearance. She wants to be 'taken' – but she does not want to be taken seriously, to be taken for what she really is: a human person in all her uniqueness and singularity. She wants to be taken as a member of a sex, and therefore she puts her body, with all its unspecific quality, in the forefront. She wants to be impersonal and to represent whatever type happens to be the fashion, happens to be going well in the market place of erotic vanities. As slavishly as possible, she will attempt to imitate that popular type, and in so doing she must necessarily be unfaithful to herself, to her self.

She may, for example, choose her type from the world of the film stars. She compares herself again and again with the type – which represents her own or her male partner's present ideal woman – in order to make herself as like it as possible. She has no urge at all to assert the personality which is unique and incomparable in all human beings. She does not even long to create a new type of woman herself, has no ambition to set the fashion. Instead of creating a type, she is content to represent one. Gladly, of her own free will, she presents herself to the man as the type he prefers. She never gives herself, never lovingly surrenders her self. Proceeding from such assumptions, proceeding along such a course, she wanders further and further from true, fulfilling erotic experience. For the man who chooses her does not want her at all; he is in reality choosing only her type. Submissive to the man's desires, she readily gives him what he needs and wants to 'have'. And both part empty-handed. Instead of seeking one another and so finding each other's selves, finding the uniqueness and singularity which alone make each other worth loving and their own lives worth living, they have settled for a fiction. For in his creative work each man displays his uniqueness and singularity, but in loving he takes the uniqueness and singularity of his partner into himself. In the mutual surrender of love, in the giving and taking between two people, each one's own personality comes into its own. The love impulse breaks through to that layer of being in which every individual human being no longer represents a 'type', but himself alone, not comparable, not replaceable, and possessing all the dignity of his uniqueness. This dignity is the dignity of those angels of whom some scholastics maintained that they do not represent a kind; rather, there is only one of each kind.

If the attitude of true love represents the directing of the core of one person toward another, that is also the sole guarantee of fidelity. In other words, out of love itself comes the assurance of its duration. But something more comes out of it: it's 'eternality'. Love can only be experienced *sub specie æternitatis*. The real lover, in the moment of loving, in his surrender to that moment and to the object of his love, cannot conceive that his feeling will ever change. This is understandable when we consider that his feelings are directed toward the essence of the beloved person and that person's worth, just like any other spiritual act – like, say, cognition or the recognition of values. Once I have comprehended that $2 \times 2 = 4$, I have comprehended it once and for all. 'That's all there is to it.' And once I have truly comprehended the inner nature of another person by seeing that person in the illumination of love, that is all there is to it: I must abide by the truth of it, must abide by this love, and this love must abide with me. The moment we experience true love, we experience it as valid forever, like a truth which we recognize as an 'eternal truth'. In exactly the same way, as long as love lasts in ordinary time it is necessarily experienced as 'eternal love'.

Yet in all of his searchings for truth, man can make mistakes. And in the matter of loving, individuals may deceive themselves. A person may think that love has made him see, when in fact he may be blinded by mere infatuation. But no one can start out assuming that a subjective truth is a possible error because it is 'only subjective'; it can turn out to be an error only later on. Similarly, it is impossible for anyone to love 'for a while', temporarily; it is impossible to intend a temporary state as such and to set a definitive term to love. A person can at most love at the risk of having the object of his love turn out to be unworthy afterward, so that his love 'dies' as soon as the worth of the beloved is no longer there in the lover's vision.

A mere possession can be changed. But since true love is not directed toward the aspect of the other person which can be 'possessed', toward what the other 'has'; since true love is rather directed toward what the other 'is' – such real love, and it alone, leads to a monogamous attitude. For the monogamous attitude presupposes comprehension of the partner in all his uniqueness and singularity, comprehending the core and the worth of his personality, going beyond all bodily and temperamental peculiarities, since these are not unique and singular and can be found in other persons of more or less the same cast.

The obvious conclusion from this is that mere infatuation, being by its nature a more or less fleeting 'emotional state', must be considered virtually a contra-indication to marriage. This is by no means the equivalent of saying that real love in itself is a positive indication for marriage. Marriage is more than a matter of personal experience. It is a complex structure, an institution of social life legalized by the state or, as the case may be, sanctioned by the church. That is, it reaches deep into the societal realm, and certain societal conditions ought to be met before a marriage is sealed. In addition there are biological conditions and circumstances which in given cases may make marriage inadvisable. Eugenic considerations may enter into the decision. These factors may not disqualify the love as such, but the parties to such a marriage should be content to view their marriage as a spiritual partnership and to stop short of the usual concomitant of marriage – i.e., reproduction.

On the other hand, if motives in themselves extraneous to real love determine a marriage, the marriage can at most partake of the nature of 'eroticism' – eroticism as we have defined it : as being directed toward 'having', toward possession. In particular, where economic motives play a major part in the decision, the materialistic desire to 'have' is preponderant. It is to such motives that institutions like marriage-brokerage owe their existence. For matchmaking of this sort the social factor of marriage is considered in isolation, is in fact considered the paramount and single issue. The degradation of human relationships that this entails is visited, as it were, upon the next generation. We know a young man who left home to escape the continual quarrels between his parents, who always dragged him into their disputes. With the naïveté and earnestness of youth he planned to devote his life to setting up some kind of institution whose sole purpose would be to prevent marriages between incompatible people like his parents.

Real love in itself constitutes the decisive factor of a monogamous relationship. But there is another factor, that of exclusiveness (Oswald Schwarz). Love means a sense of inward union; the monogamous relationship, in the form of marriage, is the outward tie. Being faithful means maintaining this tie in all its definitiveness. The exclusiveness of the tie, however, makes it the more imperative that a person form the 'right' tie; not only must he be prepared to bind himself, but also he must know whom he is binding himself to. It becomes supremely important that he decide in favor of the right partner. Erotic maturity in the sense of being inwardly mature enough for a monogamous relationship thus involves a dual requirement: the ability to select a partner; and the ability to remain definitively faithful to that partner.

Youth is a time of preparation for one's erotic life as well as for life in general. Youth must explore, seek for the right partner, and find one. Youth must also 'learn' in good time to be faithful. These two demands sometimes run counter to each other. For on the one hand, in order to develop the ability to choose a partner, the young person must acquire a degree of erotic insight and erotic practice. On the other hand, in developing the ability to be faithful, the young person must endeavor to grow beyond mere shifts of mood, stick to one person, and maintain the relationship. In some cases he (the pronoun is arbitrary here and stands for both sexes) will not know whether to abandon a particular relationship in order to have the experience of as many different relationships as possible so that he can finally choose the right one; or whether to preserve the given relationship as long as possible in order to learn fidelity as soon as may be. In practice the best advice to give a young person confronting this dilemma is to suggest that he formulate the question negatively. Let him ask himself whether he wishes to 'drop' an existing and valuable relationship because he is afraid of being tied down and is trying to escape responsibility; or in the other case let him ask himself whether he is frantically clinging to an already moribund relationship because he is afraid of having to be alone for a few weeks or months. If he looks into his subjective motives in this way, he will find an objective decision easy to make.

Scheler defines love as a spiritual movement toward the highest possible value of the loved person, a spiritual act in which this highest value – which he calls the 'salvation' of a person – is apprehended. Spranger makes a similar comment: that love perceives the value potentialities in the beloved person. Von Hattingberg expresses it differently: love sees a person the way God 'meant' him.

Love, we may say, reveals to us the valuational image of a human being. In so doing, it performs a metaphysical act. For the valuational image revealed to us in the course of the spiritual act of love is essentially the 'image' or something invisible, unreal – unrealized. In the spiritual act of love we apprehend a person not only as what he 'is' in his uniqueness and singularity, his *hæcceitas* in scholastic terminology, but also as what he can and will be: his *entelechy*. Let us call to mind the definition of human reality as a possibility – the possibility of realizing values, of self-realization. What love sees is therefore no more and no less than this 'possibility' of a human being. We may remark parenthetically that psychotherapy also must aim to see the human beings with whom it deals in their own most personal possibilities, to anticipate the potential values in them. It is part of the metaphysical mystery of the spiritual act we call love that out of the beloved's essential image it succeeds in reading the potential image. For to discover potential values on the basis of essential facts is not a matter of calculation. Facts can be calculated; potentialities are by their nature incalculable.

Awareness of values can only enrich a person. In fact, this inner enrichment partly constitutes the meaning of his life, as we have seen in our discussion of experiential values. Therefore, love must necessarily enrich the lover. This being so, there can be no such thing as 'unrequited, unhappy love'; the term is self-contradictory. Either you really love – in which case you must feel enriched, whether or not the love is returned; or you do not really love, do not actually intend the inner being of another person, but rather miss it completely and look only for something physical 'about' him or some (psychological) character trait which he 'has'. In such a situation your feelings may well be unrequited, but you are then not a lover. We must remember this: that infatuation makes us blind; real loves enables us to see. Love permits us to see the spiritual core of the other person, the reality of the other's essential nature and his value potentialities. Love allows us to experience another's personality as a world in itself, and so extends our own world. While it thus enriches and 'requites' us, it also does the other person good in leading him to those potential values which can be seen and anticipated only in love. Love helps the beloved to become as the lover sees him. For the loved one wants to be worthier of the lover, a worthier recipient of such love, by growing to be more like the lover's image, and so he becomes more and more the image of 'what God conceived and wanted him to be'. While, therefore, even 'un-

49

requited' love enriches us and brings happiness, 'requited' love is distinctly creative. In mutual love, in which each wishes to be worthy of the other, to become like the other's vision of him, a kind of dialectical process takes place in which each outbids the other and so elevates the other.

We have shown that unrequited or unhappy love is a contradiction in terms. From the psychological point of view, the expression is fraught with self-pity. The pleasurable or unpleasurable significance of an experience is simply being overestimated. In erotic matters, above all, the hedonistic point of view has no justification. Like spectators in the theater, life's actors generally find that tragedies are more profound experiences than comedies. Even when our experiences in love turn out unhappily, we are not only enriched, but also given a deeper sense of life; such experiences are the chief things which foster inner growth and maturity.

Of course the inner enrichment which a person experiences in love may be accompanied by tension. Neurotics fear these tensions and shy away from anything which may tend to produce them. The experience of unhappy, unrequited love has a definite use – the end being to protect the burned child from the fire of Eros. For those who have once had this unpleasant experience, there is a tendency not to repeat it. The phrase 'unrequited love' is therefore not only an expression of self-pity, but of perverted enjoyment of misery. In an almost masochistic fashion the thoughts of the infatuated wretch circle round and round his unhappiness. He barricades himself behind his first – or last – failure so that he will never have to burn his fingers again. He hides behind his lack of success; he escapes into the unhappiness of the past to avoid the possibility of happiness in the future. Instead of continuing to look until he finds, he gives up the search. Instead of remaining open-eyed to the wealth of opportunities that love can offer, he puts on blinkers. Spellbound, he fixes his eyes on his unhappy experience in order not to have to see life. He wants to be secure, not receptive. He cannot recover from his one unhappy experience because he does not want to chance another.

Such a person must be re-educated; he must learn to be always ready and receptive to the multitude of opportunities that may come his way. For the probability is that in the life of the average person there will be nine unhappy love affairs to a single happy one. He must simply wait for that one, not put obstacles in its path by perversely using unhappiness as a pretext for shutting out happiness. Psychotherapeutic treatment of so-called unrequited love must therefore consist in bringing this flight tendency into the open and in demonstrating the task quality not only of life in general, but of the love life in particular.

Even love which is reciprocated is not always free of unhappiness. Among other things, there are the torments of jealousy. Jealousy is an aspect of the erotic materialism we have spoken of. At its root is the attitude toward the object of love as property. The jealous man treats the person he allegedly loves as if this person were his possession; he degrades her to a piece of property. He wants to have her 'only for himself' – thereby proving that he thinks of her in terms of 'having'. There is no room for jealousy within a real love relationship. It is ruled out by very definition, since real love presupposes a mutual feeling of the uniqueness and singularity of the partners. The rivalry so feared by the jealous lover assumes the possibility that he can be replaced by a competitor, assumes that love can be transferred to another. But that is impossible in real love, for the beloved one cannot be compared with any other person.

There is another well-known type of jealousy which is jealousy of the partner's past, of predecessors. Persons plagued by this kind of jealousy always want to have been the 'first'. There is more modesty in those who are content to be the 'last'. But in another sense this is not greater modesty; rather, it is a more demanding attitude. For such a lover, while not worried about priority with respect to all his predecessors, nevertheless regards his love as a proof of his sovereign position. All who are prey to any of these forms of jealousy overlook the fundamental fact that each human being is not comparable with any other in his innermost being. To compare yourself with anyone else is to do an injustice either to yourself or to the other person. That, incidentally, is true outside of the love life also. For everyone has a different kind of start. But the person whose start was more difficult, whose fate was less kind, can be credited with the greater personal achievement, other things being equal. Since, however, all aspects of the situation imposed by fate can never be assessed, there is simply no basis and no standard for a comparison of achievements.

Where a relationship does not reach the level of real love, where therefore a person is not loved so that his incomparability is part of the relationship, there is absolutely no place for jealousy at all. For in that case the love relationship really is not present. Jealousy is consequently foolish in every case, since it comes either too soon or too late. Either it is unjustified because the partner is committed to faithfulness, or it is well founded because the partner is actually unfaithful. In the latter case jealousy is certainly pointless, since the exclusive partnership exists no longer.

It may be added that from a tactical point of view jealousy is a dangerous emotion. The jealous person engenders the very thing he fears: the withdrawal of love. Doubting himself because of previous failures brings to the doubter more and more failures (just as confidence not only comes from inner strength but leads to still greater strength). The jealous person, doubting his ability to hold his partner, may actually lose out, may actually drive his partner into the arms of another, forcing infidelity because he has cast question on the beloved's fidelity. Thus he brings about what he believes to be true. Certainly fidelity is one of love's tasks; but it is always a task only for the lover and can never be a demand directed at the partner. Posed as a demand, it will eventually be taken as a challenge. It will drive the partner into an attitude of protest from which sooner or later infidelity may well result. Trust in another makes for self-confidence just as much as trust in oneself, so that in general this trust will prove to be justified. On the other hand, distrust makes for a lack of mutual confidence, so that in the end distrust will also prove justified.

Trust must have its counterpart, on the partner's side, in honesty. But just as trust follows a dialectical law in making true what it believes to be true, so honesty is also paradoxical: one can lie with truth and, on the other hand, tell the truth with a lie – even make something true by a lie. An example familiar to every doctor can serve to illustrate this. Suppose we take a patient's blood pressure and find it slightly high. The patient asks us to tell him the reading. But if we do, he will be so alarmed that his blood pressure will rise, will actually go higher than it already is. If, however, we do not tell the truth but give him a lower figure than the true reading, we will reassure him and his blood pressure will actually drop – so that in the end our sham lie (not white lie) will be an exact statement. Throughout life in general, and especially in the love life, fanatical adherence to truth at all costs is affected by this paradox. Consider the following example: A patient asked her doctor for advice on whether or not to confess to her husband a wholly harmless and abortive instance of infidelity. The doctor was of the opinion that she should not mention it. In the first place he knew that she wanted to confess her 'infidelity' only for neurotic reasons – that in fact she had had her little adventure only to provoke her husband, to 'test' him. In the second place, objectively (that is, on the merits of the matter and disregarding motivation and psychogenesis) the doctor thought that by telling the 'truth' the patient would only be deceiving her husband. For her confession would be misleading, in that the husband would be forced to believe that there was more behind the matter than she was willing to admit, since otherwise she would not have felt impelled to confess anything. The woman did not follow her doctor's advice, and the result was a divorce which was legally and humanly needless.

Let us turn now from the problem of suspected infidelity to that of actual unfaithfulness. We at once encounter the double standard of morality: marital infidelity by the man and by the woman are commonly judged in different terms. A woman is generally blamed much more harshly for adultery than a man. Perhaps the injustice of this double standard is only apparent. For psychologically the attitude of the sexes toward sexual life differs considerably. Allers, for example, has pointed out this difference in the formula: the man lends himself to love; the woman gives herself in love.

Finally, we must not overlook the sociological reason for the double standard. For a woman who has 'had affairs' with several men can never know for certain who the father may be if she has a child; whereas a husband who has been unfaithful to his wife, but to whom his wife has remained faithful, can be perfectly sure of the paternity of his child.

The conclusions which may be drawn from the partner's infidelity are numerous. The variety of possible attitudes toward infidelity makes it an occasion for actualizing attitudinal values. One person will avenge the hurt which has been inflicted on him by breaking up the relationship; another will forgive and make up; a third will try to conquer the partner anew, to win him back.

A materialist eroticism not only makes the partner a possession, but the sex act itself a commodity. This emerges most plainly in prostitution. As a psychological problem, prostitution is as much the affair of the prostitutes as of the 'clients'. What we have said earlier in another connection is relevant here also: that economic necessity forces a particular type of conduct upon no one. That is, necessity would not force a psychologically and morally normal woman to prostitution. On the contrary, it is amazing how frequently women resist the temptation to prostitution in spite of economic necessity. That solution for economic distress simply is out of the question for them, and their resistance seems as natural to them as soliciting seems to the typical prostitute.

53

As for the prostitute's client: he is seeking precisely the sort of impersonal and non-binding form of love life which the relationship to a commodity will give him. From the standpoint of psychological hygiene, prostitution is as dangerous as it is from the standpoint of bodily hygiene. The psychological dangers, however, are less easily guarded against. The chief peril is that it nurtures precisely the attitude toward sex which wise sex education tries to prevent. This is the attitude that takes sex to be a mere means to the end of pleasure – a thoroughly decadent sensualism. Sexuality, which should be the means of expression for love, is made subservient to the pleasure principle, and gratification of the instincts, sexual pleasure, becomes an end in itself.

Faulty upbringing is often to blame when a young person yearning for love develops into a sex-starved adult. We know of a case in which a mother sent her son to prostitutes in order to wean him from his love for a girl whom the mother considered economically and socially 'beneath' him. Turning the impulses of love into the bypath of prostitution, degrading sex to mere instinctual gratification and reducing the partner to a mere instinctual object, is likely to block the way to the right kind of love life, in which sex is no more than the expression – and no less than the crowning glory – of love. When through habituation to prostitutes a young man becomes fixated upon sexual pleasure as an end in itself, his whole future marital life may be damaged. For then when he really loves, he can no longer go back – or, rather, he can no longer go forward, can no longer attain the proper attitude of the real lover toward sex. For the lover the sexual act is the physical expression of a psychospiritual union. But when a man has been accustomed to sex not as a means of expression but as an end in itself, he divides women sharply into two classes – the class of the madonna and that of the whore – with consequent psychological difficulties. Such cases are well known in the annals of psychotherapy.

For the woman, too, there are patterns which hinder her normal development toward experiencing sex as an expression of love. And here, too, the damage done is hard to correct. In one such case a girl at first had a platonic relationship with her young man; she refused to enter into sexual relations with him because she did not feel any impulse to do so. Her partner insisted more and more, and let fall the remark: 'I guess you must be frigid.' Whereupon she began to worry that he might be right. Troubled by this fear, she decided to give herself to him – in order to prove to him and to herself that he was wrong. The result of this experiment was, inevitably, a total inability to experience pleasure. For the impulse had not yet germinated; it had not awakened and could not be aroused. Instead of waiting for it to develop gradually and spontaneously, the girl entered into this first sexual act with the desperate intent to prove her capacity for pleasure, but at the same time with the secret fear that she might turn out to be incapable of it. The very artificiality of the situation would in itself have inhibited any instinctual impulses that might have been aroused. Under such circumstances it is hardly surprising that the girl, anxiously keeping watch on herself, could not possibly be yielding and responsive. The possible effect of such a disappointment on a woman's future love life or marriage may well be psychogenic frigidity of the anticipatory-anxiety-neurosis type.

The 'mechanism' of what is termed anticipatory anxiety is all too familiar to the psychotherapist. Something goes wrong when the consciousness attempts to regulate acts which normally take place, so to speak, without thought. The stutterer is acutely conscious of the way he speaks – he concentrates on saying, not on what he wants to say; he observes the how instead of the what. And so he inhibits himself – as though his speech were a motor into which he attempts to poke his fingers when he should simply start it up and let it run of its own accord. It is often sufficient to teach the stutterer that he need only switch over, so to speak, to thinking aloud. If only he will think aloud, the mouth will talk of its own accord – the more fluently when the least observed. If he can be taught this, he is well along on the way to a cure. As will be demonstrated in the more systematic setting of a later, clinical chapter, the psychotherapy of insomnia works along analogous lines. If a person mistakenly fixes his mind upon the process of falling asleep, if he desperately wills sleep, he creates an inner tension which makes sleep impossible. Fear of sleeplessness is an anticipatory anxiety which in such cases hinders falling asleep, thus confirming the fact of insomnia, which in turn reinforces the anticipatory anxiety – a vicious circle.

A similar process takes place in all persons who have become insecure sexually. Their self-observation is sharpened and they start out with the fear of not succeeding. This anxiety itself leads to sexual failure. The sexual neurotic no longer fixes his mind upon his partner (as does the lover), but upon the sexual act as such. Consequently the act fails, must fail, because it does not take place 'simply', is not performed naturally, but is willed. In such cases the task of psychotherapy is to break the hapless vicious circle of sexual anticipatory anxiety by eliminating this fixation upon the act itself. The patient should be instructed never to let himself feel obligated to perform a sexual act. Everything which the patient might feel as a 'compulsion to sexuality' must be avoided. Such a compulsion might arise from his partner (if she is an 'impulsive', sexually demanding woman) or from his own ego (making a 'resolution' to have sexual intercourse on a certain particular day) or from a situation (accompanying others to a brothel, etc.).

When all these types of compulsion which affect the sexual neurotic adversely have been eliminated, the patient must learn spontaneity until he has achieved naturalness in his sexual practices. But even before such psychotherapy is undertaken, the effort should be made to show the patient that his original 'sick' response was quite understandable in human terms. Thus the patient can be freed of the feeling that he is suffering from a fated pathological condition. In other words, he must learn to recognize the unwholesome influence of anticipatory anxiety and the vicious circle in which he has been caught, and he must learn that his reaction is a common human failing.

A young man came to a doctor because he was worried about his virility. It seemed that after a conflict lasting for years he had finally persuaded his partner 'to be his'. She promised to give herself to him during the Whitsun holidays. This promise was made two weeks before Whitsuntide. During all those two weeks the young man could hardly sleep for tension and anticipation. Then the two set out on a week-end excursion; they were going to spend the night in an Alpine shelter hut. At night, when the patient climbed the stairs to their common room, he was so agitated – by anticipatory anxiety, not by sexual excitement – that as he later described it his heart was pounding so hard and he was trembling so violently that he could scarcely walk. How in the world could he possibly have been potent!

The doctor had to explain how impossible sexual success was in such an outer and inner situation, and how understandable the patient's reaction had been. His reaction had been normal, not pathological, behavior. The patient finally saw that his was not a case of real impotence, as he had feared (the fear creating an anticipatory-anxiety neurosis and thus becoming the starting-point for a fateful vicious circle). Understanding this was enough to restore his self-confidence. He realized that it was not the sign of a very grave sickness for a man to be unable to do two things at once: to be lovingly devoted to his partner (the prerequisite for the capacity to respond and perform sexually) and at the same time to be watching himself with anxious anticipation.

The function of such a psychotherapeutic procedure is to put to flight anticipatory anxiety when it is just getting started. The dangerous autosuggestion which comes from such anxiety is not permitted to develop, is arrested right at the start.

Again, then, in this realm of sex life, in the psychology and pathology of men's sexual behavior, we see how misguided all striving for happiness is, how the desperate attempt to achieve happiness, to achieve pleasure as such, is condemned to miscarry. We have already said in another connection that the striving for happiness is not one of man's basic drives; that, in general, life is not directed toward pleasure at all. Kant has remarked that man wants to be happy, but that what he ought to want is to be worthy of happiness. We hold, however, that man does not want to be happy. Rather, he wants to have a reason for being happy. Which is to say that all deflection of his desire from the object to the desire itself, from the aim (the reason for being happy) to the pleasure (the consequence of attaining the aim), represents a derivative mode of human striving. This derivative mode lacks immediacy. It is such lack of immediacy that characterizes all neurotic experience. We have already seen how it can lead to neurotic and especially to sexual disturbances. The immediacy and therefore the genuineness of sexual intention is the indispensable prerequisite for potency in the man. In connection with sexual pathology Oswald Schwarz has coined the word 'exemplariness' to express the genuineness of an intention. Typical of the exemplary person is that he does not easily become embarrassed; with characteristic sureness of instinct he avoids all situations which he could not cope with, keeps out of all environments into which he might not fit. Strikingly non-exemplary, on the other hand, would be the behavior of a sensitive man who visits a prostitute and then finds himself impotent. There is nothing pathological about this behavior in itself; it is not yet characteristically neurotic. Sexual failure in such a situation is rather to be expected of a cultured man. But that such a man gets himself into this kind of situation where his impotence is the only way to get out of it again – that is evidence that he is not 'exemplary'.

We have dealt so far with questions of the nature of love. We turn now to its origins. Psychosexual maturity first begins in puberty. With physiologic maturation, sex (in the narrower sense of the word) enters the human consciousness so suddenly that – in analogy to Schilder's formulation in regard to psychosis – we can speak of an 'invasion of the psyche by the organic realm'. The adolescent child is unprepared for this sudden invasion of sexuality into his psyche, and the natural reaction is often some sort of shock. The psychological troubles of adolescence which follow are therefore not pathological.

At the time sexuality makes this invasion into the adolescent personality it is not as yet anything intrinsically psychological. It ought rather to be termed a psychic reaction to a somatic event, merely a psychic consequence of an endocrine upheaval, or the psychic expression of glandular tensions. This physiologically determined sexuality is originally amorphous, has not yet been shaped by the personality. In other words, it is not yet *integrated*. Only with increasing psychosexual maturity is sexuality organized by the personality, and assimilated into the life of the individual. At the beginning sex is not yet a personal tendency; rather, it is a mere urge without aim or direction. In the course of further development and maturity this urge becomes more and more directed; there is an increase in intentionality. Sexuality is brought closer and closer to the personal center, more and more within the field of force generated by personal strivings. The first step is when the sexual urge acquires a goal: detumescence, discharge of the state of tension by 'contrectation' (A. Moll) with a partner of the other sex – any one will do. Thus the aimless sexual urge becomes the real sex instinct directed toward an instinctual aim. Later an additional directional factor enters in: the sex instinct is directed toward a definite person, a particular representative of the opposite sex: there is now a specific object. The aimless drive has first become aim-directed; then the aim-directed impulse has become person-directed. To the unspecific instinctual aim (genito-sexual in nature) has been added the specific object: the partner as a – beloved – person. Sexual urge, sexual instinct, sexual striving thus mark the phases of psychosexual maturing, each phase being characterized by increasing intentionality. Thus, in the course of the individual's maturation, sexuality grows increasingly expressive of the personality.

What is the origin of this directional factor? What furnishes the instinct with its direction toward a particular person? That cannot possibly come out of itself. The instinct, sexuality in general, acquires its intentionality from a tendency different in nature and origin (that is, not merely the result of sublimation), from an immanent erotic striving. It must be called 'immanent' because its presence can always be shown, no matter how deeply buried it is. Even in cases where it is no longer conscious, the germs of it can be discovered in the past. This striving must at the same time be termed 'erotic' because it presents a contrast to all sexual strivings. In young people, for example, it appears in the form of a longing for comradeship, tenderness, intimacy, and mutual understanding. Young people yearn for companionship in a psycho-spiritual sense – an entirely different thing from real sexual strivings. Thus the erotic striving is 'erotic' in the narrower sense of the word. It is primary, and is not derivative from sexuality.

Even a man who is apparently interested in sexual pleasure alone has at some time or other experienced those finer strivings which Freud has called aim-inhibited tendencies, but which we consider to be properly erotic tendencies and more likely to attain the goal of true satisfaction than the unqualified sex drive. At some time or other even the devotee of mere sexual gratification made higher demands upon his partner, demanded qualities of the mind as well as the body. And all such impulses and requirements come to the fore even when buried deep in the rubble of vulgar sexual debauchery. Interesting in this connection is what a night-club dancer once reported : that when she brought a drunken man home with her he would typically propose that the two of them should pretend they were happily married and the husband was just coming home from work and the wife was being sweet to him – all this absolutely in conscious contrast to sexuality, and not even intended as a prelude. Here an element that has been all but repressed breaks through. For love had been repressed, the erotic tendency thrust into the background by the sexual instinct. And even in this debased, crippled form of erotic life – the relationship between a night-club dancer and her partner – the inborn yearning for a higher type of eroticism breaks through.

The immanent erotic tendency, then, is what impels sexuality to move from the merely physical urge via the psychological impulse to the spiritual striving which emanates from the self and is directed toward the self of another. In the normal or ideal course of psycho-sexual maturation there is a gradual conversion of sexual desire into the erotic tendency, until at last sex merges with eroticism and there is a congruency of the contents of the erotic tendency with the sexual desires. A successful synthesis of sexuality and eroticism is achieved. The instinct which has acquired its goal from the erotic tendency – namely, its direction toward a particular person – then fastens itself to this person.

59

This process of maturing therefore leads by logical steps to a monogamous attitude. The sexual desire has been turned toward one single partner, as the erotic tendency dictates. The really mature person, therefore, will feel sexual desire only when he loves; he will consider a sexual relationship only where sex is the expression of love. In this sense, then, the inner capacity for a monogamous relationship is the real criterion of sexual-erotic maturity. The monogamous attitude is at once the culmination of sexual development, the goal of sex education, and the ideal of sexual ethics. As an ideal it is achieved only seldom; usually it is only approached closely. Like all ideals, this one too is only a governing principle; 'It is set up like the bull's-eye of the target, which must always be aimed at even if it is not always hit' (Goethe). Just as it is the rare person who is capable of real love, so it is the rare person who attains to the highest developmental state of the mature love life. But, after all, every human task is an 'eternal' one and human progress is endless, an advance into infinity, toward a goal located in infinity. And even then it is a matter only of each individual's progress in his own personal history. For it is questionable whether and in what sense there is true progress within humanity's history. The only kind we know for certain is technological progress, and perhaps this impresses us as an advancement only because we happen to live in a technological age.

It is easier for women than for men to realize this ideal goal of the normal process of maturation. That, of course, is true only as a generalization and under present conditions. For a woman to feel sexual desire only where the physical longing is conjoined with a desire for psycho-spiritual union is the height of normality. Every 'unspoiled' woman knows that this is how she feels. A man, on the other hand, does not attain this stage without some struggle. The woman is aided by a further factor: if she remains virginal until she has physical union with the man she finally and really loves, a monogamous relationship is henceforth easier for her, since – from the inception of sexual relations with her husband – both her eroticism and her sexuality are almost automatically centered on her partner's personality, and her sexual reactions are released almost like a conditioned reflex exclusively by him.

Normal psychosexual maturing is subject to various types of disturbances. Three different kinds of disturbed development can be distinguished, the presence of each one marking a different type of sexual neurotic.

60

The first type is represented by young people who are already well on the way to accomplishing the transformation of the formless sexual urge into a person-directed erotic tendency. They have achieved successively higher forms of eroticism and increasingly deep attitudes towards their partners until they are almost at the culminating point where sexual drive and erotic tendency merge and are directed toward a single goal: the inner personality of the beloved. At this last stage of development a setback occurs, produced perhaps by some disappointment. An unhappy love affair may so discourage a young person that he is blocked from continuing his normal development to the highest form of love life. He can no longer believe he will ever, or ever again, find someone whom he can at the same time respect as a person and desire sexually. And so he plunges into pure sexual pleasure; in sexual intoxication he tries to forget his erotic unhappiness. Quantity of sexual pleasure and instinctual gratification must take the place of quality: deeper fulfillment in the love life. Accent is shifted from eroticism to sexuality. The sex instinct suddenly demands gratification, as much of it as possible. In procuring such satisfaction for himself, the young man departs more and more from the goal of psychosexual maturation, becomes less and less capable of mastering the synthesis of eroticism and sexuality. The disappointing experience drives him down to the lower plane of mere sexuality; he reverts to an earlier stage of development. Since this type of disturbance of psychosexual maturation derives from an experience with disappointment, we call it the 'resentment type'.

The diary of a delinquent which we happen to have read reveals much about the inner workings of the 'resentment type'. While still a young boy, he was led into taking part in sex parties. At these sexual orgies he was also subjected to homosexual abuse. (Considering the essential aimlessness of the sexual urge, it is quite understandable that in this stage of psychosexual development perverse instinctual goals and instinctual objects are also accepted.) The young boy associated with the worst kind of companions, including criminals – and not sexual deviants alone – until one day he happened to meet up with a club of young people who were enthusiastic mountaineers and political idealists. Here he met a girl with whom he fell in love. Instantly his whole life changed, and especially his sex life. From the first he had no sexual aims toward this girl he loved. An abrupt shift of accent from sexuality to eroticism had taken place. In spite of his premature experiences with sex, he now took the step forward to the stage of non-sexual eroticism. One day, however, when this girl rejected him, he plunged back into his former life of crude pleasure-seeking, sexual and otherwise. His social as well as his sexual behavior retrogressed. The words he wrote in his journal ring out like a cry of despair, words imaginarily addressed to his girl: 'Do you want me to be again what I once was, to go back to my former life, sitting around in dives, drinking and whoring?'

The second type of aberrant psychosexual maturing is represented by persons who have never achieved a truly erotic attitude or relationship. People of this type restrict themselves from the start to mere sexuality. They do not even attempt to unite sexual demands with erotic (in our sense) demands; they do not try to respect or love the sexual partner. They consider it impossible to have a real love relationship; they do not expect to experience love – or be able to inspire it. Instead of undertaking the task of synthesizing sexuality and eroticism, they resign themselves. In contrast to the resentment type we will call this type the 'resignation type'. Because people of this type do not believe in the possibility of love for themselves, they do not believe in love at all. They maintain that it is an illusion. In reality, they say, all is sex; love occurs only in novels and is an unrealizable ideal.

The so-called Don Juan type belongs to this class. Simple souls are impressed by him, think of him as an erotic hero. But in reality he is a weakling who has never dared to attempt a truly fulfilling love life. For all the amount of sexual pleasure and the numbers of sexual partners he can total up, he remains inwardly empty. His world is emptier than that of the real lover and his life more unfulfilled than other lives.

The third and last type we will call the 'inactive type'. Persons of the resentment type and the resignation type never achieve more than sex; the inactive type does not even achieve that in the sense of sexual contact with a partner. While the resentment type experiences, at least initially, erotic partnership, and the resignation type at least experiences sexual partnership, the inactive type experiences no partnership at all, shunning it entirely. He is neither erotically nor sexually active. He remains in isolation, as it were, with his sex instinct, and the expression of this isolation is masturbation. That is the form that sex life takes in lonely people. Sexuality is experienced in an undirected way; the act of masturbation entirely lacks any object outside of the self, any directedness toward a partner.

Masturbation is, to be sure, neither a disease nor a cause of disease; rather, it is the sign of a disturbed development or misguided attitude toward the love life. Hypochondriacal ideas about its morbid consequences are unjustified. But the hangover which generally follows the act of masturbation has a reason, quite aside from these hypochondriacal theories. The underlying reason is that guilt feeling which comes upon one whenever one flees from active, directional experience to passive, non-directional experience. We have already named this kind of escape as the underlying motif of intoxication. It therefore seems all the more significant that masturbation – like drunkenness – is followed by a mood of hangover.

Aside from the practitioners of masturbation, the inactive class also includes all those young people who suffer from so-called sexual frustration. Sexual frustration should be understood as the expression of a more general psychological distress. It is the problem of a person who is 'alone' with his drive and therefore experiences intense frustration – but only so long as he is alone with it. Whenever the erotic element is dominant, as it is in normal development, sexuality does not build up to any dangerous extent, and the conflict between the erotic element and sexuality does not occur. Only when a displacement arises in the course of deviant development – when, for example, the above-mentioned shift in accent from eroticism back to sexuality occurs – do there arise those conflicts and psychic tensions which make up sexual frustration. The phrase is deceptive in that it sounds as if the unsatisfied sex instinct were the source of the frustration, as if frustration therefore were necessarily bound up with sexual abstinence. In reality, abstinence as such is far from equivalent to frustration. We shall have more to say on this subject later on. That is true only of maturing young people, not of adults. But insofar as a young person suffers from sexual frustration, this is an indication that his sex instinct is not yet (or is no longer) subordinated to an erotic tendency and so integrated into the total system of his personal strivings.

The shibboleth of sexual frustration is occasionally called forth for purposes of sexual propaganda. In this sense it is a misconception and vulgar misinterpretation of psychonalysis. The implication is that the ungratified sex instinct itself – rather than the repression of that instinct – must necessarily lead to neurosis. The harmfulness of sexual abstinence has been preached to youth. Such doctrines have done a good deal of injury by nourishing neurotic sexual anxiety. The slogan has been sexual intercourse at any cost, even among young people, when, on the contrary, sexuality should be permitted to mature tranquilly and to advance toward a healthy and meaningful eroticism consonant with human dignity, eroticism in which the sexual element is the expression and crown of a love relationship. This kind of eroticism must necessarily precede the commencement of sexual relations. But if the realm of mere sexuality is entered prematurely, a young person is incapable of proceeding to the synthesis of sexuality and eroticism.

Let us consider what can be done in the way of therapy for the so-called sexual frustration of youth. This question is relevant if only because a successful method of treating such sexual frustration throws light upon its psychogenesis. The therapy is of the simplest. It suffices to introduce the young person in question into a mixed company of people his age. There the young man will sooner or later fall in love – that is, he will find a partner – in the erotic and not in the sexual sense. Once this happens, his sexual frustration promptly vanishes. Such young men often admit that, for example, they have literally 'forgotten' to masturbate. Their longing to be together with the girl of their choice is quite free of sexual promptings; not in their boldest daydreams, or even in their actual dreaming about her, do they have a direct desire for sexual gratification. The moment they fall in love, crude sexuality automatically drops into the background. Eroticism moves into the foreground. There is an abrupt shift in accent from sexuality to eroticism, a sudden alternation in dominance between the sexual and erotic tendencies which are to some extent antagonistic in young people. In treating young people suffering from sexual frustration we must take note of the reciprocal relationship between sexuality and eroticism. This reciprocal relationship and the resultant diminishing and cessation of suffering from the ungratified sex instinct in spite of sexual abstinence seems to be, as far as young people are concerned, a phenomenon governed by definite laws. The broad experience of psychological counsellors who have worked with young people has confirmed the regularity of this phenomenon, as have discussions with large numbers of young people in connection with talks on sex education to youth groups. Among many thousands of young persons who have been questioned, not a single one failed to admit the effect of this shift in accent from sexuality to eroticism.

As we have suggested, the problem takes a different form with mature people. In adults sexual desires go hand in hand with the erotic tendencies, since as a result of that synthesis of sexuality with eroticism which comes with maturity, the two have become fused. Nevertheless, sexual abstinence need by no means lead to neurotic symptoms in the adult. If we do actually find neurotic symptoms in the sexually abstinent adult, we need not take these as the direct consequence of continence, but rather as co-ordinate with it. For in such cases it usually turns out that the abstinence is itself a symptom, one among others, of an underlying neurosis.

Among those young people who have been liberated from sexual frustration as a result of the accentual shift from sexuality to eroticism, the sex instinct will sooner or later come to the fore again, with the growth of maturity, and will make its claims felt. The question of sexual gratification has only been thrust into the background temporarily. But something vital has been achieved by this postponement, for the young person has been given time to mature. Now, under the dominance of the erotic tendency, he can build up an erotic relationship within the framework of which sexual relations can then be considered. A love relationship now exists for which eventual sexual intercourse may signify a means of expression – which is precisely the goal we were aiming at. But something has been accomplished even beyond that. The young man's sense of responsibility has meanwhile matured to the point where he can decide on his own and his partner's behalf whether and when he ought to enter into a serious sexual relationship with her. We can then turn this decision over to him with an easy conscience. For if such a relationship is reached, its sexuality will assume its appropriate form – that of physical expression of a spiritual content, the expression of love.

Let us then sum up the doctor's position on the problem of sexual intercourse between young people. What should he recommend in regard to continence or intercourse for the young? We find the following general guiding principles.

In the first place, from the somatic, medical point of view, neither continence nor intercourse is contraindicated – given a degree of physical maturity. In this respect the doctor ought to be entirely neutral, since he knows that neither sexual relations nor sexual abstinence can do any physical harm. But in terms of mental hygiene he ought not to be neutral; from this point of view he must take a stand. He must oppose sexual relations, must veto them if he can, whenever young people want sexual intercourse without real love. Where this is the case (and only where this is the case) he must take a negative stand. Sexual intercourse between young people who are sexually but not psychosexually mature is contraindicated.

Another point of view from which this question of sexual intercourse between young people can be evaluated (the other two being the somatic and the psychohygienic points of view) is that of sexual ethics. And from this point of view the doctor can never say yes, can never directly recommend sexual intercourse in a given case. For here is drawn the line beyond which advising cannot go. As a counsellor it is not the doctor's function to relieve of responsibility the person seeking advice; on the contrary, the doctor's task is to teach him to be responsible. The young person will have to decide himself on his own responsibility. The question of whether a young person who really loves his partner should enter into a sexual relationship cannot be answered by the doctor and counselor; it remains a personal, moral problem for the individual himself. The most the doctor can do is to point out that there is nothing to fear from abstinence – in case an individual should freely decide upon such a course for whatever reason (perhaps because he conceives it as a sacrifice necessary to his love).

Responsibility, when attained, covers not only the partner as an individual. For, particularly if a monogamous relationship is to culminate in marriage, there are social, economic, and eugenic responsibilities to be considered by the young person. As we have already seen in another connection, marriage involves a number of independent areas of existence and thus transcends the psychological field. The psychotherapist, however, is asked to deal only with the problems of the psyche; his concern can only be with the inner capacity for a monogamous relationship, and with ways of promoting this monogamous attitude. In dealing with young men, the psychiatrist must encourage them to accept all the difficulties which youth, being a period of erotic preparation, imposes upon them. The young man must have the courage to fall in love, to fall out of love, to court, to be alone, and so on. Where sexuality threatens to take precedence over eroticism and become dominant, the psychiatrist or the sex educator must raise his warning voice. A large-scale statistical psychological study of the Charlotte Bühler School has shown that serious sexual relationships of very young girls (in whom we may assume no proper erotic relationships have yet developed) led to a distinct shrinking of general interests, a limitation of the mental horizon. Within the structure of a still incomplete personality the sex instinct, holding out the promise of easy pleasure-gains and vehemently demanding gratification, swallowed up, as it were, all other concerns. As a result of this deviant development, inner preparation for the generally esteemed and culturally valuable state of marriage must naturally suffer. For the happiness and duration of marriage are guaranteed only by attainment of the ideal aim of normal development: the maturity for a monogamous relationship, which means successful synthesis and congruence of sexuality and eroticism.

Human existence as a whole is fundamentally grounded in responsibility. The counsellor, the psychiatrist, bears an additional responsibility, for he is also responsible for the patient who comes to him seeking advice. His responsibility grows even greater when he is asked to give advice in sexual matters. For this responsibility transcends the present and may well extend to the fate of a future generation.

All those concerned with adolescent sex education must bear in mind the greatness of their responsibility. In carrying out their task, they will have to hold fast to the general principles of adolescent education. The factor of trust is perhaps the most important one in such a relationship. The trust is threefold. First, there is the trust of the young people in the educator, whether he be parent or teacher, youth leader, family physician, or counselor. The adult must make every effort to win and to keep the confidence of the young people. This is especially important when it comes to instructing the young in the 'facts of life'. On this subject we will say only the following : such sex information should never be given to a group. For if that is done, the revelations will come too soon to some, and only dismay them, while for others they will come too late and only seem ridiculous. To instruct each boy or girl individually is the only sensible way. Here the young person's confidence in the educator is of supreme importance. Having that confidence, a young person troubled by a question about sex will ask the adult whom he trusts at the right time, neither too soon nor too late.

The second kind of trust which must be the aim of adolescent education is the young person's trust in himself, which will keep him from becoming discouraged on the steep road to the mature personality. The third kind of trust must be our own trust in the young person – a trust which is ideally designed to increase his self-confidence and provide a foundation for his trust in us. In trusting him (or her) we aid him in developing independence in thought and action and help him on the way to freedom and responsibility.

From *The Doctor and the Soul*

THE VIRTUE OF CHASTITY

John Macmurray

M Y task in this lecture is not to defend any recognized view of sex morality, either orthodox or unorthodox. I shall come to no definite conclusions about the questions that people are asking so insistently nowadays about marriage and divorce and free love and so on. I want to do something, if I can, much more honest and, therefore, much more valuable. I want to try to understand and try to help you a little to understand.

On such a subject this is very difficult; because it is very difficult to be honest or even to know whether you are being honest or not. Prejudice and bias, the heat of unreal emotions generated by associations of ideas, are everywhere – in ourselves. The very words we have to use are tainted and spoiled by overtones of feeling which blind us. So I must ask you to be patient with me and with yourselves; not to expect me to answer questions to which I do not know the answer, nor to undertake the defence or the destruction of positions of which I am not sure.

Our greatest need is for a deep inner sincerity that will not let us plead a case which we should like to see prevail. I shall try – I cannot promise to succeed in this – to be sincere; to say what I think, leaning on experience rather than on logical argument; and to tell you when I feel convinced, when I feel that I can only reach a balance of probabilities, and when I am guessing and groping in the dark.

I shall begin with one thing of which I feel quite sure. The problem of the relations between men and women with which we are faced in modern civilization is an urgent one and a new one. It is perhaps the most important of all the problems which this generation is called upon to face. But it is also a new problem in the history of civilization. Many people fail to see this, and it is vitally important to recognize it.

The development of civilization depends on the interplay of two factors, individual initiative and social cohesion. If the forces which maintain social cohesion manage to overcome individual initiative civilization stagnates and deteriorates. If the forces making for individual independence and initiative – for individualism, in fact – become overmastering, they disrupt social unity and produce a catastrophe. Roughly speaking, the intellect is on the side of individualism, while emotion is on the side of unity.

Now, it is roughly true that when civilization began to develop, it was through the rise of individuals standing out from the mass who showed the capacity to act and think for themselves and so to become spear-heads of initiative. That development of individuals has gone on with increasing speed and effect. But it has been until recently almost completely confined to men. We might say with very great truth that when men took to being individuals – in thinking and fighting, and inventing, and creating – women took charge of the maintenance of social unity. So the sexes were differentiated in their social functions – man towards individuality and intellect, woman towards unity and emotion. These, of course, are rough statements, but sufficiently correct for their purpose.

It is this specialization of the sexes which has governed the social organization of marriage and the family, and so determined our sex-morality. When people say that 'woman's place is the home', this is, in fact, what they mean. To allow men to specialize, assert their individual initiative, and stand on their achievements as individuals, women must guard the inner springs of personal unity and love. Of all the great thinkers of Europe until nearly our own time, Plato was the only one who dared to challenge that differentiation of the sexes with a full knowledge of what it might mean – the extinction of the family as the focus of social unity.

In our own day, however, it has been challenged with increasing success, not in theory but practically. Women have increasingly insisted that they too are individuals, and must be permitted to stand upon their own achievement; to realize their own capacities as individuals; to exercise their own initiative in the development of civilization. They have entered the world of literature and art, of politics, of the professions, of industry and commerce. And this is, I think, bound to continue and increase. We cannot do other than look upon it as a momentous advance in culture and civilization; and to be afraid of it is surely to fail in faith and courage. But it means in principle the disappearance of a differentiation of function which has governed the relation of the sexes from the dawn of history. No longer can we look to women to guard the delicate spiritual attitudes which maintain the unity of persons in the face of the differentiating forces of individualism – of private self-realization. No longer can men specialize in the intellectual life while women specialize in the emotional. The social unity – which is necessarily a matter of emotion – must be maintained, if we are not to perish, but it can no longer be maintained through the differentiation of the social functions of the sexes. Women, if they are to develop their intellectual initiative will necessarily demand the right to stand side by side with men as equal, independent individuals. That is the crisis we are facing. That is why I insist that *our* problem of sex-morality is a new one in the history of civilization, and not to be solved by any insistence on traditional forms of social organization.

There is, however, one assumption which I make, and cannot help making. It is that in trying to find a clue to the reconstruction of social relations between men and women under the new circumstances we must approach it as members of a Christian tradition. To abandon Christianity would be to turn out the light before beginning our search. Do not imagine, however, that this means that we must declare ourselves upholders of so-called 'Christian views'. I am strongly of opinion that most of our so-called 'Christian' morality, particularly in the field of sex, has little fundamental relationship to the outlook and spirit of the founder of Christianity. Let me try and explain what I mean. The orthodox European morality – usually called Christian – is intellectual and, therefore, external. It is a matter of rule or principle applied to the organization of life. Take first its externality. When we say that a man and woman are 'living in sin' or have 'immoral relations', what do we mean? We mean simply that they are living together without being married. Now, marriage is a social institution, that is to say, a generally recognized arrangement involving a contract between two people. It is constituted by a promise made before witnesses that they will confine their sexual relationships to one another. The making of that contract confers upon them the right to have sexual intercourse, and makes such intercourse not immoral. Now, to use the existence of such a contract as a test of morality is to use an external standard. That is all we are concerned with at the moment. On such a ground the virtue of chastity consists in refraining from all sexual experience except within the institution of marriage. To say that sex-relationships are moral *because* a man and woman are married, immoral *because* they are not married, is to base morality upon something external.

But, you will say, there is much more in it than this. Undoubtedly there is. But before we go deeper let me remind you of the enormous extent to which we do use this external test, and nothing more, in our moral judgments, and of the strength of the feelings which

70

are aroused and calmed by merely applying the external test. What, then, does lie behind? A moral principle. It is a matter of moral principle for us that the sex-life should be confined within marriage, and within monogamous marriage. That is, I think, the proper way to put it, instead of saying that our principle is one of sexual fidelity. Because if a man and woman lived together in perfect fidelity without being married, the European tradition and conscience would still insist that they were guilty of immorality, though when pressed we might have difficulty in justifying our feeling on moral grounds. I cannot help feeling that though when we reflect and try to justify our judgments to ourselves on grounds of principle, we feel bound to go deeper than marriage as an institution, yet in the main it is the external fact – married or not married – that controls our practical judgments and our practical conduct.

Let us grant the principle, then, without further enquiry. Now, any principle is an intellectual thing. It is a universal judgment upon which we base our conduct. It is a rule defining how we ought to behave; and we apply it in particular cases to approve or forbid particular actions. A morality based on principle, therefore, is a morality based on thought, on judgment, on laws governing conduct and determining intellectually what is right and what is wrong. Such a morality is based on *will*; and I want to draw your attention to the idea of *will* and its implications. The idea of will originated with the Stoics. It turns upon the idea of a struggle between reason and the passions. For the Stoics passion, impulse, desire – the emotions in the widest sense – were the source of evil. To live rightly was to dominate the emotional life by reason, and so to act by will; that is to say, in the way that you have rationally decided to act, whether you want to or not. Now that opposition between will and impulse has gone deeply into our European moral tradition. Stoicism was the dominating philosophy of Rome. It made Roman law. And the Roman tradition, which is by far the strongest element in European civilization, is a Stoic tradition. It lies at the root of our moral conscience, particularly as regards sex. The mediaeval idea of chastity, which went so far as to identify chastity with complete lifelong sexual abstinence, is pure Stoicism. Sexual desire is held to be in itself evil; and 'virtue' consists in dominating and suppressing it on principle, by force of will, in a lifelong struggle. We have given that up in its extreme form, though I think there is far more of it in our attitude to sex still than we dare or care to acknowledge. But we still retain the main idea – that morality means the control of desire by reason; suppression of inclination in favour of purpose, i.e. of action willed

71

in accordance with rational decisions. This yields us the idea of duty – the distinction between what we ought to do and what we want to do. Indeed, Kant – the greatest of our European moralists – rested his whole moral theory upon the clear-cut distinction between acting from inclination and acting from duty; and identified will, which is the source of dutiful action, with practical reason.

I need not argue this further. I think you will agree with me that what we call 'Christian' morality, at least in the field of sex, does mean the control of emotion by principle, signifies the capacity to say 'no', on grounds of rational principle, to desire and emotion, and so depends upon will for the suppression of emotion as the source of action. For 'Christian' morality, in sex, the right thing to do is to bring our emotions and desires under the control of principle and harness them to the service of universal purposes. Intellect, that is to say, not emotion, is the governing source of good conduct, particularly in regard to sex. That is what is ultimately meant by saying that morality is a matter of principle.

I hope that this has made clear what I meant when I said that the orthodox European tradition of sex-morality, what we refer to as 'Christian' morality, is essentially external and intellectual. It is external *because* it is intellectual, for the intellect is essentially external, objective, outward looking, dealing with external situations and the external world, and so *organizing* life in terms of external situations. But that point I have no time to elaborate. Rather let me call your attention at once to the fact that what Jesus did was to substitute an inner and emotional basis of behaviour for an external and intellectual one. It was the externality of the Pharisee morality which he condemned. And his basis for morality was not rules, principles or laws, but love. And love is emotional, not intellectual. We are driven to the conclusion that our so-called 'Christian' morality is not Christian at all in the true sense, but Stoic, and that this is particularly true in our morality of sex. The true Christian morality will be quite different from our orthodox one in its basis and in its outlook. It will be emotional and in terms of love; not intellectual and in terms of purposes and principles.

Now, of course, our orthodox sex-morality does relate love and marriage very closely, and we do insist that love is the only proper basis for marriage. In that case are we not being unfair to the orthodox position? On the whole I think we are not, because I think that on the whole this common insistence on love is neither very effective nor very sincere. In fact it is largely sentimentalism. I must give you some of my reasons for thinking so.

In the first place, the love that is looked for is neither considered in itself moral or immoral, but a passion; something that happens or does not happen between two people; an instinctive and violent attraction. It is not considered the real basis of morality. It may be beautiful, natural, a source of joy and delight, the loveliest and most exciting experience of human life – but not either right or wrong in itself. It is rather regarded as a potent source of happiness or unhappiness, of morality or immorality. Everything depends on whether or not it can be controlled and directed along the lines of a social purpose, used to establish and strengthen the social institution of marriage.

The nineteenth century idolized and deified sexual love, and at the same time feared and dreaded it. The Victorian age was the age of Romance in which no praises were too fulsome or sickly sweet for the experience of physical passion. Yet when we now talk of Victorianism, what is uppermost in our minds? Prudery, Mrs Grundy, and the suppression of frankness about sex. The romantic views about love were fanatically prevented from being brought to the test of fact. Now, that is the essence of sentimentality. It is emotional insincerity. And to this day, though with less and less effect among young people, romantic sentimentality has held the field. The real morality of the nineteenth century was the morality of principle, but it was poisoned by sentimentality so that it appeared a Social Utility. And we are suffering under the curse that it laid upon our fathers. Love was, in effect, made a talking horse for social success, in all its multiform varieties; unconsciously, no doubt, but none the less effectively.

It worked like this. We kept young men and women in careful ignorance of the facts of sex. We instilled a sense of shame about them to this end and at the same time filled their minds with vague colourful ideas and emotions – romance. We kept a close guard over the meeting of boys and girls by a policy of segregation. When the time was ripe, we engineered a meeting of selected couples under conditions which would be likely to lead to a 'match', and made sure that nothing could come of it until they were safely married. Then with a sigh of relief we sent them off on a 'honeymoon' to discover the real facts for themselves. I do not believe that history can show an example of more barbarous duplicity and trickery than this. We are still too close to it to feel the grossness and vulgarity of deceit of which it is constituted. To talk of that sentimentality as a belief in love as the basis of morality is nonsense.

I have spent too long in sketching a background. Let me come straight away now to the one really positive thing I have to say about sex-morality. Its true basis is the virtue of chastity. And I want to explain what I think chastity really is. That I can make it very exact and clear I am not sure; but perhaps I can put you on the track of something that is absolutely vital. In a word, then, chastity is emotional sincerity.

We know pretty well what we mean by honesty, or *intellectual* sincerity. You will remember that I insisted earlier that the moral standard of Europe was an intellectual one. On the intellectual side our moral development has made us very sensitive to the intellectual virtues – the virtues of the mind. Telling the truth – the honesty of the mind – is I think the virtue to which we are most sensitive. We hate and despise the liar, and we recognize his duplicity easily. We feel in our bones that lying is shameful, despicable and immoral. What, then, is lying? It is expressing what you do not think, pretending to believe what you do not believe. That is what I mean by intellectual insincerity, the dishonesty of the mind. By emotional insincerity I mean the parallel of this in the emotional life. We are emotionally insincere when we express a feeling that we do not feel. If honesty is expressing what you think, chastity is expressing what you feel.

Let us go into the parallel a little more closely. Negative untruthfulness is simply expressing what you do not think; that is lying. But sincerity in the mind is much more than this. It is positively expressing what you do think and believe. To refrain from expressing what you think or believe or know to someone, if it is to his advantage or to someone else's advantage that he should know it, is positive dishonesty. We call it dissimulation – the suppression of the truth. In the same way, there is a positive and a negative insincerity of the emotions. The negative insincerity is to express a feeling that you do not feel. The positive is to fail to express what you do feel when it makes a real difference to the person from whom you conceal it. It is, then, a failure in chastity to express a feeling to someone that you do not feel; to express love for a person, for instance, when you do not feel it. It is equally unchaste to conceal your feelings from someone to whom it makes a real difference.

Now, of course, it is difficult to be sincere – much more difficult than we usually imagine. But the point I wish to draw your attention to is this: that though we are sensitive to the moral need for intellectual sincerity, we are very insensitive to the need for emotional sincerity. We may excuse mental insincerity under certain circumstances, but we never, I think, would praise it as a virtue. Yet we constantly inculcate emotional insincerity as a duty, and praise people for concealing their real feelings, or pretending to feelings that they do not possess. We pretend to like the things that we are told we ought to like; we pretend that we feel sympathy for a person in distress, when we do not, and we not only see no harm in this, but we positively encourage it as a social virtue. In reality emotional sincerity is far more important than the sincerity of the mind, because it lies nearer to the heart of life and conduct. It is vicious to pretend about our feelings. It is something of which we ought to feel ashamed.

One other point we must notice. We know that a man who habitually trifles with the truth tends to lose the capacity to distinguish between truth and falsehood. It is dangerously easy to deceive ourselves about what we believe. If we keep repeating a story that is not true we come to believe in its truth ourselves. Now this holds good with even greater force in the emotional life. If we habitually cheat others about our feelings, we soon become unable to know what we really feel. If we act as though we love a person when we do not, we will come to believe that we do love him. If there is any truth about life that experience and modern psychology have together driven home to me it is this – that any pretence about our feelings results in self-deception. We become incapable of knowing what we really feel. I have heard Christian moralists say that the way to learn to love people whom you dislike is to behave to them as if you loved them. This, I am certain, is completely and dangerously false. Emotional pretence leads to emotional insensibility. If you express systematically to anyone, in word or action, a love which you do not feel, you will undoubtedly come to believe that you love him. But you will hate him without knowing it. That is what the psycho-analyst discovers. To tamper with the sincerity of your emotional life is to destroy your inner integrity, to become unreal for yourself and others, to lose the capacity of knowing what you feel. There is nothing more destructive of all that is valuable in human life. I am certain of this; not on theoretical grounds but because I discovered it in my own experience.

Now let us go a step further. What is called Christian morality today is based upon a Stoic tradition; upon intellect and will, upon the suppression of the emotional basis of conduct in the interest of 'principles'. The result of that is inevitable. Though Europe has developed itself intellectually with a steady growth upwards, has progressed in its grasp of principle, in scholarship and understanding, in the organization and control of life and of the world, it has remained all but completely barbarous on the emotional side. Our civilization, for all its scientific and administrative capacity, has remained emotionally vulgar and primitive, unchaste in the extreme. We do not recognize this, of course, because it is simply the reflection of our own inner insensibility. That insensibility is the inevitable result of a morality based upon will and reason, imposing itself upon the emotions and so destroying their integrity. Until we insist upon emotional sincerity, until we cease playing ducks and drakes with our feelings in the mistaken desire to dragoon them into conformity with what we conceive to be our 'duties', until we begin to trust our emotional life, this state of affairs will necessarily go on. Our sex-morality, in particular, will remain blind, barbarous and unreal, a vulgarity and a scandal.

Chastity, then, is emotional sincerity – sincerity in the expression of what we feel; and it is the fundamental virtue, from one point of view, of a Christian morality. It is the emotional guide to good conduct, the proper determinant of personal relations. It is the condition of personal integrity. I am obviously using the word 'chastity' in a wider sense than is usual. I think myself that this is the proper use of the word – that it explains what an artist means when he says that a picture is chaste – that there is no striving after effect, and so no vamping of emotion; that it explains what Jesus meant when he said 'Blessed are the pure in heart for they shall see God'. I can think of no other word which will express what I feel about the majority of cinema films and of modern novels. They are unchaste; they arouse feelings that one doesn't really feel, by pretending emotions that the author doesn't feel. The use of the term in reference to sex is merely a special case, I think, like the similar restriction of the term 'morality' to mean sexual morality. But we shall not argue about words, especially as our main theme is the application of this guiding rule of emotional sincerity to the relations of men and women.

Let us return to the new phenomenon of modern society, the disappearance of the differentiation of the social functions of the sexes. Women are demanding that they should be individuals in the same sense that men are, that they should be independent, granted the same free initiative that men have in the choice of a vocation; in a word, that their social functions and duties should not be determined by their sex. This is a demand that in social relationships and activities sex should not count as a determining factor. Is that a right demand? Undoubtedly. It is, firstly, just as much a consequence of the teaching of Christ as that slavery is wrong. 'In Christ Jesus there is neither male nor female . . . neither bond nor free.' The gospel cannot admit functional distinctions as a basis of moral distinctions. The morality of the relations between men and women has nothing to do with the differences of sex, which belong to the physical and organic, not to the personal plane. The proper relations between human beings are personal relations, in which organic differences have no essential standing. Differences of sex is on the same level as differences of natural capacity. Therefore, men and women must meet and enter into relationships on the personal level – not as male and female, but as human beings, equally made in the image of God. They must determine their relations to one another for themselves, as human persons, and not allow organic differences to determine their relations for them. There is only one proper ground of relationship between any two human beings, and that is mutual friendship. Difference of sex may make the friendship easier or more difficult of achievement, but it cannot make any difference in principle.

Further, if difference of sex is made an essential difference in human relations, then men and women are treated as complementary to one another. Each, then, has meaning and significance only in terms of the other. Neither is a real individual. Now this is a denial of human personality. It destroys the possibility of true friendship between them. Complete individual integrity is the condition of personal relationship. Otherwise you inevitably subordinate persons to their function. Moral relations are dependent on the absolute value of the human being, as a free human spirit, not as a man or a woman. It was this, I imagine, that Paul was feeling after when he advised Christians not to marry if they could help it, because, 'the husband will care for the things of this world, how he may please his wife'. If the relation is an organic one that is inevitable. And when you begin to live to please people, you destroy emotional sincerity. Love is ruled out because chastity is ruled out. Inner integrity is impossible. This is the recurrent tragedy of so many marriages that start with fair promise. The husband and wife are specialized in different directions, and the further each develops in his or her own function the wider the gulf between them becomes. They come to depend upon one another, and so lose their integrity – the very basis of personal unity. Dependence and freedom are incompatible. Yet freedom is the basis of all moral conduct.

Let me put this in another way because I feel that it is all-important. A mutual sexual attraction is no proper basis for a human relationship between a man and a woman. It is an organic thing, not personal. What, then, is a proper basis? Love is, between any

77

two persons. Love may or may not include sexual attraction. It may express itself in sexual desire. But sexual desire is not love. Desire is quite compatible with personal hatred, or contempt, or indifference, because it treats its object not as a person but as a means to its own satisfaction. That is the truth in the statement that doing what we want to do is not the same as doing what we ought to do.

But notice this – that mutual desire does not make things any better. It only means that each of two persons is treating the other as a means of self-satisfaction. A man and a woman may want one another passionately without either loving the other. This is true not merely of sexual desire but of all desires. A man and a woman may want one another for all sorts of reasons, not necessarily sexual, and make that mutual want the basis of marriage, without either loving the other. And, I insist, such mutual desire, whether sexual or not, is no basis of a human relationship between them. It is no basis of friendship. It is the desire to obtain possession of another person for the satisfaction of their own needs; to dare to assert the claim of another human being – 'You are mine!' That is unchaste and immoral, a definite inroad upon the integrity of a fellow human being. And the fact that the desire and the claim are mutual does not make a pennyworth of difference. Mutual love is the only basis of a human relationship; and bargains and claims and promises are attempts to substitute something else; and they introduce falsity and unchastity into the relationship. No human being can have rights in another, and no human being can grant to another rights in himself or herself. That is one of the things of which I am deeply convinced.

Now take another point. There is only one safeguard against self-deception in the face of desire, and that is emotional sincerity, or chastity. No intellectual principle, no general rule of judgment is of any use. How can a man or woman know whether they love another person or merely want them? Only by the integrity of his or her emotional life. If they have habitually been insincere in the expression of their feelings, they will be unable to tell. They will think they love when they only want another person for themselves. What is usually known as 'being in love' is simply being in this condition. It blinds us to the reality of other people; leads us to pretend about their virtues, beauties, capacities, and so forth; deprives us of the power of honest feeling and wraps us in a fog of unreality. That is no condition for any human being to be in. If you love a person you love him or her in their stark reality, and refuse to shut your eyes to their defects and errors. For to do that is to shut your eyes to their needs.

Chastity, or emotional sincerity, is an emotional grasp of reality. 'Falling in love' and 'being in love' are inventions of romantic sentimentality, the inevitable result of the deceit and pretence and suppression from which we suffer. Love cannot abide deceit, or pretence or unreality. It rests only in the reality of the loved one, demands the integrity of its object, demands that the loved one should be himself, so that it may love him for himself.

This indicates the true basis for *any* intimate personal relationship and applies universally between persons, whether they are of the same or of different sexes. What then of the morality of sexual intercourse? It falls, in the first place, within the wider morality of personal relationship of which we have been speaking, and is governed by it. Any intimate human relationship must be based upon love and governed by that emotional sincerity which is the essence of chastity. Real personal love is the basis in the absence of which specifically sexual relations are unchaste and immoral. This holds inside marriage just as much as outside it. The fact of marriage cannot make chaste what is in itself unchaste. I would hazard the guess, without much fear that I was wrong, that there is as much sexual immorality inside marriage as outside it. Morality does not rest on externals.

In the second place, between two human beings who love one another, the sexual relationship is one of the possible expressions of love, as it is one of the possible co-operations in love – more intimate, more fundamental, more fraught with consequences inner and outer, but essentially one of the expressions of love, not fundamentally different in principle from any others, as regards its use. It is neither something high and holy, something to venerate and be proud of, nor is it something low and contemptible, to be ashamed of. It is a simple ordinary organic function to be used like all the others, for the expression of personality in the service of love. This is very important. If you make it a thing apart, to be kept separate from the ordinary functions of life, to be mentioned only in whispers; if you exalt it romantically or debase it with feelings of contempt (and if you do the one you will find that you are doing the other at the same time; just as to set women on a pedestal is to assert their inferiority and so insult their humanity); if you single out sex in that way as something very special and wonderful and terrible, you merely exasperate it and make it uncontrollable. That is what our society has done. It has produced in us a chronic condition of quite unnatural exasperation. There is a vast organization in our civilization for the stimulation of sex – clothes, pictures, plays, books, advertisements and so on. They keep up in us a state of sexual hyper-sensitiveness, as a result of which we greatly overestimate the strength and violence of natural sexuality. And the most powerful stimulant of sex is the effort to suppress it. There is only one cure, to take it up, simply, frankly and naturally into the circle of our activities; and only chastity, the ordinary sincerity of the emotional life, can enable us to do so.

Sex, then, must fall within the life of personality, and be an expression of love. For unlike all our other organic functions it is essentially mutual. If it is to be chaste, therefore, it must fall within a real unity of two persons – within essential friendship. And it must be a necessary part of that unity. The ideal of chastity is a very high and difficult one, demanding an emotional unity between a man and a woman which transcends egoism and selfish desire. In such a unity sex ceases to be an appetite – a want to be satisfied – and becomes a means of communion, simple and natural. Mutual self-satisfaction is incompatible with chastity, which demands the expression of a personal unity already secured. Indeed, it seems to me, that it is only when such a unity in friendship has reached a point where it is shut up to that expression of itself that it is completely chaste. How can two people know that their love demands such an expression? Only through a mutual chastity, a complete emotional sincerity between them. That alone can be the touchstone of reality. Only that can save us from self-deception where strong feelings are engaged, and preserve our emotions unsullied by organic excitement, free for their personal function, to grasp the realities of value in persons and in the world outside us. That is the crux of personal relation always. In sex it is only more difficult to maintain. Sex-love, if it is love at all, is a personal communion in which a man and a woman meet in the full integrity of their personal reality. And the law of reality in the relationship of persons is this. 'The integrity of persons is inviolable. You shall not use a person for your own ends, or indeed for any ends, individual or social. To use another person is to violate his personality by making an object of him; and in violating the integrity of another you violate your own.' In all enjoyment there is a choice between enjoying the other and enjoying yourself through the instrumentality of the other. The first is the enjoyment of love, the second is the enjoyment of lust. When people enjoy themselves through each other, that is merely mutual lust. They do not meet as persons at all; their reality is lost. They meet as ghosts of themselves and their pleasure is a ghostly pleasure that cannot begin to satisfy a human soul, and which only vitiates its capacity for reality.

Does the distinction between enjoying yourself in your friends' company and enjoying your friends seem a too subtle philosopher's distinction? I assure you, from experience of friendship – not from study of logic – that the distinction is the root of the difference between morality and immorality, between love and lust. It is a distinction not to be argued, but to be felt; and chastity is the capacity to feel it and to live by it. For it is the distinction between reality and unreality in the emotional life, which controls the springs of conduct, and chastity is the sincerity of the emotions.

That is the positive thing I have to say. I have no doubt that it leaves you perplexed and puzzled. It seems to have no definite bearing upon practical problems. You want to ask me: 'Will it preserve the sanctity of marriage?' So far as marriage has a sanctity it will preserve it; so far as it has not it will destroy it. This may look like dodging the issue, but I cannot help it. If you ask me 'Will chastity prevent men and women from having sexual intercourse outside marriage?' I can only answer 'I don't know.' 'But that is surely the really important point,' you may urge. I answer: 'It is *not* the important point. Compared with the importance of personal reality, of chastity, it is a point of no significance.' There could only be one reason for wanting to answer it, the desire to substitute a social rule for spiritual chastity. We want to be able to approve and condemn other people by the externals of their conduct, and to approve and condemn ourselves by the conformity of our actions to a rule. To that Christ answers: 'Judge not, that ye be not judged.' You say, perhaps, that it is a very dangerous position; there is no security in it. Since when has the truth become the line of least resistance, an insurance against danger and insecurity and the need of faith and courage? The danger is merely the danger of life, and there is only one way of escape from that danger, and that is to die. There is a spiritual death; and it is possible to commit spiritual suicide from fear of the terrors of spiritual reality. That is the only *real* danger. If you wish for 'security' you can have it at the price of spiritual death. You can fence in your soul with bulwarks of rules and forms, trenches of prohibitions and exhortations, to protect it from the inroads of the armies of the spirit. You can refuse to traffic with men and women in the sterling gold of your own precious life. Like the man in the parable, you may wrap up your capital in a clean handkerchief and bury it, for fear of the risks of trading with it in a world where even banks go bankrupt. You may hope so to render it up at last and say: 'I have kept it safe; see how clean my soul is, unspotted from the earth.' And the judge will say: 'Take it from him, and cast him into outer darkness.' If you choose security you will have your reward: you may gain the whole world. You may escape all the dangers of reality. All but one! In the long run – and for those of us who are fortunate, it comes before the hour of death – a voice will say: 'Thou fool! This day thy soul shall be required of thee. Then whose will these things be? For what shall it profit a man if he shall gain the whole world and lose his own soul?'

From *Reason and Emotion*

PSYCHOLOGICAL ASPECTS OF
THE MIS-USE OF SEXUALITY

Sexual love can be the gateway to values and meaning. By contrast, the subjugation of sex to the 'bondage of the human will' is tending, in our time, to depersonalize sex, and to reduce it to a meaningless function. Men and women, in this, become mere bearers of sensation, objectified, and made into something like machines. These processes are found in 'sexology' and its effects, in voyeurism as a manifestation of the disordered consciousness, and in pornography – which tends towards subversion, and rage, and is inherently fascistic.

A fundamental problem in our thinking here is explored by Erwin Straus – whether shame is an inhibitory manifestation, of which we should rid ourselves, or whether it is a device that protects creative love. Dr Farber sees deep dangers in our sexual knowledgeableness.

SEX IN BONDAGE TO THE MODERN WILL: 'I'M SORRY DEAR'

Leslie H. Farber

And the eyes of them both were opened, and they knew that they were naked; and they sewed fig leaves together, and made themselves aprons.

— Genesis

Lust is more abstract than logic; it seeks (hope triumphing over experience) for some purely sexual, hence purely imaginary, conjunction of an impossible maleness with an impossible femaleness.

— C. S. Lewis[1]

THE modern dialogue that furnishes me my title is practiced throughout the Western world. As a theme with only a limited number of variations, it cannot sustain much repetition: familiarity breeds silence; although never really abandoned, the script quickly becomes implicit. When reduced to a dumb show – or perhaps no more than a monosyllabic token – it still remains faithful to its pathetic premise. However, for the purposes of introduction, I shall try to represent its essence in a wholly explicit manner. The man speaks first.

'Did you?'
'Did you? You did, didn't you.'
'Yes, I'm afraid I – Oh, I'm sorry! I am sorry. I know how it makes you feel!'
'Oh, don't worry about it. I'm sure I'll quiet down after a while.'
'I'm so sorry, dearest. Let me help you.'
'I'd rather you didn't.'
'But, I ...'
'What good is it when you're just – when you don't really want to? You know perfectly well, if you don't really want to, it doesn't work.'
'But I do really want to! I want to! Believe me. It will work, you'll see. Only let me!'
'Please, couldn't we just forget it? For now the thing is done, finished. Besides, it's not really that important. My tension always wears off eventually. And anyhow – maybe next time it'll be different.'
'Oh, it will, I know it will. Next time I won't be so tired or so eager. I'll make sure of that. Next time it's going to be fine! ... But about tonight – I'm sorry, dear.'

Unhappily, no end to talking and trying for our pathetic lovers. To deaden self-consciousness, they may turn to alcohol or sedatives, seeking the animal indifference that is unencumbered with hesitations, reservations, and grievances – in short, all those human tangles that create the sexual abyss they will themselves to bridge. To delay his moment, to quicken hers, they may try to assist the chemicals by thinking of other matters – football games and cocktail parties – in order finally to arrive at that mutual consummation that, hopefully, will prove their sufficiency unto each other, if not their love. All the strategies and prescriptions of sexology that have often failed them in the past are not cast aside, but stubbornly returned to, if only because in such an impasse there is nothing else. Instead of alcohol or drugs or irrelevant reveries they may – in solitude or mutuality – resort to sex itself as their sedative, intending in the first try to spend their energies just enough to dull self-consciousness and thicken passion to the 'spontaneity' necessary for their second and final attempt. Although normally truthful people, our lovers are continually tempted by deception and simulation: he may try to con-

84

ceal his moment, she to simulate hers – as they stalk their equalitarian ideal. It can happen that they will achieve simultaneity by means of one or several or none of these devices. But their success – in the midst of their congratulations – will be as dispiriting as their failures. For one thing, the joy the lovers sought in this manner will be either absent or too fictitious to be believed. Furthermore, once the moment has subsided they must reckon with the extraordinary efforts that brought it about – efforts that appear too extraordinary for ordinary day-to-day existence. Thus does it happen that success may bring as much as, or more, pathos than failure. And, always lying between them will be the premise borrowed from romanticism : if they *really* loved each other, it would work. Small wonder, then, as self-pity and bitterness accumulate, that their musings – if not their actions – turn to adultery : a heightened situation that promises freedom from the impingements of ordinary sexual life. Or, pushed gradually past heightening, past hope, they may even come to abstinence, which can seem – with some irony – the least dishonourable course.

My conviction is that over the last fifty years sex has, for the most part, lost its viability as a human experence. I do not mean that there is any danger it will cease to be practiced – that it will be put aside like other Victorian bric-a-brac. The hunger will remain, perhaps even increase, and human beings will continue to couple with as much fervor as they can provoke, while the human possibilities of sex will grow ever more elusive. Such couplings will be poultices after the fact : they will further extend the degradation of sex that has resulted from its ever-increasing bondage to the modern will. To those first pioneers at the turn of the century – sexologists, psychoanalysts, political champions of woman's suffrage – 'sexual emancipation' seemed a stirring and optimistic cause. Who could have imagined then, as the battle was just beginning, how ironic victory would be : sex was emancipated, true, but emancipated from all of life – except the will – and subsequently exalted as the measure of existence.

At this point I think it only fair that I commit myself, even if briefly, on how sex was, is, or could be a viable human experience. My view is not that of St Augustine – that man, by reason of the Fall, is necessarily subject to the lust of concupiscence. Nor can I subscribe, at the other extreme, to the position of the Church of England, as reported at the Lambeth Conference in 1958 : 'The new freedom of sexuality in our time is . . . a gate to a new depth and joy in personal relationship between husband and wife.'² Of the erotic life, Martin Buber has remarked that in no other realm are dialogue and monologue so mingled and opposed. I would agree that any attempt to offer a normative description would have to include precisely such mingling and opposition. Even if we place it optimally within an ongoing domestic world of affection, in which sex bears some relation, however slight, to procreation, our task is still the difficult one of maintaining that sex is both utterly important and utterly trivial. Sex may be a hallowing and renewing experience, but more often it will be distracting, coercive, playful, frivolous, discouraging, dutiful, and even boring. On the one hand, it tempts man to omnipotence, while on the other, it roughly reminds him of his mortality. Over and over again it mocks rationality, only to be mocked, in turn, at the very instant it insists its domain is solely within the senses. Though it promises the suspension of time, no other event so sharply advises us of the oppressiveness of time. Sex offers itself as an alternative world, but when the act is over and the immodesty of this offering is exposed, it is the sheer worldliness of the world we briefly relinquished and must now re-enter that has to be confronted anew. Residing no longer in the same room that first enclosed us, we now lie in another room with another topography – a room whose surfaces, textures, corners, and knobs have an otherness as absolute and formidable as the duties and promises that nag us with their temporal claims. What began as relief from worldly concern, ends by returning us to the world with a metaphysical, if unsettling, clarity.

Though sex often seems to be morality's adversary, it more often brings sharply in its wake moral discriminations that previously had not been possible. Because the pleasure of sex is always vulnerable to a split into *pleasuring* and *being pleasured*, the nature of pleasure itself, as well as the relation between pleasure and power, are called into question. If pleasuring is the overpowering concern, intimations of the actual and immediate experience of slavery or peonage will appear. On the other hand, if being pleasured is the most compelling, tyranny and oppression will invade experience with some urgency. And, finally, should the lovers will equality between these two concerns in their effort to heal the split, they will personally suffer the problematic character of democratic forms. To some extent, our political past influences our sexual negotiations, but in equal measure sexual pleasure itself is a source of political practice and theory.

The list of oppositions and minglings could easily be extended, but such an extension would not change the fact that human sex inevitably partakes of human experience, for better or for worse, and through its claim on the body simultaneously asserts its particular difference, for better or for worse.

Its particular difference from everything else in this life lies in the possibility which sex offers man for regaining *his own* body through knowing the body of his loved one. Should he fail that *knowing* and *being known*, should he lapse into all those ways of *knowing about* which he has proudly learned to confuse with knowing – both bodies will again escape him. Increasingly, as D. H. Lawrence understood, man has become separated from his body, which he yearns to inhabit, such yearning understandably bringing sentimental and scientific prescriptions for the reunion eluding him. Yet, it is through the brief reconciliation with his own and his loved one's body that he can now grasp – and endure – the bodily estrangement which has always been his lot, without succumbing to the blandishments that would betray the realities of both sides of this duality.

In order to develop more concretely my conviction that sex for the most part has lost its viability as a human experience, I wish to consider the Sex Research Project, directed by Dr William H. Masters at the Washington University School of Medicine. Through the use of women volunteers, Dr Masters is endeavoring 'to separate a few basic anatomic and physiologic truths' about 'the human female's response' to what he calls 'effective sexual stimulation'. The subject, he believes, has been hopelessly beclouded by 'literary fiction and fantasy', 'pseudoscientific essays and pronouncements', and 'an unbelievable hodgepodge of conjecture and falsehood'. His debt to Kinsey is clear, though qualified. He acknowledges his 'complete awe' for Kinsey's 'time-consuming efforts', which have made his own research not only 'plausible, but possible'. On the other hand, he finds that the work of his predecessors, including Kinsey, has unfortunately been 'the result of individual introspection, expressed personal opinion, or of limited clinical observation' – rather than 'a basic science approach to the sexual response cycle'.[3] Therefore, he has done what was indeed inevitable: he has moved the whole investigation into the laboratory.

I should make clear that Dr Masters' project itself interests me far more than his exact findings. This project strikes me as one of those occasional yet remarkable enterprises that quite transcends, despite its creator's intentions, its original and modest scientific boundaries, so that it becomes a vivid allegory of our present dilemma, containing

87

its own image of man – at the same time that it charts a New Jerusalem for our future. Such an enterprise, when constitutive, is apt to be more relevant and revealing than deliberate art. Because no actual artist is involved, it is not particularly rewarding to ask how this matter acquires its revelatory, even poetic, power. Often its director merely pursues the prevailing inclination in his field. Yet the pursuit is so single-minded, so fanatical and literal, that part of the power of the enterprise as constitutive symbol must be credited to the director's unflagging lack of imagination and his passionate naïveté, which stay undeterred by all the properties, traditions, and accumulated wisdom that would only complicate his course.

I shall not linger over the anatomical and physiological detail in Dr Masters' reports, except to say it concerns the changes observed on the various parts of the bodies of his volunteers as they approach, accomplish, and depart from sexual climax. Of all the mechanical, electrical, and electronic devices at his command in this research, it is movie-making which seems to give Dr Masters the clearest edge over the subjective distortions of his predecessors.

Since the integrity of human observation of specific detail varies significantly, regardless of the observer's training or good intent, colored motion-picture photography has been used to record in absolute detail all phases of the human sexual response cycle. The movie is a silent one. Wisely, I think, the director has omitted a sound track, for the tiny events of the flesh he wishes to depict are not audible. Moreover, had there been sound equipment, all one would have heard would have been those adventitious rustlings of any well-equipped laboratory, and perhaps the quickened breathing and gasping of the subjects.
The movie opens quite abruptly with a middle-distance shot of a naked woman, standing, her head and lower legs deliberately outside the movie-frame. One arm hangs at her side, the other is stretched toward her genitals in an Eve-like posture, except that it is immediately apparent she is caressing, rather than covering, her parts. More in the service of decorum than science, there are no close-ups of her hand. This opening scene of a faceless woman silently playing with herself against a neutral antiseptic laboratory background quickly sets the tone for what is to follow. The naked, yet faceless, body informs us this is a 'human female' we are observing. The other bodies that will subsequently appear in the film will also be faceless; the viewer may momentarily wonder, as cuts are made from one

body to another, if it is the same body he is looking at, until he becomes used to distinguishing one body from another by differences in shape of breasts, distribution of pubic hair, and the like. At no time do any scientists or technicians appear; they may be presumed to be standing fully clothed behind the camera. In any large dramatic sense, the arm manipulating the body's private parts furnishes the only real movement and cinematically asserts, even when not in view, that it will continue to fondle during the photographing of more microscopic and glandular events. Since what is to follow will focus on relatively small and minute areas of flesh that ordinarily would not be cinematic, the first shot of the moving hand heightens the dramatic effect of the oozings, engorgements, and contractions this flesh will undergo as climax approaches.

Following this middle-distance shot that is extended a bit in time to give the illusion of mounting excitement, the camera moves in on the skin of the abdomen and back, so that the film can record the first fine rash beginning to appear over the lower body.

Through the use of cuts, several bodies exhibit their rashes until the phenomenon is safely established. Now the camera moves to the breasts to portray distention, venous engorgements, and changes in the nipples. As these changes are repeated on a number of breasts, we must remind ourselves that the initial arm or arms are continuing their work, although it is obvious that views of such action must be suspended from time to time to allow for certain close-ups. Up to this point, all that occurs in the movie could take place on that lonely, upright body that appeared in the opening scene. Now, quite suddenly and without preparation, that body is no longer upright but supine, and the scene is a brilliantly lit close-up of the opening of the vagina. At this point, something of an operating-room atmosphere intrudes, largely because a speculum spreads the lips of the vagina apart to permit an unobstructed view of all that will occur during orgasm.

It is obvious from this portion of the movie that the source of vaginal lubrication is of special interest to the project, as evidenced by a series of ingenious shots of the wall of the vagina showing the formation of individual drops of secretion. The movie then proceeds with a rush to the point that has been imminent since the beginning – namely, orgasm – objective orgasm, displayed visually in the contractions around, and the dilations within, the vagina. The film ends, as might be anticipated, with a succession of photographs of other bodies undergoing similar spasms. With some shrewdness, the director has withstood the tempting aesthetic impulse to conclude his movie with a final shot of the upright naked body with both arms now hanging limply down.

This movie is often referred to in Dr Masters' writings and, I am told, has been exhibited at a number of scientific institutes throughout the country. So fond is he of this medium that there seem to be occasions when his scientific prose seeks, however incompletely, to emulate, not only the objectivity, but the aesthetic brilliance of his movie sequences:

If the bright pink of the excitement phase changes to a brilliant primiparous scarlet-red, or the multiparous burgundy color, a satisfactory plateau phase has been achieved.[4]

There is even a point at which the movie medium itself becomes the inventor: like the accidental solution or the contaminated culture, which have heroic roles in older scientific romances, moviemaking allows Dr Masters to uncover 'the vascular flush reaction to effective sexual stimulation' that had not been previously described in the scientific literature.

With the aid of artificially increased skin surface temperature, such as that necessary for successful motion-picture photography, the wide distribution of this flush becomes quite apparent.... With orgasm imminent, this measle-like rash has been observed to spread over the anterior-lateral borders of the thighs, the buttocks, and the whole body.[5]

Probably it was this discovery of the 'measle-like rash' that inspired a more Pavlovian venture which, if read slowly, will be seen to have quite eerie dimensions:

One observed subject, undergoing electroencephalographic evaluation, had been trained for four months to attain orgasm without producing concomitant muscle tension in order to provide significance for her tracing pattern. Yet, this patient repeatedly showed a marked flush phenomenon over the entire body during plateau and orgasm, and during resolution was completely covered with a filmy, fine perspiration.[6]

If movie-making is his main laboratory device, 'automanipulative techniques' constitute his 'fundamental investigative approach' to 'the sexual response cycle of the human female.' His frankness here is to be commended, particularly since some scientists might feel that such automanipulation was inadequate to the verisimilitude necessary for laboratory demonstration. Dr Masters himself does not discuss the issue, but his obvious preference for this approach over coitus does not appear to be ascribable to decorum. To some degree, I imagine, it was the laboratory procedures and devices – particularly motion-picture photography – which determined the approach, automanipulation being clearly more accessible to scientific inspection than coition. But, more important, there is evidence that Dr Masters regards automanipulation to be a more reliable[7] – that is, a more predictable – technique than 'heterosexual activity' in the pursuit of 'the more intense, well-developed, orgasmic response' cycle.

This type of total pelvic reaction is particularly true for an orgasmic phase elicited by manual manipulation, but it also occurs, although less frequently, with coition.[8]

Yet even this approach, so admirably suited to laboratory research, must share part of the blame for Dr Masters' inability to measure the 'clitoral body' during sexual excitement.

The attempts to measure increases in clitoral size objectively have been generally unsatisfactory due to the marked variation in size and positioning of the normal clitoral body, and the multiplicity of automanipulative techniques employed by the various subjects under observation.[9]

Little is told us about the volunteers in this research. Apparently the project began with prostitutes. But when objections were made that such a profession might not yield the best 'normal' sample, subjects were chosen among medical students and medical students' wives who volunteered and were paid a modest fee for their activities. Naturally no studies could be made on those who, for whatever reason, would not volunteer. And, presumably quickly eliminated were those young women who offered themselves out of their enthusiastic wish to contribute to science, only to discover they could not sustain their sexual excitement in the setting of the laboratory, with the paraphernalia, the cameras, the technicians, and the bright lights. Even more quickly eliminated were those women who on initial interview were not sure whether or not they had climax: 'Our rule of thumb is if they're not sure about it, they probably haven't had it.'

Other circumstances surrounding the study can only be guessed at. Like much scientific research, this particular project must have been an orderly affair. It can be assumed that the investigators did not wait on the whim of their volunteers; that is, they were not subject to call day or night whenever the volunteer felt in the mood.

No, the women were given regular appointments during the working day when the entire research crew was available. Doubtless, too, the directors of the project considered it scientifically unseemly to encourage sexual titillation in their volunteers – certainly out of the question would have been anything resembling a physical overture. Should suggestive reading matter be required by the research – as it indeed occasionally was – it would have to be offered the volunteers in a spirit of detachment; not even the hint of a smirk could be allowed to disrupt the sobriety of the occasion. On the whole, the erotic basis would have to be provided by the scientific situation itself, in addition to the actual manipulation: that is, the prospect of arriving at the laboratory at 10.00 a.m., disrobing, stretching out on the table, and going to work in a somewhat businesslike manner while being measured and photographed, would have to provide its own peculiar excitement. (Thank you, Miss Brown, see you same time next week. Stop at the cashier's for your fee.) So, back to one's ordinary existence.

If these speculations have any truth, what can be said about the qualities that the ideal subject for such experiments would have? In a general way, her sexuality would have to be autonomous, separate from, and unaffected by, her ordinary world. 'World' here would have to include, not only affection, but all those exigencies of human existence which tend to shape our erotic possibilities. Objectively, her sexuality would be mechanically accessible or 'on call' – under circumstances which would be, if not intimidating, at least distracting to most bodies. Hers would have to be indifferent to the entire range of experiences, pleasant and unpleasant, whose claim is not only not salacious but makes us forget there is such a thing as sexuality. Her lust would lie to hand, ready to be invoked and consummated, in sickness or in health, in coitus or 'automanipulation', in homosexuality or heterosexuality, in exasperation or calm, hesitancy or certainty, playfulness or despair. (This would be the other side of that older, though not unrelated, romanticism which just as willfully insisted on soft lights, Brahms, incense, and poetical talk.) In other words, her sexuality would be wholly subject to her will: whenever she determined – or the project determined – that she should reach a climax, she would willingly begin those gestures that would lead to one. To use the modern idiom, all that would be unavailable to her sexological dexterity would be frigidity. Or, to speak more clearly, all that would be unavailable to her would be a real response to the laboratory situation. Insofar as her sexuality was under her will's dominion, she would resemble those odd creatures on the old television quiz programs – also ideal subjects in their own way – who were led from boarding houses to stand in a hot soundproof isolation booth, and when the fateful question was delivered from the vault, answered correctly and without a tremor how many words there were in *Moby Dick* – answered correctly in a loud clear voice under circumstances in which most of us could not even mumble our name. The popularity of these programs (at least until skulduggery was revealed) suggests the audience looked with envy and/or admiration at this caricature of knowledge – a knowledge equally responsive to its owner's will, regardless of contingency or trapping.

A truly constitutive symbol should embody both an accurate rendering of contemporary life and a clear indication of what that life should be. Taking, for the moment, only the ideal contained in my description of the volunteer in these experiments, I would say that she is a latterday Queen of Courtly Love, a veritable Queen Guinevere. For most modern men and women, who grow ever more discouraged by their bodies' stubborn refusal to obey their owners' will, this Lady of the Laboratory has long been the woman of their dreams: men long to channel or claim this creature's prompt and unspecific response for their own specific overtures, while women dream of rivaling her capacity to serve her body's need whenever she so wills.

And what of those self-effacing scientists behind the camera who conceived and guided this research? Do they too reflect who we are and who we would become? We know as little about this research team as we know about the volunteers. How the scientific boundaries were staked out and protected against trespass is not described in the reports. Once again, we can only surmise, but that there was difficulty is suggested by a remark Dr Masters made in one of his lectures – namely, that he preferred to have a woman scientist alongside him in these investigations because she helped to make him or keep him more 'objective'. I assume he meant that having an actual woman present, fully clad in the white coat of science, reminded him, not only of the point of the matter at hand, but of the more hazardous life to be lived with women outside the laboratory – of the difference between the ideal and the actual. It would be a ticklish problem how to maintain the proper detachment to protect the scientists without at the same time inhibiting the volunteers. Here, the equipment and rituals of research would help. And, very possibly, there would be a deliberate effort to eliminate

93

even the ordinary frivolity that sometimes overcomes a surgical team in the midst of the most delicate operation, because frivolity in this sort of research might be only a way-station en route to the lubricious. Any falling-away into the most ordinary locker-room talk, in or out of the laboratory, would have to be regarded as a danger signal. I imagine each scientist, with all the resolution at his command, would remind himself continually that it was just an ordinary day's work in the laboratory, no different from the work next door with the diabetic rats. At the end of the day, when his wife asked, 'How were things at the lab today?' he would reply, 'Oh nothing, just the same old grind.' And, if she pressed him in a jealous fashion, his justifications might resemble those of a young artist explaining his necessity to sketch nude models. Of course, there would be strict rules forbidding dalliance between scientist and volunteer after hours. But, should they happen to run into one another in the cafeteria, each would keep his conversation casual, trying not to allude to those more cataclysmic events of a few hours before. Mindful of his professional integrity, the scientist would have to guard against prideful thoughts that he knew her, if not better, at least more microscopically than those nearest her. Most troublesome of his self-appointed tasks, it seems to me, would be his effort to prevent his research from invading his own ordinary erotic life, particularly if it were worried by the usual frustrations. In this regard, he would be indeed heroic to withstand the temptation of comparing his mate's response to those unspecific, yet perfectly formed, consummations of the laboratory.

Again, if these imaginings have any truth, how may we characterize the ideal scientist in research of this immediate order? First of all, he would have to believe, far more than the volunteers, in a 'basic science' approach to sex. This is not to say that he would consider the practice of sex a possible science, even though his practice might eventually be informed by his scientific theories. But it would have to be an article of faith for him that the visible, palpable reactions of the organs themselves, regardless of whatever human or inhuman context they might occur in, would speak a clear, unambiguous truth to all who cared to heed. In his hierarchy of beliefs, these reactions would take precedence in every sense. The questions we are apt to ask about human affairs, not excluding lust, ordinarily have to do with appropriateness, affection, and the like – in other words, right or wrong, good or bad, judged in human terms. On the other hand, the Ideal Sexologist, as he presses his eye to his research, finds another variety of drama – inordinately complicated in its comings and goings, crises and resolutions – with its own requirements of right and wrong, good and bad, all writ very small in terms of 'droplets' and 'engorgements' and 'contractions'.

The will of the Ideal Sexologist seems different from the will of the Lady of the Laboratory, but it may be that the opposition is more illusory than actual. The latter wills orgasm through physical manipulation. Certainly the sexologist supports and approves her willing, such sexual promptness being ideal for laboratory study. However, while his approval may be invented by his will, it is by no means the most important expression of his will. As a scientist, his will must be given to the systematic inspection of the sexual response of the 'humane female', literally portrayed. To this end he persists in his gadgetry, always at the expense of any imaginative grasp of the occasion. His will to be a scientist requires his further commitment to any number of willful enterprises; in the present circumstance he finds it necessary to will his own body to be unresponsive – not merely to the events on the laboratory table, but to any fictional construction of these events his imagination might contrive, because imagination, at least in this arena, is his opponent in his pursuit of science. On the surface his dilemma may seem a familiar one, being comparable to older ascetic ventures, particularly of the Eastern yoga variety. But the sexologist's task is actually more difficult: asceticism is not his goal – the very nature of his enterprise points in an opposite direction. He wishes indifference, which he can invoke at will: it may be the project that demands his not responding, but – as we shall see later – it may be other moments, unofficial and unscientific, which seem to call forth his willed lack of response. The will not to respond and the will to respond are related possibilities of the will. In this sense, the Lady of the Laboratory and the Ideal Sexologist are collaborators rather than opponents. Of course, I speak in ideal terms – whether these ideals can be achieved is another matter. But, if the Lady of the Laboratory is a latter day Queen of Courtly Love, then our Ideal Sexologist is the modern Sir Galahad, and together – separately or commingled – they rule our dreams of what we should be.

Let us remind ourselves that most of us could not hope to qualify for this research – either as volunteers or scientists. But this does not mean the differences are great between us and them. True, compared to ours, their lives have an oversized quality, and true, they are in the vanguard. But, in a real sense our fleshly home is that laboratory. Whatever room we choose for our lovemaking we shall make into our own poor laboratory, nothing that is observed or undergone in the real laboratory of science is likely to escape us. At this stage, is there any bit of sexology that is not in the public domain, or at least potentially so for those who can read? Whatever detail the scientific will appropriates about sex rapidly becomes an injunction to be imposed on our bodies. But, it is not long before these impositions lose their arbitrary and alien character and begin to change our actual experience of our bodies. Unfortunately, our vision of the ideal experience tends to be crudely derived from the failure of our bodies to meet these imperatives.

Our residence in the laboratory is recent: really only since the turn of the century has the act of sex been interviewed, witnessed, probed, measured, timed, taped, photographed, and judged. Before the age of sexology, objectifications of the sexual act were to be found in pornography and the brothel, both illicit, both pleasurable in purpose, both suggesting the relatively limited manner in which will – given absolute dominion – could be joined to sexual pleasure. However else the Marquis de Sade may be read, he at least offered the most exhaustive inventory yet seen of technique for exploiting the pleasure of the body's several parts, if one wholeheartedly put one's will to it. As a moralist, he seemed to say, Why our particular rules? What if there were no limits? More recently, yet still before sexology, it was possible for shy erotomaniacs, disguised as greengrocers, to visit brothels, there to peek at the antics of the inmates. The bolder ones could join the sport. When the performance reached its final gasp our tradesmen, now satiated, would slink back to the propriety and privacy of their own quarters, convinced their ordinary domestic world was discreetly separate from the world of the peephole which they paid to enter. In fact, or so it seemed, the separateness of these two worlds heightened the erotic possibilities of each. The emancipation which sexology enforced gradually blurred this distinction, making it unclear whether each home had become its own brothel, or whether every brothel had become more like home. The truth is that sexology eventually not only blurred the distinction, but by housing us all in laboratories, made both the brothel and pornography less exciting dwellings for our erotic investigations.

When last we left our pathetic lovers, I suggested that as their self-pity and bitterness mounted, they might – in desperation – turn to adultery. Yet even for the person who believes himself to be without scruples, adultery – in fact or fantasy – is difficult to arrange, exhausting to maintain. Requiring, as it does, at least two persons and two wills, this illicit encounter risks the danger of further pathos. But, if we heed our laboratory drama carefully, we can see that there is another possibility preferable to adultery. According to the lesson of the laboratory, there is only one perfect orgasm, if by 'perfect' we mean one wholly subject to its owner's will, wholly indifferent to human contingency or context. Clearly, the perfect orgasm is the orgasm achieved on one's own. No other consummation offers such certainty and, moreover, avoids the messiness that attends most human affairs. The onanist may choose the partner of his dreams who very probably will be the Lady of the Laboratory, or he may have his orgasm without any imagined partner. In either case, he is both scientist and experimental subject, science and sex now being nicely joined. In his laboratory room, he may now abstract his sexual parts from his whole person, inspect their anatomical particularities, and observe and enjoy the small physiologic events he knows best how to control. True, this solitary experience may leave him empty and ashamed. But, as a citizen of his times, he will try to counter this discomfort by reminding himself that sexology and psycho-analysis have assured him that masturbation is a morally indifferent matter. As a true modern, he tells himself that it is not as good as what two people have, but that does not make it bad. Superstitious people of other ages thought it drove one crazy, but he knows better; he knows that the real threat to *his* sanity is unrelieved sexual tension. In fact – he may decide – were it not for certain neurotic Victorian traces he has not managed to expunge from his psyche, he could treat the matter as any other bodily event and get on with his business. So we must not be too harsh with our pathetic lovers, if they take refuge in solitary pleasures – even if they come to prefer them to the frustrations of sexual life together. Nor should we be too surprised if such solitary pleasure becomes the ideal by which all mutual sex is measured – and found wanting.

Let us now turn to the phenomenon being inspected and celebrated in our laboratory – the phenomenon which contributes most of all to our lovers' impasse. Of all the discoveries sexology has made, the female orgasm remains the most imposing in its consequences. De Tocqueville's prediction of life between the sexes in America[10] might not have been so sanguine, could he have anticipated first, the discovery of sexology and psychoanalysis, and second, their discovery of the female orgasm.

In the second half of the nineteenth century, Western man began to see nature in a new and utilitarian way as a variety of energies, hitherto unharnessed, which could now be tamed and transformed

97

into industrial servants and which, in turn, would fashion never-ending progress and prosperity. The health of the machine, powered by steam and electricity, and the sickness of the machine, if those energies were misdirected or obstructed, were obsessive considerations of the period. It was entirely appropriate to regard the human body as still another natural object with many of the vicissitudes of the machine: this had always been medicine's privilege. But, for the first time, the scientists, in their intoxication, could forget the duality previous centuries knew: namely, that the body is both a natural object and not a natural object. Once it was decided that the dominant energy of the human machine was sex, the new science of sexology was born. With the suppression of the second half of the dialectic, sexology and psychoanalysis could – with the assistance of the Romantics – claim the erotic life as their exclusive province, removing it from all the traditional disciplines, such as religion, philosophy, and literature, which had always concerned themselves with sex as human experience. Such qualities as modesty, privacy, reticence, abstinence, chastity, fidelity, and shame could now be questioned as rather arbitrary matters that interfered with the health of the sexual parts. In their place came an increasing assortment of objective terms like *ejaculatio praecox*, foreplay, fore-pleasure, and frigidity – all intended to describe, not human experience, but the behavior of the sexual parts. The quite preposterous situation arose in which the patient sought treatment for *ejaculatio praecox* or impotence, and the healer sought to find out whether he liked his partner.

If the Victorians found sex unspeakable for the wrong reasons, the Victorian sexologists found it wrongly speakable. (To what extent Victorian prudery was actually modesty or reticence, I cannot say. It has become habitual for us to regard Victorian lovemaking as an obscenity.) Science is usually democratic, and since sex now belonged to science, whatever facts or assumptions were assembled had immediately to be transmitted to the people, there to invade their daily life. Writing of the Kinsey Report, Lionel Trilling finds – correctly, I believe – a democratic motive for the study:

In speaking of its motives, I have in mind chiefly its impulse toward acceptance and liberation, its broad and generous desire for others that they be not harshly judged. . . . The Report has the intention of habituating its readers to sexuality in all its manifestations; it wants to establish, as it were, a democratic pluralism of sexuality. . . . This

98

generosity of mind ... goes with a nearly conscious aversion from making intellectual distinctions, almost as if out of the belief that an intellectual distinction must inevitably lead to a social discrimination or exclusion.[11]

If we disregard Kinsey's scientific pretensions, we still must recognize his eminence as an arbiter of sexual etiquette. Like the lexicographer who finds his sanction in usage, Kinsey discovers his authority in practice: his democratic message is that we all do – or should do – more or less the same things in bed. And, any notion lovers retain from an older tradition that what they have together is private and unique is effectively disproved by his cataloguing of sexual matters, providing they join him in equating behavior with experience. As a fitting disciple of Kinsey, Masters actualizes the 'pluralism of sexuality' within the democratic unit of the laboratory and enlarges behavior to include the more minute physiological developments which, too, should belong to every citizen.

The political clamor for equal rights for the woman at the turn of the century could not fail to join with sexology to endow her with an orgasm, equal in every sense to the male orgasm. In fact, Freud went so far as to stipulate two female orgasms, clitoral and vaginal, the latter clearly superior. (It was not many years ago that an anatomist demonstrated that there were as many nerve endings in the clitoris as in the penis.) It was agreed that, just as she was entitled to the vote, she was entitled to her orgasm. Moreover, if she were deprived of such release, her perturbation would be as unsettling to her nervous system as the frustration of orgasm was thought to be for the man. Equal rights were to be erotically consummated in simultaneous orgasm. On the one hand, it was unhealthful for her to be deprived of orgasm, and, on the other hand, psychoanalysis decreed that an important sign of her maturity as a woman was her ability to achieve orgasm. In other words, without orgasm she was neurotic to begin with, or neurotic to end with.

Though simultaneous orgasm seemed to be a necessary consequence of equal rights, the problem remained that, in matters of lust, more than a decree or amendment was required for such an achievement. True, the sexologists were most generous with instruction, but each citizen has had to discover over and over again the degree to which he is caught in the futile struggle to will what cannot be willed – at the same time that he senses the real absurdity of the whole willful enterprise. The lover learns, as his indoctrination progresses, to observe uneasily and even to resist his rush of pleasure, if it seems he is to be premature. When no amount of resolution can force his pleasure to recede, he learns to suffer his release and then quickly prod himself to an activity his body's exhaustion opposes. In other words, he learns to take his moment in stride, so to speak, omitting the deference these moments usually call forth, and without breaking stride get to his self-appointed, and often fatiguing, task of tinkering with his mate – always hopeful that his ministrations will have the appearance of affection. While she is not likely to be deceived by such dutiful manipulation, she nevertheless wishes for both their sakes that her body, at least, will be deluded into fulfilling its franchise. Still, it cannot be easy for her to ignore the irony that her right to orgasm may perhaps depend for realization upon her willingness to be diddled like a perverse underwater edible whose shell refuses to be pried open.

As far as I know, little attention was paid to the female orgasm before the era of sexology. Where did the sexologists find it? Did they discover it or invent it? Or both? I realize it may seem absurd to raise such questions about events as unmistakable as those witnessed in our laboratory. But I cannot believe that previous centuries were not up to our modern delights; nor can I believe it was the censorship imposed by religion which suppressed the supreme importance of the female orgasm. My guess, which is not subject to laboratory proof, is that the female orgasm was always an occasional, though not essential, part of woman's whole sexual experience. I also suspect that it appeared with regularity or predictability only during masturbation, when the more human qualities of her life with her mate were absent. Further, her perturbation was unremarkable and certainly bearable when orgasm did not arrive, for our lovers had not yet been enlightened as to the disturbances resulting from the obstruction or distortion of sexual energies. At this stage, her orgasm had not yet been abstracted and isolated from the totality of her pleasures, and enshrined as the meaning and measure of her erotic life. She was content with the mystery and variety of her difference from man and, in fact, would not have had it otherwise. Much that I have said, if we leave aside the erotomanias that have always been with us, applies to the male of previous centuries. For him, too, the moment of orgasm was not abstracted in its objective form from the whole of his erotic life and then idealized. He, too, preferred the mystery of difference, the impact of human contingency, becoming obsessed with the sheer anatomy and mechanics of orgasm only when all else was missing, as in masturbation.

Theological parallelism is a treacherous hobby, especially when we deal with flagrantly secular movements. Nevertheless, the manner in which lovers now pursue their careers as copulating mammals, adopting whatever new refinements sexology devises, covering their faces yet exposing their genitals, may remind us of older heresies which, through chastity or libertinism, have pressed toward similar goals; one heretical cult went so far as to worship the serpent in the Garden of Eden. But the difference between these older heresies and modern science – and there is a large one – must be attributed to the nature of science itself, which, by means of its claims to objectivity – if we accept such evidence as the Lambeth Conference, can invade religion and ultimately all of life to a degree denied the older heresies. So, with the abstraction, objectification, and idealization of the female orgasm, we have come to the last and perhaps most important clause to the contract which binds our lovers to their laboratory home, there to will the perfection on earth that cannot be willed, there to suffer the pathos that follows all such strivings toward heaven on earth.

1 C. S. Lewis, *The Allegory of Love* (New York: Oxford University Press, 1958), p. 196.
2 Dorothea Krook, *Three Traditions of Moral Thought* (Cambridge: Cambridge University Press, 1959), p. 336.
3 William H. Masters, 'The Sexual Response Cycle of the Human Female', *West. J. Surg., Obst. & Gynec.*, 68 (Jan.–Feb. 1960), p. 57.
4 *Ibid.*, p. 63.
5 *Ibid.*, p. 61.
6 *Ibid.*, p. 61.
7 In a later investigation of contraceptive devices, Dr Masters is led to develop a research technique of 'artificial coitus.' (See William H. Masters and Virginia E. Johnson, 'Intravaginal Contraceptive Study,' *West. J. Surg. Obst. & Gynec.*, 70 [July–Aug. 1962], particularly pp. 202–203). Since it is not described in any detail, we cannot know whether the old limerick was its inspiration. (The one that goes, 'There was a young man from Racine, Who invented a fucking machine,' ending with 'And was terribly easy to clean.') However, it does seem to involve an 'artificial penis,' whose principal virtue is that it 'affords direct observation of the vaginal barrel during the entire female sexual response cycle.' Its disadvantage, admittedly surmountable, lies in the fact that his volunteers did not immediately take to the method. 'The technique of artificial coitus necessitates conditioning of these individuals to assure definitive research results. In every instance, all thirty members of the subject population . . . underwent three separate sessions to establish familiarity with, and effective response to, the artificial coital technique.' Once again, the problem of verisimilitude is presented: how much threat of impregnation can this machine pose?

8 William H. Masters and Virginia E. Johnson, 'The Artificial Vagina: Anatomic, Physiologic, Psychosexual Function,' *West. J. Surg., Obst. & Gynec.*, 69 (May–June 1961), p. 202.

9 Masters, *op. cit.*, p. 62.

10 '. . . I never observed that the women of America consider conjugal authority as an unfortunate usurpation of their rights, or that they thought themselves degraded by submitting to it. It appeared to me, on the contrary, that they attach a sort of pride to the voluntary surrender of their will. . . . Though their lot is different, they consider both of them as beings of equal value. . . . If I were asked . . . to what the singular prosperity and growing strength of that people ought mainly to be attributed, I should reply: To the superiority of their women.' Alexis de Tocqueville, *Democracy in America* (New York: Alfred A. Knopf, 1945), Vol. II, pp. 212–214.

11 Lionel Trilling, 'The Kinsey Report,' in *The Liberal Imagination* (New York: Doubleday Anchor Books, 1954), pp. 232–233.

IS SHAME BENEFICIAL? SHAME AS A HISTORIOLOGICAL PROBLEM

Erwin Straus, M.D.

THE term 'historiological' has not yet been accepted as a natural-ized citizen by psychology. Nevertheless, I have used it to define my subject, first, because I do not know of a better word and, second, because it denotes that the immediate experience of shame can only be understood with the help of historical-psychological categories. This is so because the experiencing person understands himself historiologically, i.e., as continuously emergent (*Werdend*). Of course, this kind of self-understanding is not a conceptual knowledge but a more elementary form of self-disclosure.

One may think that I have chosen a poor subject to demonstrate the importance of historical categories in psychology, for, as far as psychology has been concerned with the problem of shame at all, it has attempted to interpret it statically. The definitions given by Lipps (1907) and others illustrate in a striking way this nonhistorical way of looking at things in psychology. Therefore, if we can demonstrate the necessity for a historical method in this instance, we will have gained two points: a more intimate acquaintance with the pheno-menon itself and, at the same time, a clarification of the problem of method in psychology. While normal psychology, and particularly experimental psychology – with its formulations so alien to every-day life – have been able to treat the problem of shame as trivial, pathopsychology, especially in the treatment of neuroses, urgently requires development of our theme, if only to avoid the errors of psychoanalysis. Our position forces us to fight on two fronts: against the static interpretation of shame in normal psychology and against the genetic interpretation of psychoanalysis.

I shall begin by contrasting my view with the theory of Freud (1963). Freud often speaks of the barriers of shame and disgust and how they have been set up by the disciplinary measures of those to whom the child's education has been entrusted. This genetic interpretation of shame and disgust rests on a group of significant assumptions and leads to remarkable consequences.

1. Shame and disgust merely inhibit the actualization of innate drives and demands. The actions prevented by shame and disgust stem from more primary drive impulsions.

2. Shame and disgust are acquired modes of behavior. They do not originate at the same level as the drives whose actualization they block. Shamelessness or unashamedness is primary according to Freud; shame is secondary.

3. Shame and disgust are basically prohibitive. They call for abstention from certain *specific* actions.

4. From such *specific* abstentions, with the help of the Unconscious, feeling-toned attitudes and chronic traits gradually develop.

5. Shame and disgust are peripheral activities. Basically, they represent an abstention that is demanded and imposed but one that is no more able to affect the continuity and character of the original attitude than any forced renunciation or confession is able to modify one's real character. Man would be happy only if he could live without shame or disgust.

6. There are certain partial drives whose actualization is interfered with by the barriers of shame and disgust. But, in the perversions, the partial drives are active in an unmodified way, showing themselves without disguise. In shame, it is the drive to consume by looking (scoptophilia) that has suffered a painful restriction. Therefore, in Freud's view, we ought to be most successful in explaining shame genetically by relating it to voyeurism. But this certainly needs testing.

Freud does not consider perversions as deteriorations or distortions of human existence. On the contrary, the original drive impulsions appear in them nakedly. The psychoanalytic theory of perversions, so closely tied to the doctrine of partial drives, assumes and must assume the ultimate aim of all libidinal drives to be the gain of pleasure. All the various partial drives agree in this aim; thus, they can function vicariously for one another, and, thus, there is a quantitative equilibrium among them. In each instance, the world is but an object, i.e., a means toward the end of drive gratification. Man has no real and actual relation to the world; the world is a source of disturbances from which man turns away to himself. Psychoanalysis not only makes use of a mechanistic terminology out of a historically contingent accident but is, in its basic concept, a mechanistic psychology. Its object is the individual viewed in isolation. All experiences are to be understood, in the last analysis, as events in an isolated organism. Psychoanalysis is a solipsistic doctrine; it is not a solipsistic theory of knowledge but – and this has even farther reaching implications – an anthropological solipsism.

Yet, the perversions are pervasive modifications of and disturbances in man's communication with the world. The concept of *communicative mode* is of fundamental importance for anthropological psychology. The voyeur does not become a voyeur out of an exogenous or endogenous heightening of his 'urge to look'. Anyone who draws his sexual gratification from looking at another lives continuously at a distance. If it is normal to approach and unite with the partner, then it is precisely characteristic of the voyeur that he remains alone, without a partner, an outsider who acts in a stealthy and furtive manner. To keep his distance when it is essential to draw near is one of the paradoxes of his perversion. The looking of the voyeur is of course also a looking at and, as such, is as different from the looks exchanged by lovers as medical palpation from a gentle caress of the hand. In viewing, there is a transition from the immediate I–thou encounter, i.e., mutual participation, to a unilateral intention – a transition from the I–thou relationship to the subject–object relationship proper. All looking and being looked at is a lapse from immediate communication. This is demonstrated in everyday life by our annoyance and irritation at being observed. The psychotic experience of being looked at is also based on a change in communicative mode. 'Looking at' objectifies. Objectification is the second and essentially perverse action of the voyeur, along with his keeping his distance. Both are closely linked together. Objectification is only possible with a keeping of distance, and, conversely, it is only the keeping of distance that makes objectification possible. The peculiar mode of existence of the voyeur directs his curiosity toward the sexual organs, the sexual function, and the sexual word, continually in search of both clarity and closeness, whereas lovers search for concealment, half-light, and silence.

Thus, the voyeur does not participate in reality in any direct sense but only by way of the objectifications, i.e., reflected knowledge. He makes the Other into an object in and for itself. His objectification, then, permits arbitrary re-enactments in fantasy. The behavior of the voyeur is not an inherently meaningful surrender to fate, like that of lovers. The perversion of the voyeur, like all perversions, reveals a fundamentally different kind of attitude toward the world, toward himself, and toward his partner. The voyeur reveals, in his objectifying attitude and in his furtive entry into the Other's most intimate experience, the antinomy of two modes of being – the public mode and that of immediate being.

These two modes of being, the public and the immediate, are separated by shame, which, at the same time, protects immediate experience from invasion by the public sphere. We will call this latter form of shame, our main interest at present, protective shame. We may now define our subject very generally as the antithesis between public and immediate experience. It is our aim to give an adequate understanding of this antithesis and, from this, to show how immediate being could be threatened by the public.

The public sphere is only found among humans. We cannot speak of 'the public' in the plant kingdom or among other animals. The public emerges simultaneously with language or the production of symbols. From a functional psychological point of view, it is linked with perceiving, thinking, and thoughts. Incidentally, what we call the private sphere is a delimited public sphere and not the polar opposite to 'public', which we call 'immediate'.

We belong to the public in the ways we are described – e.g., by our name, title, position, status, profession, etc. Everyone is assigned a particular role in the public sphere, but this role is not merely 'played'. Both the assumption and performance of the role assigned to the individual is linked to a certain way of being human. If we meet a stranger in public, we usually ask two questions: 'Who is he?' and 'What is he?' The name identifies someone in the social space of the family, of the birthplace, of the chronicles. To the question of the What of his being, we answer by stating his profession, position, etc. The specification points to something general and repeatable. (*Le roi est mort. Vive le roi.*) These are general and repeatable functions that the individual assumes in public. The intimate person is always initially concealed by his public figure. It is possible to participate in the public figure with a noncommittal, one-way kind of general interest; but the intimate person opens and reveals himself to understanding only in mutual and immediate participation.

The public originally constitutes itself through objectification, i.e., reflection. The logical features of identity, generality, and repetition here assume an anthropological significance. What is conceived as definite in a logical sense has the significance of finite and, thereby, finished in an anthropological sense. Conceptual determination, rationality and the past, and completion and accomplishment are closely and reciprocally related. Now, to the extent that a man becomes identical with his public position, i.e., to the extent he is what

106

he has become – and no one is exempted from this fate – he loses the possibility of immediate becoming. As a man ages, he tends increasingly to turn toward the past and live in repetition.

Public being is characterized, as we have seen, by objectification or reflection, generality, repetition; the outcome is noncommittal, one-way participation. Immediate being, on the other hand, is not objectified, it is singular, unique becoming and calls for reciprocal sharing.

Shame divides what is immediately becoming from the finished outcome and protects whatever is in becoming from violation by the completed. The temporal and historical moment, an important feature of any anthropological approach, is implicit in this antithesis between immediate becoming and completion. This antithesis between *natura naturans* and *natura naturata* should make clearer our reference to shame as a historiological problem.

Shame is basic to human existence and is continuously active; it is not made up of many isolated occurrences of shame separate from one another in time. Shame is not merely active at certain times and under certain circumstances. When someone is ashamed, it is a sign that the permanent safeguard of shame has been breached, that immediate experience has been jeopardized by the entry of public experience. But the need for protection in immediate becoming is still imperfectly explained by the antithesis between the two modes of being. It is conceivable that the two modes of being could alternate. Experience, however, shows that immediate becoming – whether erotic, religious, or spiritual – generally seeks protection against the profane and safeguards against the presence of the non-participating stranger. The stranger is of necessity an observer. He is, thus, at odds with the shared unity of the group, and his mere presence tends to introduce some objectification into every immediate relationship.

The phenomenon of the comic will help to elucidate the peculiar linkage of the stranger with objectification, one-way participation, repetition, and the destruction of immediate becoming. We will state this as several theses:

1. What is strange tends to be comic, e.g., that which is old-fashioned or the the customs of other countries and peoples.
2. Only the strange is comic. The traditional figures of comedy – the stutterer, the dullard, the cuckold, etc. – are comic only as long, as sympathy is denied, i.e., when communication is in one direction only. We suffer with the hero, but we laugh about the clown.

3. What is different beyond all comparison is not strange; there is always similarity in what is strange. Neither the plant nor the worm are comical, but the ape is.

4. Repetition, or the element of parody, is essential to the comic. Repetition, repeatability at will, annuls the seriousness of a word, an act, or a person. Hence, the comic effect of children's miming and aping of adults, the comic effect of twins, and the uncanny effect of the double. Note, in addition, the repeatability of the comic figure in contrast to the singularity of the tragic hero: a joke can be repeated, while a word is serious only at a particular time.

Repetition, sacrilege, or profanation; the comic; the strange; one-way participation, and outcomes are all linked together on the one hand; on the other are singularity, seriousness, decision, mutual participation, and immediate becoming. To the stranger, our doings seem just so much to-do, even in the cool detachment of historical perspective. In the presence of the detached observer, we are in danger of experiencing our own doing as so much to-do. For this reason, we are inclined to keep strangers at a distance.

Whatever is in becoming must gradually emancipate itself from what has already become. The terminated prevails in tradition, the family, language, and knowledge; they are with us everywhere. To come into our own immediacy, we must unloosen ourselves from the outcomes, as in crisis, revolution, solitude, or *Wanderjahre*. Maturity, like all coming to oneself, requires a break with what has been inherited. We come to ourselves only in confrontation with the other. The incest prohibitions that prevent the individual from lingering in the sphere of the terminated enounce the essential laws of becoming as positive injunctions. Shame is a safeguard for immediate experience against the world of outcomes. It does not constrain the erotic, as is assumed in psychoanalysis, but makes the erotic possible for the first time. Shame is a protection against the public in all of its forms. The stranger, of course, is a perfect expression of the public threat of invasion to immediate experience, but it is not the only one. The word, in the form of 'dirty joke', vivid representation as pornography, and self-observation in the mirror shows the objectifying character of a self-representation. Those who are in love have no use for the 'dirty joke', pornography, or the mirror, for these all belong to the shrunken existences of persons no longer capable of being immediately touched. Words of affection tend to exclude the language of everyday life, giving rise spontaneously to an idiom that is personal and jealously guarded, one that names rather than describes. The secret that shame protects is not, however, as prudery makes the mistake of believing, one that is already in existence and only needs to be hidden from outsiders, for those who are in becoming are also hidden from themselves. Their existence is first made explicit in their shared immediate becoming. Youth keeps its secret still, while age has become knowing. Thus, youth is impelled to youth. Here, again, incest prohibitions are to be understood as essential laws of becoming.

One of the important forms of shame, in addition to the protective, is that of concealing shame. Most writers on shame have mostly chosen examples of concealing shame while claiming to treat the topic generally. Concealing shame judges the individual in terms of the group ideal, primarily attempting to conceal the deficiencies and deviations from the group ideal before a third person. The power of concealing shame diminishes as distance from the group increases. While protective shame safeguards immediate becoming, concealing shame acts on behalf of social prestige. It addresses itself directly to the onlooker and is oriented to the objectified public image. Thus, honor and disgrace, like medals of honor and stigmata, are both thing-like; like any possession, they may be transferred or inherited.

The group ideal changes in time and varies also according to country, people, class, and generation. And the form taken by concealing shame varies according to the prevailing group ideal.

The essential character of shame, preservative and concealing, discloses itself in a variety of ways, just as the idea of justice finds its situationally valid actualization in positive legal norms. While language does not provide us with different terms for distinguishing protective from concealing shame, it actually does for the privative forms of shame. The negative of protective shame we term 'shamelessness', and the negative of concealing shame we term 'unabashedness'.

Psychology has limited itself for too long to be an analysis of the contents of experience in terms of objective states. In so doing, man has been turned into a rubber-stamp subject, much like a thing. But a phenomenon such as shame can only be fully revealed within a perspective in which man is understood in terms of becoming or being actively engaged with his world, a perspective which grants sufficient significance to temporality and historicity in experience. Only a historiological psychology suited to such phenomena can comprehend and clarify the antitheses between singularity and repetition, immediate becoming and outcome, and temporal character and points on a time coordinate. Such a psychology reveals shame as an original feature of human existence and shamelessness as acquired behavior.

REFERENCES

Freud, S. *Three essays on the theory of sexuality*. New York: Basic Books, 1963.
Lipps, T. *Vom Fühlen, Wollen und Denken*. Leipzig: Barth, 1907.

PORNOGRAPHY AND PERVERSION

Robert J. Stoller, M.D.

PORNOGRAPHY is a daydream in which activities, usually but not necessarily overtly sexual, are projected into written or pictorial material to induce genital excitement in an observer. No depiction is pornographic until an observer's fantasies are added; nothing *per se* is pornographic. There is always a victim, no matter how disguised : no victim, no pornography. The use of such matter is an act of perversion with several components. (Perversion is defined for the present purpose as indefinitely repeating conscious preference for a genitally stimulating exciting act which is not genital heterosexual intercourse.) The most apparent is voyeurism. The second, hidden (unless the person is an overt sexual sadist), is sadism; sadism is, however, rather easily demonstrated. The third, more hidden (unless the person is an overt sexual masochist), is masochism; masochism is hard to demonstrate, since it is hidden in an unconscious identification with the depicted victim.

These above components are universal for users of pornography. To be dwelled on more in this paper is a fourth component which is specific to each user – his own style or perversion; thus, for example, a sadist will choose depictions of sadistic acts and a fetishistic transvestite depictions of acts of cross-dressing. As with all perversions, pornography is a matter of aesthetics: one man's delight is another's boredom. Also, as with all perversions, at its heart is a fantasied act of revenge, condensing in itself the subject's sexual life history – his memories and fantasies, traumas, frustrations, and joys. Pornography is for restitution; in men, the main producers and consumers, its creation and its use are ritualized acts, for deviation from a narrow, prescribed path will produce decreased sexual excitement. At these moments, it reveals the function of perversion as a necessary preserver of potency.

So much for positive, unverified introductory statements.

The main purpose of this paper, which takes off from thoughts expressed in an earlier paper,[1] is to show how pornography can help

B

one investigate the dynamics of perversions. The several genres of pornography, each created for a specific perverse need by exact attention to detail, define an area of excitement that will have no effect on a different man. These details commemorate historical events as well as past fantasies. I shall attempt to demonstrate that the unconscious memory of these historical events exists in the conscious fantasies expressed in the pornography.

The development of the manifest complex daydream which the pornography exteriorizes is a chronicle of fantasies, each elaboration occurring at the moment when a piece of pain (or of incomplete pleasure) is converted into (greater) pleasure, until all these fantasies, like building blocks, have been assembled to create the adult perversion that presents itself overtly. But, as just noted, there is, I believe, a grain of historical reality embedded in each fantasy, and the differences in that historical reality account in good part (though not completely) for the minor variations found even in a group of men homogeneous for a particular perversion.

A Particular Example: Transvestite Pornography

Let us examine pornography of the perversion transvestism to find these bits of historical reality. (For our present purpose, transvestism is defined not simply as any dressing in the clothes of the opposite sex but that wherein the clothes themselves cause sexual excitement. That is a criterion which helps separate a distinct syndrome from other conditions in which cross-dressing also occurs.[2]) There should be an advantage for us in using such an odd condition for our example, for it is rare and its pornography does not stir anyone but a transvestite. (One might suggest, not quite seriously, that a test to establish the diagnosis of transvestism or any perversion in men would be to show its pornography to a subject: only those with increased penile blood flow would fit the diagnosis. One cannot ask for a more rapid, precise diagnostic procedure. Such a test would also demonstrate most concretely that the psychodynamics of transvestites are different from those of other people.)

In the pornographic literature catering to transvestites, there are repeated stories with the same theme – a frightened, pathetic, defenseless boy–man finds himself, through no doing of his own, trapped by powerful, dangerously beautiful women, who bully and humiliate him. The poor victim – the peak of whose victimization is illustrated by the women physically forcing him to put on women's clothes – hardly seems a subject created for inducing sexual excitement. Yet the men who need such material find their greatest anticipation just at this point in the story, when the humiliated man is illustrated being exposed to his greatest anguish. The typical picture and accompanying text show him seated, cowering, while standing over him with threatening gestures and looks are the very phallic women. (The term 'phallic' here is not simply the application of a concept: the drawings show repeated themes of phallic-shaped objects – stiletto heels, table and chair legs, whips, pens.)

Clinical Data

Here are excerpts from the pornography. Fraternity pledge Bruce King, as part of his initiation, has to raid the clothesline of a sorority house, when 'squeals and bubbling laughter suddenly enveloped him'. He is caught and bound by sorority girls. 'All were shrieking with joy.'

He tried to protest but his gag was too tight; he wiggled but only succeeded in getting the brunt of their sharp fingernails into the muscular flesh of his flanks and thighs. This brought much raucous laughter from the victorious vixens who thrilled at the helpless struggles of their male captive. . . .
The girl named Lori, apparently the group leader, was a silver-blonde Amazon. She must have stood a statuesque six feet tall, proudly erect, her heaving bosom thrust forth with a strange form of arrogance which demanded obedience and respect. Lori was garbed in a tight fitting buckled beauty of a pure satin dress; it featured a permanently pleated skirt which shivered like so many leather strings with each movement. The turquoise blouse boasted floral and fruit decorations. Lori's waist was captivated [sic] by a huge patent leather belt of shining black; the contrasting silver buckle resembled a lock, with a tiny keyhole which defied entrance and exit. Her hips were forced into a figure-training position so that she walked with some difficulty, but with greater pride. And Lori's shoes: they were the heavenly dream of any clothes raider. The unbelievably thin match-stick high heels must have been a perfect seven inches long! Made of shiny white patent leather – believe it or not – the shoe featured a slinky sling back which was a silvery chain, a *peau de sole* trim, an open toe through which peeped a gleaming red nail, the toe almost grateful to be liberated from its confinement. The vamp was charmingly decorated with a pair of gleaming glass eyes! Yes, the eyes even winked wickedly as Lori moved her slender legs. Such white patent leather, polished to milky perfection, deserved respect as they were held in awe and esteem! As

Lori stamped her dainty but powerfully shod foot, tiny sparks escaped from the stiletto seven-inch heel!

Bruce flinched, struggling against the bonds of the robe belts. 'Lori,' his voice tried to be fierce and confident, 'will you cut me loose? All right, so I didn't succeed in my panty raid. I lost! The frat brothers will give me a real paddling,' he squirmed at the thought, 'and that'll be that. So let's just forget it.'

'Oh, we don't want you to be paddled out of your fraternity, no sir!' another girl said. 'Lori, what say we give him . . . what's your name. . . .'

'Bruce . . . Bruce King.'

'. . . let's give Bruce a complete feminine outfit to bring back to his frat brothers. This will be something he shall long remember!' Lori smiled. As she folded both of her slender swan-like arms across her chest, Bruce caught sight of her blood-red fingernails, extended like the talons of a wicked vulture! 'Very well, Sandra. We'll give Bruce a nice frilly outfit . . . bloomers, slip, bra, dress, silk stocking which attach to the garter straps of the garter belt we'll also let him have, and a nice pair of high-heeled shoes. . . .'

Before Bruce could protest, he found himself descended upon by the girls, who ripped off his simple white business shirt, cotton khaki trousers (he was grateful he wore protective boxer shorts), off went his moccasins, wool socks. 'It's cold : . .' he shivered, feeling more embarrassed and humiliated than the elements of the weather in early spring. To be stripped, bound and in the captivity of four domineering types of females was certainly an experience that shattered his manhood. There was no telling what they could do to make good a threat that Lori now voiced: 'We'll teach him that the female of the species are the *real* aggressive members of the human race! . . .'

'We're going to dress you, Bruce,' purred Lori, her green eyes glittering with a strange fascination of the spectacle of a man being held in her captivity. 'Now, girls – get those boxer shorts of his and throw them out . . . good boys shouldn't wear such sloppy things. We'll teach our Brucie how to dress.'

'No! No!' he protested, but four sets of female hands yanked down his boxer shorts. With a sigh of relief, he remembered he wore his tiny athletic supporter which the girls ridiculed by giggling, 'Look – he wears a G-string!'

Lori then said, 'Okay, girls, untie him. It'll be easier to get his clothes on. But Brucie-boy,' she said in a falsetto tone, 'you won't get very far – in your G-string. So behave yourself, or we'll take that away from you, too.'

Bruce flushed and no sooner were his arms and legs freed than he tried to cover himself with his hands but his awkward knock-kneed position and round shouldered position of embarrassment only provoked more laughter. 'Very funny! Very funny!' he gasped.

'Come on, girls,' laughed Lori. 'I can hardly wait to see what he looks like in some *really* dainty clothes. Let's start with this panty....'

Lori held up a few brassieres and finally made her selection of a charming item. 'See, Bruce,' she dangled it before him, as if threatening his manhood, 'this brassiere has in-up pushup pads and foam rubber shapemakers. This low plunge front gives real cleavage; to a girl, it's breathtakingly sinful. To you,' and she made a throaty laugh, 'it'll be very wicked....'

He would make no protest. It would only infuriate the girls and they might intensify their hatred upon him. And now ... yes ... here it was: the gown to be worn by Bruce King.

'Do you like it?' asked Lori, already joining in giggling with the other girls at the anticipation of seeing him wear a dress. 'It's a French import. It's an exclusive design.' The color was Vampire Red! The gown featured a gossamer silk sheer V-insert lined in nude, exciting 'nail-heads' and a braid trim. The back was plunging. The sleeves were made of transparent net-like soft silk of smoke-red. The waist was captured with a very tight suede belt, its buckle a huge replica of Satan, with twin fangs for an insert. A tiny Devil's pitchfork pointed at the buckle which was polished silver. The skirt of this unusual gown was scintillating in its three rows of six-inch fringes made of leather. Each fringe was as delicate as a shoe lace but as strong as the reins used to compel a team of horses to do the bidding of the driver. With each movement of the hips, the three rows of fringes would dance in all directions, as would a group of frenzied primitive worshippers before a weird fetish-God.

As the dress was lowered upon Bruce, he found his heart was pounding, his emotions were stepped up and he was breathless with eager anticipation. He dared not admit his true feelings to anyone; even to himself! After all, he had been FORCED into this whole thing ... by his frat brothers and then he was CAPTURED and BOUND BY FEMALES and compelled to follow their orders....

(We do not quite know how sexual excitement is produced in anyone, not just the perverse. How does a woman('s body) excite a heterosexual man? What has he learned from infancy on and how do the nongenital responses of infancy and childhood become converted into the adult genital response? Is the explanation simply physiological? (Not likely.) Does anxiety play a role in normals as in the perverse?)

How can humiliation produced on being forced to put on women's clothes by hostile women cause sexual excitement? There are several explanations that can (almost) account for this excitement.

First, although the man in the illustration is humiliated, the man reading the book is humiliated only in effigy; while he identifies with the illustrated man, he is very clearly also safely not so identified. He knows this experience, taking place via pornography, is only a fantasy.

Second, the excitement is accompanied by a guilt-removing device inherent in the story: since the pathetic boy–man is being forced to dress by the cruel women, he cannot be accused of wanting to do this himself. (In pornography, as in humor, there is always a device for reducing guilt. This could be true for many other sublimated activities with hostile components, such as the theater, visual arts, and normal sexual relations. . . . Imagine considering sexual intercourse a 'sublimated activity'!)

Yet these two reasons above are only secondary devices to *protect* the excitement and are not causes in themselves. We come closer if we study the life history that is present in the pornography in such condensed fashion.

The man who first showed me these dynamics, who also brought in the above pamphlet, had been forced to dress thus by women in childhood.

Fortunately for the research (and disastrously for him), he was posed for snapshots, placed quite openly in the family album, tracing the development of his cross-dressing. In addition, the women who did it to him are alive; though I could not interview them, they gave information to him and his wife, filling in the story indicated by the snapshots.

Each historical event now to be recounted appears in the pornography.

History. – From birth to age 3, he developed in a masculine manner.

PORNOGRAPHY. – The story starts with a masculine heterosexual man, who has shown no fetishistic interest before in women's clothes or any feminine or effeminate mannerisms.

History. – At age 3, his mother left the family and his 'mothering' was turned over to an aunt and older cousin, who despised males.

PORNOGRAPHY. – The man is trapped by a group of females, who make fun of his maleness and immediately overpower him.

116

History. – His father was almost never home day or night, for years, and in effect abandoned the boy to the women.

PORNOGRAPHY. – There is no other man in the story.

History. – These two women designed and fashioned new clothes, ruffled and effeminate looking, for the little boy. Later they dressed him, not just effeminately, but in girls' clothes 'as a joke'.

PORNOGRAPHY. – The dangerous women force the man, who is filled with shame and humiliation, to put on women's clothes. Yet they are portrayed as joking and laughing.

History. – The women, being older and bigger, were psychologically immensely powerful and physically overpowered him without a struggle.

PORNOGRAPHY. – The man does not have the strength to struggle, much less escape.

History. – Nevertheless, the little boy needed and wanted, even loved, these women. What choice did he have at 3, or 4, or 5 years? They served not only as models for identification but as desired heterosexual objects, for they were now his 'mother'.

PORNOGRAPHY. – The women are drawn as phallic and dangerous but also beautiful and feminine.

History. – Despite dressing him on occasion in girls' clothes, these women always left him the knowledge he was male and had masculinity. Except for the rare occasions when he was cross-dressed, he wore masculine clothes. His games and hobbies have always been masculine. He is now a leader of men in a masculine business. To make their own satisfaction exquisite, they had to prove that masculinity was worthless, far beneath their desire. To accomplish this, they had to be sure not to destroy it, only make it foolish. So he was not feminized to the degree that he wished his body changed to female or lost the pleasure of his penis.

PORNOGRAPHY. – The man is clearly identified as a male; this is never denied. His name is strongly masculine and is not changed by the women during the story. The women express recognition that he is masculine. The attack is specifically aimed, not at damaging his maleness, but at his identity, his masculine attributes, of which the most visible are clothes. Never in transvestite pornography is a male turned into a female.

History. – The disaster became a triumph. By age 6, he was sexually excited putting on a woman's garment.

PORNOGRAPHY. – After the trauma, the man senses in himself an intense, growing sensualness for the women's clothes that had at first been forced on him.

History. – His fetishistic cross-dressing gradually increased in frequency and completeness to dressing quite like a woman, so that added to it was a nongenitally exciting pleasure in being fully dressed as a woman.

PORNOGRAPHY. – The man, near the end of the story, is dressed completely as a woman.

History. – He found an apparently benign, gentle woman, who married him although knowing of (in fact, I learned after a few years, because of) his transvestism. She enjoyed helping him buy women's clothes and wigs and taught him to dress stylishly, apply makeup properly, and carry himself like a woman.

PORNOGRAPHY. – The harpies are now gentle, friendly, and accepting, fully feminine, and rather girlish.

History. – He presently goes into the world, passing intermittently as a woman.

PORNOGRAPHY. – All leave together, the man looking like a normal woman; he is promised that they will all do it again soon, next time as friends.

All that is missing in the pornography, but which occurs in transvestites, is a latency period after the trauma, a matter of months or years, during which there is no evidence of overt transvestism, following which the first surface manifestation of the perversion appears (that is, sexual excitement produced by women's clothes.) This latency period, being silent, has never been studied. One can, therefore, only surmise that during it the boy is developing a system of fantasies to preserve his masculinity against the onslaught to his identity by the hating female who, *in reality*, jeopardized his sense of maleness and masculinity.

It is not coincidental that he creates his success exactly at the point of disaster. That is, he uses agents of the trauma – women's clothes and the appearance of femininity – to preserve his masculinity and potency. This is not to say that this is all that is needed to create the perversion, for, while the fear of being unmanned is crucial, so also is the (defensive) construction that the powerful women have penises and the power of supermen.[3-5] As noted, this too is indicated in the pornography. (I prefer to use the term 'unmanned' at this point rather than the term 'castration anxiety' because what is feared in this case is not just organ loss but identity loss, i.e., of no longer being a man and a male.)

Some such mechanism (the conversion of sexual trauma into triumph) may be at work not only in transvestism but in other perversions and even in aspects of sexual excitement in nonperverse people.

I have tried to detail the nature of this specific trauma (attempted feminization by older, powerful females) by reporting case material showing the contributions made by mothers (and their substitutes) and fathers in helping create a transvestite. These data suggest that in *fetishistic transvestism there is not only denial of the threat of castration and invention of phallic women but also the use of historical reality*. In these patients, it really did happen that the boy was threatened with loss of masculinity and humiliated by females more powerful than he, not just in some general way, but very precisely by putting him into women's clothes.

Just where are we to find this supposed triumph that preserves the transvestite's potency? It cannot come simply from reliving a trauma. I presume, as with other episodes of mastery, it comes from such sources as finding that one has actually, over and over, survived the trauma, or from the infinite uses to which repression and denial can be put. More specifically, however, the following are suggested: (1) Conversion of a sense of being damaged and inferior into exhibitionistic fantasies ('See what a lovely woman I make'). (2) 'Self-realization', the gradual self-conscious creation of a fully evolved 'feminine' role: Some transvestites learn to act so much like a woman that they can pass as such undetected publicly. (3) More important, fantasies (conscious, preconscious, and unconscious) of actual acts of revenge against women, which create an exultant sense of redressing the balance. (4) Identifying in the pornography and other fantasy life not only with the humiliated male but with the masterful aggressor, the phallic woman.

This brings us back to the earlier remark that an essential quality in pornography (and perversion) is sadism (revenge for a passively experienced trauma). I am not only referring to well-known revenge fantasies and sexual acts found also in nontransvestite men such as those of poisoning or humiliating one's partner with ejaculate or of physical damage to someone by one's phallic onslaught. I suppose these are present in transvestites, but, additionally and more important, the transvestite revenges himself just by being able to get an erection. That is, he succeeds with a woman when he was supposed to have failed. Even more triumphantly, he succeeds at exactly that moment that should be the moment of greatest failure, when he is dressed as a woman and should be humiliated. Of course, one crucial fact sustains him when he is so dressed – his constant awareness that he has a penis under the woman's clothes, which makes him, too, a phallic woman. In the pornography, the moment of greatest pleasure is just when the story describes how the victim is told by the powerful women that he must put on women's clothes. It is no coincidence, therefore, that the fantasy picks out the moment of greatest trauma for its now moment of greatest thrill. There is no more perfect triumph than to succeed after running the precise risks that had undone one in childhood. (The reader may have already noted the similarities between this and semiperverse pleasures built on reaction formations, such as automobile racing, stage-acting, parachute jumping, competition in sports, and so many other acutely anxiety-provoking situations of potential triumph.)

Who is the victim in this transvestite fantasy? In the manifest daydream, it is the pictured transvestite-in-the-making with whom the observing transvestite consciously identifies. But additionally and unconsciously the victim is the pictured cruel phallic woman, for the transvestite, in the reality of his masturbation, is having the final victory over such a woman. Despite all she did to him in his childhood to ruin his masculinity, he has escaped her – though barely, and at the price of a severely compromised potency that can succeed only by means of perversion.

But he does win; he has survived. His penis is not only preserved, but now, as he celebrates his sacrament, he feels himself no longer split but concentratedly unified in his sexual excitement.

He identifies with the aggressor and, then (as may often be the case with the use of this mechanism), he believes (tries to believe) he is better than the aggressor: he says he is a better woman than any woman. He says this because, he rationalizes, he possesses the best of both sexes. He is always aware of his masculinity (an essential part of transvestism), and he is aware of his femininity. He feels that, having been a man and living intermittently as a man, he has a keen eye for what is most to be appreciated in women and being a 'woman' permits him to put this into action. At a deeper level, he believes himself a better woman than any woman because he is the only woman who surely has a penis.

Yet transvestites are, in the great majority, overtly heterosexual and yearn for heterosexuality (having to work against a pull from the unconscious toward identification with women). Considerable intimacy with a living woman to be desirable but dangerous, they substitute her inert clothes for her living skin. Note these descriptions of women's clothes taken from the above booklet: 'The straps were milky-way white; the sheer fabric was bewitching'; 'pure silk'; 'pure satin'; 'panties virginal white in color'; 'skin tight'; 'transparent green, like sea foam'; 'cool, silky-soft, sensuously intimate'; 'filmy'; 'smoothly formed'; 'blushing pink'; 'deliciously molded'; 'transparent net-like soft silk,' etc., for many pages.

One can see that the experience is a bisexual one, for not only is the transvestite making contact fetishistically (safely, indirectly) with women's skin (taking the woman as a heterosexual object), he is also putting it on (taking the woman as an object with whom to identify).

Comment

The reader may ask if this is a paper on pornography or on transvestism, for the matter herein shifts from the one perspective to the other. This in itself makes, then, an obvious point – that pornography, as the perverse subject's key daydream, is psychodynamically about the same as his perversion. It is the highly condensed story of his perversion: its historical origins in reality, its elaborations in fantasy, its manifest content which disguises and reveals the latent content. Without pornography, one can obviously still study the dynamics of perversions, but with pornography one has an additional tool which at times will give clues one might otherwise miss. Especially helpful is the fact that since pornography, for its creator, is produced for money-making, he will be motivated in the highest to develop a daydream which is not idiosyncratic. If his pornography is to pay, he must intuitively extract out of what he knows about his audience those features which they all share in common. If he does not, he runs the risk of selling only one copy. He, therefore, has to create a work of 'art' which is precise enough to excite and general enough to excite many. Thus, pornography is for the researcher a sort of statistical study of psychodynamics – though a more colorful, and perhaps more powerful, methodology.

With the relaxation of laws that restricted the production of pornography, the market has increased, and so it has been financially possible for the producers to cater more precisely to the taste of selected readers. And so, where formally all transvestites, regardless of varying interests within the over-all genre, had to settle for a very limited and standardized story, each now has variant forms designed more precisely to the specifics of his own perversion. Thus, not all men who intermittently cross-dress and become sexually excited by women's clothing find the pornography quoted earlier as their first choice. They say that in the past they settled for it, purchased every book that came out illustrating it, but did not feel it quite fitted *their* case. So, for those transvestites who find the overt sadomasochism in that story too intense there are now available more charming stories of the happy shy man and the happy competent woman happily buying women's clothes and then the happy woman putting the lovely clothes on the happy man.

The following is a story from a transvestite magazine. A masculine man with no previous transvestic interests has been told to dress up by a woman he knows.

It was now time to get ready for the barbecue and Lynn [the man who is to become a transvestite] selected a flowery shift and a pair of minimal heels for the occasion. More time than usual was given to application of her makeup to her eyes and mouth. How she enjoyed shaping it into the delightful bow that nature had endowed her with. Unusual attention was given to her hairdo to make certain it was perfect and in selection of beads of just the right length for her colorful outfit. Millie [the woman who is encouraging him to cross-dress] dressed similarly, but added two artificial flowers just above her ears.

'You look simply wonderful,' complimented Millie, 'and a more beautiful girl just does not exist. However, try not to talk too much this evening, but rather observe what the others do and say. O.K.?'

Soon the two girls were mingling with the other tenants at poolside, and Lynn's first evening out was underway. Millie noticed as she watched Lynn moving about, how graceful and feminine her friend appeared. . . .

(Later)

'What a wonderful evening,' exclaimed the enthusiastic Millie. 'Bill is sure a charmer and knows his way with women! Did you enjoy yourself too?'

'Yes and no,' replied Lynn. 'To be honest, I felt left out of things and did not want to get myself too involved and possibly give myself away.'

'Don't be silly, just be sure and be yourself the next time we are out. Still I can see why you might be uncomfortable,' Millie replied, 'though no one could possibly suspect that you are not what you appear to be.'

'It's easy enough for you to tell me to be myself, but remember that the me that existed till two months ago was all man. Business and sports would not be the conversation expected of me with the men, would it?' retorted Lynn. 'I can get along well enough with the women alone. God knows I've probably read as much feminine material these past months as they have in the past ten years . . . and the conversations that you and I have had give me confidence with them, but not with the men.'

'Don't worry your pretty little head about it now,' Millie said. 'We will solve that problem also in time. Get some rest for we do have a busy schedule tomorrow.' And planting a kiss on Lynn's forehead she left. . . .

(Later)

Millie was fully dressed and soon they were chatting about the many small things that most women enjoy. When they were finished, Millie insisted on doing the dishes, so that Lynn could hurry and get dressed. 'Wear the beige suit and that darling coral blouse you like so much,' she commanded. 'I don't want you to look too overbearing today since we will be out most of the day.'

(Later)

The ladies were soon seated and Lynn was delighted with the assistance of the waiter in seating them. During their light meal Millie told Lynn of her plans for them for the balance of the day.

'We are both going to enroll in the John Robert Powers Charm School where they will not only instruct you on makeup and clothes which you are coming along very well with now, but also in the art of conversation and development of your feminine personality. Most women who attend these courses are weak in this area also, and if we are to be in mixed groups again such as the barbecue, I want you to be at ease, and this should do it.'

On the opposite end of the spectrum are the stories in which the sadomasochism is intense, placed even more in the foreground than is the cross-dressing. In this form, the story is so slam-bang instantaneous that it is often represented simply by photographs without text. These show a 'woman' tied up in ropes and chains in uncomfortable positions, in fact a man in woman's clothes; but what excites in this pornography is not just the male in women's clothes but the fact that 'she' is chained. With pornography becoming specific enough for each type of man, there is less need to buy the pornography of the past which was acceptable but not ideal.

I have the impression (i.e., there are too few cases for sureness) that those who, in their childhood, were treated less cruelly by a woman (or women) prefer a happier pornography in which frank humiliation or even open physical sadism is not a part of the overt story.

123

As has been suggested, each sexually deviant person will have his own pornography and will be untouched by the pornography created for a different person. In addition to the obvious sexual excitement, however, all share in common the essential factor that the pornography will illustrate danger (humiliation, anxiety, fear, frustration) surmounted. In this sense all pornography contains the psycho-dynamics of perversions. The above is noted to introduce the idea that there is no nonperverse pornography. Most pornography is aimed at heterosexual men, however, and since there are so many customers and since there is so much of this minor-league pornography, such literature is 'normal' in the statistical sense of being congenial to many men. Thus, for most men in our society pornography consists of pictures of nude women and of heterosexual intercourse. That these forms are very common does not mean that they do not arise as solutions to conflict, distress, frustration, and anger. If they were 'normal' (now used in the sense of a universal, biological expression of unconflicted pleasure-seeking), then nudity would be sexually fetishistic in all societies, which it is not, not just in ours where it is made tantalizing by frustration.

Although it is so popular, pornography may, nonetheless not, be simply (though it may, especially in adolescence, be partly) a sub-stitute because of lack of proper sexual objects. It exists because it fills voyeuristic, sadomasochistic needs that in some people cannot be satisfied no matter how many willing sexual partners are available. And, especially, it spares one the anxieties of having to make it with another person; the people on the printed page know their place and do as directed.

At the beginning of this paper it was stated that in pornography sexual activities are somehow portrayed and that there is always a victim. These criteria are not so obvious in 'normal' pornography. Who is the victim in pictures and descriptions of heterosexual inter-course? Who is the victim and what is the sexual activity in a photo-graph of a nude?

While most of the excitement in pornography of heterosexuality probably comes quite simply from identification with the depicted participants who are displaying their agility, it is also likely that an added piquancy comes from the primal scene fantasy of a child getting away with something when he watches what he should not and perhaps a sense of superiority that is part of the dynamics of being an audience and so not exposed to risk. The victims then are the 'grown-ups' whose lack of omnipotence is proven since they do not know they are being observed.

Some of the above also is true for the nude pictures, where it is implied that the girl is calmly unaware that she is being secretly stared at and used. In fact (in fantasy) there is, however, force, something that smacks of rape, of taking from the posed girl what it is imagined she would not give the observer freely.

Very popular are descriptions of a woman who starts out cool, superior, sophisticated, and uninterested but is swept by the precisely described activities of the man into a state of lust with monumental loss of control. One easily sees therein a power struggle disguised as sexuality: the dangerous woman who is reduced to a victim and the boy who, by means of the pornography, becomes a man.

I have said that an essential dynamic in pornography is hostility. Perhaps the most important difference between more perverse and less perverse ('normal') pornography, as between perversion and normalcy, is the degree of hostility (hatred and revenge fantasies) bound or released in the sexual activity. One can raise the possibly controversial question whether in humans (especially males) sexual excitement can ever exist without brutality also present (minimal, repressed, distorted by reaction formation, attenuated, or overt in the most pathological cases). (This may be comparable to asking whether a piece of humor can exist without hostility. In humor the hostility is not simply tacked on but is a *sine qua non* [though not the only one].⁶ Is it possible that in nonperverse sexual excitement, unconscious hostility also is an essential and not simply anaclitic?)

Can anyone provide examples of behavior in sexual excitement in which, in human males at least, disguised hostility in fantasy is not a part of potency? We are already familiar with a similar situation in which hostility surmounted is essential for normal functions, for we know that normal development demands that infants be increasingly frustrated in order to permit the separation that will result in the ego functions and identity necessary for coping with the external world. This process, using frustration as an essential tool, creates a reservoir of unconscious hatred, coping with which helps determine successful or maladaptive personality development. Mastery, that most gratifying experience, often comes about through restitution from passively suffered frustration, by creating fantasies, character structures, or modes of activity which in their most primitive form are brutal, but which, filtered through a process of sublimation, may end up far removed from the original hatred.

If hostility (I do not mean here simply activity, benign aggression. but intent [even if unconscious] to harm) could be totally lifted out of sexual excitement there would be no perversions, but would normal sexuality be possible? The differences with each of the perversions, and between the different perversions and more normal sexual behavior, may lie with the specific differences in frustrations (often determined by society but applied by parents, especially mother) inflicted in infancy and childhood (e.g., the magnification of conflict in males over looking at female bodies vs. the lack of conflict in females in looking at male bodies).

Along with an increasing number of workers, I do not think that perversions are explained by permutations on castration anxiety, though these do play a part. There is growing evidence that some dangers for a boy in the oedipal situation are later versions of more fundamental problems which have to do with existence and nonexistence (that is, sense of identity). Thus, one might extend the idea that the greater frequency of perversions in males is due to having a penis which might be lost by saying that the greater frequency of perversions in males may come from males' added problem in developing a distinct identity: for the little girl, she has the process of identification working for her. Her mother is a female, so that being upon her mother's body in infancy enhances the identification process while the boy has to surmount those feminine identifications. He may even convert them into one of the sources of his masculinity. (It would be ironic if some of the forms masculinity takes *require* anlagen of femininity.) This would require a more complicated, vigorous, defensive process than in girls, with the special task that he not be swamped (as occurs in feminine men) by the original identifications with a woman. Perhaps perversions are fracture lines resulting from this process[4,5] and, while they may be cemented shut in the nonperverse, covered over in the neurotic, and kept open as channels in the perversions, these faults nonetheless run into the depths of males' identity and require greater reparative work and vigilance than in females.

A few words may be in order regarding the puzzling fact that selling pornography to women would lead one to starvation. Why? I believe in the asking itself, not just in an answer, there is information. The question is like 'the age-old mystery' of what – to put it in its ripest form – is Woman? Only men worry over the mystery of women; women do not, because they are not mystified. This does not mean that they comprehend the dynamics of their own sexuality but simply that, experiencing it, does not strike them as mysterious. If women wished (and if they were as curious as men), they would ask about the mystery of men's sexuality, which may not be so clear as some would have us think. We may take for granted that we understand male sexuality because most of the work on it has been done by males who, experiencing it, need not be so curious and mystified.

In regard to the question of why women do not use pornography, perhaps the question is wrong. Men tend to equate pornography in general with what is pornography for them in particular, but, for instance, precise depiction of sexual intercourse is less likely to be effective for women. You cannot sell pictures of nude men to women for erotic purposes; but that does not mean women do not have their own pornography. They do, but most men have not recognized it as pornographic because it would not excite a man : for instance, stories of romance, where what is emphasized is affection, closeness, courtliness, a little lovely masochism that disguises gentle triumph over a manly man, but not sweating anatomy. Thus it can appear *ad libitum*, not recognized, much less legislated against. In addition, most of us believe (cf. Kinsey[7]) that women are less voyeuristic, an essential quality of pornography. (Women are never Peeping Toms.) This may be a reflection not of a biological difference in the sexes but of our society's inhibition of a little boy's right to sexual looking and a little girl's training that she is not to permit that looking (which implies to her that it makes no big difference to anyone if she looks or not). (It may also develop that, as the routine heterosexual pornography becomes available to them in a more lenient society, more women will discover a taste for such products.)

Conclusion

I have stressed the obvious, that pornography for one person is not so for another with a different life history and psychodynamics. Looking at the repetitive, unvarying stories of transvestites, the non-transvestite finds himself quickly bored and unable to read any more. One day I asked a transvestite to bring in pornography suited to his transvestism; he told me that these stories which I had been too bored to read were in fact the pornography. Similarly, what women may find exciting in books and movies will make men in the audience restless as they wait for the story to pick up its interest again.

It is also obvious that today, with politicians legislating about pornography, they will tend to define as pornographic only those things which excite themselves.

Societies fear pornography as they fear sexuality, but perhaps there is also a less sick reason : they respond intuitively to the hostile fantasies disguised but still active in pornography. And so, pornography will be loathsome to the person responding to it (who, in

127

responding, makes it pornography rather than foolish prose); the word 'loathsome', like 'disgust', implies not only forbidden sensuality but also fear that the hostility may be released.

1 Stoller, R. J.: Transvestites' women. *Amer. J. Psychiat.* 124: 333–339, 1967.
2 Stoller, R. J.: *Sex and Gender*, New York Science House, 1968, pp. 176–193.
3 Fenichel, O.: The psychology of transvestism (1930), in *Collected Papers*. New York, W. W. Norton & Co. Inc. Publishers, 1953, vol. 1, pp. 167–180.
4 Freud, S., Fetishism (1927), in Strachey, J. (trans-ed.): *Complete Psychological Works*, standard edition. London, Hogarth Press Ltd., 1961, vol. 21, pp. 152–157.
5 Freud, S., Splitting of the ego in the process of defence (1940), in Strachey, J. (trans-ed.): *Complete Psychological Works*, standard edition. London, Hogarth Press Ltd., 1964, vol. 23, pp. 275–278.
6 Freud, S., Jokes and their relation to the unconscious (1905), in Strachey, J. (trans-ed.): *Complete Psychological Works*, standard edition. London, Hogarth Press Ltd., 1960, vol. 8, pp. 194–208, 222–227.
7 Kinsey, A. C., et al.: *Sexual Behaviour in the Human Female*, Philadelphia, W. B. Saunders Co., 1953, pp. 651–672.

PORNOGRAPHY AND THE
POLITICS OF RAGE AND SUBVERSION

Masud R. Khan

Reproduced from *The Times Literary Supplement* by permission

Pornography: obscene writings or pictures intended to provoke sexual excitement. (*The Penguin English Dictionary*.)

I ACCEPT the above as an adequate definition and shall try to
explore the nature of 'provocation' and the quality of 'sexual excitement' which is engendered by pornographic literature and
imagery. In order to make my point I offer two examples of pornographic writing, taken at random:

'*Yes, Lovely –* ' Her voice came to him, somewhere near a scream,
it seemed, as a hot, white spinning haze began enveloping him, 'Yes,
YES, LOVELY – ' she said – His arm was gliding, penetrating, he
was almost up to his elbow, he was drenching wet, nearly out of his
head, he began to stroke, he stroked and stroked, she was writhing
under it, it was a pumping stroke, he stroked more rapidly, feeling
the very depths of her meeting his loving fist, each time it thrust
home in her, he stroked and stroked, she began to scream, he was in
a wild dream, the sweat poured off him, she couldn't have been
drenched more, he plunged and stroked, up to his elbow. (F. Polini :
Pretty maids all in a row.)

A man we had never seen previously, said that amiable whore,
came to the house and proposed a rather unusual ceremony: he
wished to be tied to one side of a stepladder: we secured his thighs
and waist to the third rung and, raising his arms above his head, tied
his wrists to the uppermost step. He was naked. Once firmly bound,
he had to be exposed to the most ferocious beating, clubbed with the
cat's handle when the knots at the tips of the cords were worn out.
He was naked, I repeat, there was no need to lay a finger upon him,
nor did he even touch himself, but after having received a savage
pounding his monstrous instrument rose like a rocket, it was seen
to sway and bounce between the ladder's rungs, hovering like a

pendulum and soon after, impetuously launch its fuck into the middle of the room. He was unbound, he paid, and that was all. (Sade: *The 120 Days of Sodom.*)

Even a cursory examination of the somatic events described leaves one in no doubt of their physical impossibility for a woman and a man. To push a whole fist and arm up the genitals would entail rupture, violence and enormous damage to the organ involved. But the author disregards all that. Instead, the sensation reported is one of pleasurable ecstasy. Similarly, Sade's character, after the thrashing he receives, is in no way enfeebled or injured; he just walks robustly away after the event. And the example I have quoted is, by Sade's standards, a rather mild one. For persons to be severely injured, girls to be maimed in sexual orgies, their toes cut off, etc., is routine in the adventures undertaken in the Sadeian *écriture*. No matter what is done to the human body, it never gets really damaged or incapacitated. Every character remains the same after the event as before. Pain hinders nothing, and pain teaches nothing. Sade's Justine stays whole and innocent and ignorant from the beginning to the end of that narrative.

If the somatic events described in a pornographic *écriture* – I prefer to use the French concept of *écriture* to the English word 'writing', because it implies a specific intent in the use of words – are utterly unfeasible in terms of the actual human body and its capacities, then the question arises: from where do these 'somatic events' derive their authenticity and potential to stimulate the reader sexually? The answer lies in the specialized use of words in pornography. Here they do not describe human experience, but instead simulate or concoct a completely non-human somatic event. The very absurdity and unfeasibility of this event lends it a new power: it has transcended the innate physical limits of the human body to experience pain and excitement.

This specialized use of words has another quality: the mentalization of instinct. What are described are not spontaneous, shared, humanly sexual experiences, but highly elaborate and synthetic events which are the concoction of the mind through words. Though, overtly, the experiences are meant to be physical, and concrete, in fact these events can happen only in the mind, and in that conjuring void which is the terrain of pornography. It is this characteristic which puts pornography beyond the scope of ethics and morality. It can be evaluated only aesthetically and psychologically, not judicially or ethically.

Since pornography is exclusively a perverted mind-game that has little to do with ordinary sexual experiences, it is necessary to examine it more closely, aesthetically and psychologically. The aesthetics of pornography are a conglomerate of lacks. Rarely does it achieve the quality of literature proper. With due apologies to Apollinaire, Jean Paulhan, Geoffrey Gorer, Georges Bataille and Roland Barthes, no one can really claim any virtues for the style of Sade. One has to admit that Sade's *écriture* is boring, oppressively repetitive and without invention – the same somatic events are concocted in a claustrophobic space with an obsessive and indefatigable insistence. There is also little imagination or invention or characterization in pornography; and Sade again is the prime example. And there is never any emotion, object-relation or self-experience. But I anticipate: that belongs to the psychological examination.

It is when one considers pornography aesthetically that one discovers that it is as false in its pretensions to be literature as it is lacking in its claim to be the vehicle of heightened instinctual experiences. Here pornographic writers have struck lucky, with the hysterical outcries of outraged Europeans, reared in their puritanical traditions. The whole issue has been sidetracked. The real issue is not that pornography is immoral but that it is pathetically bad literature. An ironic and absurd situation has arisen vis-à-vis pornography in contemporary European cultures. While pornographic writers will engage in endless debate with the cultural moralists – those anachronistic and eunuched custodians of culture's failing vitality – they are dogmatically intolerant of any suggestion that pornography retails poor literature and sick psychology to those resourceless individuals who have not the means to evaluate it and can only become its hapless accomplices.

This is the first cultural area where pornography is most subversive. Since it neither draws upon nor extends the reader's imagination and sensibility, it offers him/her a limited world of omnipotent verbiage, insinuated and fabricated as somatic events, with their built-in faked climaxes and orgasms, at which the accomplice can feel both complacent and excited. The genius, if one may use that word, of pornography rests in its confidence-trick. It aligns itself with the incapacity of a given individual and a culture to actualize experiences from personal initiative – both as real life and as literature. It is the incapacitated writer's revenge on the tradition of true literature in a culture. If it takes a culture centuries to actualize, through one of its members, the *Confessions* of a Rousseau or the *Four*

Quartets of an Eliot, it entails merely a desperate addiction to personal affliction to bring about a Sade or a William Burroughs.

The chief sin of pornography – and one must use that concept since pornography has become sacred today – is that it is not literature proper. No, much worse, that its intention and achievement are to dislocate literature from its vital role in the life of the individual and the culture. Pornography negates imagination, style and the tradition of man's struggle to use language to know and enhance himself.

Now let me turn to the psychological aspects of pornography. What I am offering is a personal point of view or, to borrow a felicitous phrase of Nietzsche's, 'regulative fictions'. My psychoanalytic training and practice have naturally biased me in a certain direction and lend a specific conceptual slant to my 'regulative fictions'. I believe that pornography alienates its accomplices – one cannot talk of them as its readers – both from their self and the *other*. What masquerades as mutual and ecstatic intimacy through somatic events is in fact a sterile and alienated mental concoction. It is this characteristic which made me once remark that pornography is the stealer of dreams. In it there is neither scope for reverie nor for object-relations. Everything is imprisoned through words in a violent and tyrannical game with the own body-self and the *other*. Its time is the perpetual and static present. Hence the nostalgic atmosphere of pornography.

Anna Freud has diagnosed the essential predicament in perversion-formations as the dread of emotional surrender. One could argue that the crucial predicament in pornography resides in the incapacity for sensual surrender. Here lies the fascinating paradox at the root of pornography. Overtly it is militantly devoted to describing states of ecstatic sensuality and abandonment to a mutual orgastic pleasure. But all that it actualizes is an orgiastic expertise in the physical manipulation of the own body-self and the *other*'s bodily organs. Hence a certain manic quality, which infests the narrative. If one reads the two specimens that I have quoted, one cannot fail to sense a certain quality in it, very much like that of an apoplectic fit.

So the next question is: what is the nature of affect that these somatic events are trying to actualize, externalize and distribute (one cannot call it share). My answer to that is: *rage*. The only true achievement of pornography is that it transmutes rage into erotic somatic events. I advisedly use the word 'transmutes' and not 'sublimates'. Because of the peculiar use of words in this *écriture* there is none of that assimilation or working-through of the affect of rage, which sublimation would entail. It abreacts and encapsulates the transmuted rage into pleasurable somatic events, but with the violence of rage still wholly there. Now, as Barrington Cooper once remarked to me, violence is not a quarrelsome emotion; it entails an absolute demand for submission. What in health can be experienced as sensual surrender, in pornography becomes abject submission through violent events. Hence the perspicacity of Jill Tweedie's remark in *The Guardian*: 'The whole pattern of pornography is one long woeful saga of female degradation.' But as my example from Sade shows, it is not only female degradation but male as well. Genet too has given us this bizarre spectacle of degradation, mutilation and violent submission in vivid, hieratic and hallucinatory terms.

The capacity of pornography to transmute latent rage into violent, erotic events encapsulated in language lends it three potent functions: subversion, therapeutics and instruction. It is subversive in so far as it negates the *person* through its somatic expertise. The accomplice/reader can reach and participate in this type of *écriture* only in very specific states of depersonalization and dissociation. It is therapeutic in so far as it transmutes the threat of total violence and destruction from latent rage in the individual and the culture into manageably distributed, dosed and eroticized language. In a macabre way the therapeutics of pornography achieve Freud's demand for analytic treatment: 'where Id was there shall the Ego be'. In pornography it is all ego and only the ego; no id, no body, no person. The id, the person and the body are merely exploited to establish and actualize the machinery of somatic events. Its instruction lies in that it has to *teach* the tricks to its accomplice/reader for its peculiar reality to be participated in. And here again the Divine Marquis set the pace, when he all too awarely wrote his *Philosophy in the Bedroom*. In Madame de Saint-Ange's postulate to Eugénie:

May atrocities, horrors, may the most odious crimes astonish you the most forbidden, 'tis that which best rouses the intellect ... 'tis no more, my Eugénie; what is of the filthiest, the most infamous, that which always causes us most deliciously to discharge.

Sade most insighfully exposed the omnipotent role of intellect in these somatic events, and the absence of instinct.

This specific hyper-functioning of intellect, through the creation of somatic events imprisoned in words, not only alienates but also isolates the reader/accomplice just as much as it does the characters

133

in pornography. Geoffrey Gorer in an article on 'The Pornography of Death' accounts for this phenomenon in an interesting way:

Pornography on the other hand, the description of tabooed activities to produce hallucination or delusion, seems to be a very much rare phenomenon. It probably can only arise in the literate societies, and we certainly have no records of it for non-literate ones; for whereas the enjoyment of obscenity is predominantly social, *the enjoyment of pornography is predominantly private.*

My contention here is that this privacy, or what I call isolation, is a further subversive function of pornography. The banal fact is that pornography is largely, if not exclusively, used for masturbation.

Sartre in his mammoth study *Saint Genet – Comédien et martyr*, discussing the whole function of masturbation in Genet's books, has this to say:

Seeking excitement and pleasure, Genet starts by enveloping himself in his images as the polecat envelops itself in its odour. These images call forth by themselves words that reinforce them; often they even remain incomplete; words are needed to finish the job; these words require that they be uttered and, finally, written down; writing calls forth and creates its audience; the *onanistic narcissism ends by being stanched in words.* Genet writes in a state of dream and, in order to consolidate his dreams, dreams that he writes, then writes that he dreams, and the act of writing awakens him. *The consciousness of the word is a local awakening within the fantasy; he awakes without ceasing to dream.*

I am not so convinced as Sartre is that the phenomenon of dream is involved in Genet's writings; it strikes me that it is the other way round. All of Genet's compulsive onanistic fantasizing compensates both for his incapacity to dream and his incapacity to relate to the other. And pornography, in this sense, is an objectivization of these incapacities in its authors. One can go to the extreme and say that pornography is little more than masturbation writ large. Or, in Sartre's postulate, 'the onanist wants to take hold of the word *as an object.*'

If, aesthetically, pornography is lacking in imagination and, psychologically, in both emotion and object-relation – and if, physically, it symptomizes a lack of spontaneous instinctual impetus and desire – then one can define it as exclusively preoccupied with the mental pursuit of sensations to the exclusion of both emotions and object-relations. It aims to conjure up somatic events through words,

134

and these are its only reality. If an accomplice/reader becomes too addicted to the given reality of pornography, then there is definitely a disruption of his own inner capacities to grow and personalize as a human adult. The trouble with pornography is not that it is against God's law but against nature's law in so far as it subverts the growth of the human adult into selfhoood.

I have so far used the concept 'somatic events', and have given two sorts of example of them. But one needs to examine the character of these events in more detail. Though they purport to be sexual in nature, in fact sexuality is merely exploited, to express violence and rage, either against the self-body or the other-body. The champions of pornography and pornographic writers themselves often make out that what they are trying to remedy are the inhibitions of instinctual experience in the individual through prudish cultural prejudices. Their claim is that they are trying to free the individual, to be more vitally and sentiently his instinctual, sexual self. And yet what pornography achieves in fact is the opposite of what it claims to set out to do. As Sade and Sartre have pointed out, the mind and the word usurp in fact the natural function of instinct in human experience and misappropriate the instinctual drive to a hyper-mental concoction of often brutal imagery, in order to establish somatic events which disregard the person and being of the characters

So one sees that there is a specific type of split involved in the concoction of these events. First, the instinctual sexual drive is dissociated from natural bodily expression, sharing and gratification through object-relation. Second, this mutilation of the sexual drive is then used to create a very specific type of violence through language, a violence that is further eroticized to make it palatable. But the fact remain the same: negation of the self and object. It is in this particular redistribution of the instinctual drives of sex and aggression that the true pathology of pornography rests. It has replaced sexual freedom and sharing by a mental act of coercion on the body-self and object into extreme stances of submission and humiliation. In this context one can say that the politics of pornography are inherently fascistic.

So far, by and large, I have looked at the negative aspect of pornography. It cannot, however, be denied that a cultural revolution has been realized through pornography, from the Divine Marquis to Saint Genet. To my knowledge nobody has so far tried seriously to account for it; and one cannot write it off as a fatuous phenomenon. Pornography is both a symptom of specific processes of the devitalization of instinct in a culture as well as in the indi-

135

vidual, and an attempt at a cure of the symptom. Hence, my emphasis on the therapeutics involved in pornography. It is necessary now to understand more about the nature of the symptom and its functioning, on the one hand, and the character of the revolution that pornography has created in European cultures on the other. It is no use saying that both the symptom and the revolution can be done away with by legislation. As my quote from Geoffrey Gorer indicates, the advent of pornography is very much linked with literacy, and in recent decades advertising media have added a vast and new vocabulary of visual imagery to pornography.

All serious thinkers – be they poets or psychologists or philosophers – in this century have been concerned about a distinct dehumanization of man's relation to himself. It is my contention that with the Industrial Revolution and the advent of scientific technology in European cultures man began to consider himself neither in the image of God nor of man, but in that of a machine which was his own invention; and pornographic *écriture* and imagery try to make of the human body an ideal machine, which can be manipulated to yield maximum sensation. These sensations are derivative of instinct but essentially aggressive in intent. What David Holbrook has called 'the cult of death circuit'[1] in certain types of modern literature is only one side of the coin, the other being the pornographic circuit. Both of them are essentially nihilistic towards the realization of the individual's psychic potential, both within himself and in his relation to others.

1 See *Sylvia Plath and the Problem of Existence*, Athlone Press, 1972.

SOCIAL ASPECTS OF PORNOGRAPHY

Many observers have called our society a 'schizoid' society, meaning that the inhuman nature of our surroundings, and the meaninglessness of many of our activities, tends to reduce our sense of our uniqueness, and our potentialities. In this environment, many people tend to hide their feelings, and separate them from their activities, which become increasingly mechanical. Inevitably, this loss of emotional power and wholeness affects people's sexual lives.

Pornography, far from being a solution to this tendency towards 'affectlessness' and division of the self, is likely to make these worse. Because it is itself a form of the schizoid division of 'sex' from the whole being, it menaces the individual with distortions of attitude and new forms of inhibition. It may well be having the effect of lowering the barriers of concern, by undermining the imagination, and by reducing human beings, in one another's eyes, to the mere bearers of impersonal sensations. Its inherent sadism may well find its way into society, in forms of non-consensual acts, and the 'acting out' of primitive fantasy.

Yet the steam behind pornography is mainly economic, and it is a feature of the same economy that depersonalizes man at large.

SEX IN A SCHIZOID SOCIETY

Rollo May

FREUD'S patients were mostly hysterics who, by definition, carried repressed energy which could be released by the therapist's naming of the unconscious. Today, however, when practically all our patients are compulsive-obsessional neurotics (or character problems, which is a more general and less intense form of the same thing), we find that the chief block to therapy is the incapacity of the patient to feel. These patients are persons who can talk from now till doomsday about their problems, and are generally well-practiced intellectuals; but they cannot experience genuine feelings. Wilhelm Reich described compulsive characters as 'living machines', and in his book, David Shapiro refers to this as well as to the 'restraint and evenness in living and thinking' of these compulsive-obsessives.

Reich, here, was ahead of his time in insight into the problems of twentieth-century patients.[1]

The Emergence of Apathy

Earlier, I quoted Leslie Farber's assertion that our period should be called the 'age of disordered will'. But what underlies this disordered will?

I shall take my own leap in proposing an answer. I believe it is a state of feelinglessness, the despairing possibility that nothing matters, a condition very close to apathy. Pamela H. Johnson, after reporting the murders on the moors of England, found herself unable to shake loose her conviction that 'We may be approaching the state which the psychologists call affectlessness.'[2] If apathy or affectlessness is a dominant mood emerging in our day, we can understand on a deeper level why love and will have become so difficult.

What some of us were nonplussed to find in our patients in the 1950's has, in its predictive fashion, during the last few years, emerged as an overt issue gravely troubling our whole society. I wish to quote from my book, *Man's Search for Himself*, written in 1952 and published in the following year:

It may sound surprising when I say, on the basis of my own clinical practice as well as that of my psychological and psychiatric colleagues, that the chief problem of people in the middle decade of the twentieth century is *emptiness*.[3]

While one might laugh at the meaningless boredom of people a decade or two ago, the emptiness has for many now moved from the state of boredom to a state of futility and despair which holds promise of dangers.[4]

... The human being cannot live in a condition of emptiness for very long: if he is not growing *toward* something, he does not merely stagnate; the pent-up potentialities turn into morbidity and despair, and eventually into destructive activities.[5]

The *feeling* of emptiness or vacuity ... generally comes from people's feeling that they are *powerless* to do anything effective about their lives or the world they live in. Inner vacuousness is the long-term, accumulated result of a person's particular conviction about himself, namely his conviction that he cannot act as an entity in directing his own life, or change other people's attitudes toward him, or effectually influence the world around him. Thus he gets the deep sense of despair and futility which so many people in our day have.

And soon, since what he wants and what he feels can make no real difference, he gives up wanting and feeling.[6]

. . . Apathy and lack of feeling are also defenses against anxiety. When a person continually faces dangers he is powerless to overcome, his final line of defense is at last to avoid even feeling the dangers.[7]

It was not until the mid-60's that this problem erupted in the form of several incidents that shook us to the very foundations. Our 'emptiness' had been turning into despair and destructiveness, violence and assassination; it is now undeniable that these go hand in hand with apathy. 'For more than half an hour, thirty-eight respectable, law-abiding citizens in Queens,' reported The New York Times in March, 1964, 'watched a killer stalk and stab a woman in three separate attacks in Kew Gardens.'[8] In April of the same year, the Times said, in an impassioned editorial about another event in which a crowd urged a deranged youth who was clinging to a hotel ledge to jump, calling him 'chicken' and 'yellow': 'Are they any different from the wild-eyed Romans watching and cheering as men and beasts tore each other apart in the Colosseum? . . . Does the attitude of that Albany mob bespeak a way of life for many Americans? . . . If so, the bell tolls for all of us.'[9] In May of that year, a Times article was headed 'Rape Victim's Screams Draw 40 But No One Acts.'[10] A number of similar events occurred during the next months which awakened us from our apathy long enough to realize how apathetic we had become, and how much modern city existence had developed in us the habit of uninvolvement and unfeeling detachment.

I am aware how easy it is to exaggerate specific events, and I have no wish to overstate my case. Nevertheless, I do believe that there is in our society a definite trend toward a state of affectlessness as an attitude toward life, a character state. The anomie about which intellectuals had speculated earlier seemed now to emerge with a hideous reality on our very streets and in our very subways.

What shall we call this state reported by so many of our contemporaries – estrangement, playing it cool, alienation, withdrawal of feeling, indifference, anomie, depersonalization? Each one of these terms expresses a part of the condition to which I refer – a condition in which men and women find themselves experiencing a distance between themselves and the objects which used to excite their affection and their will. I wish to leave open for the moment what the sources of this are. When I use the term 'apathy', despite its limiting connotations, it is because its literal meaning is the closest to what I am describing: 'want of feeling; lack of passion, emotion or excitement, indifference.' Apathy and the schizoid world go hand in hand as cause and effect of each other.

Apathy is particularly important because of its close relation to love and will. Hate is not the opposite of love; apathy is. The opposite of will is not indecision – which actually may represent the struggle of the *effort* to decide, as in William James – but being uninvolved, detached, unrelated to the significant events. Then the issue of will never can arise. The interrelation of love and will inheres in the fact that both terms describe a person in the process of reaching out, moving toward the world, seeking to affect others or the inanimate world, and opening himself to be affected; molding, forming, relating to the world or requiring that it relate to him. This is why love and will are so difficult in an age of transition, when all the familiar mooring places are gone. The blocking of the ways in which we affect others and are affected by them is the essential disorder of both love and will. Apathy, or a-pathos, is a withdrawal of feeling; it may begin as playing it cool, a studied practice of being unconcerned and unaffected. 'I did not want to get involved,' was the consistent response of the thirty-eight citizens of Kew Gardens when they were questioned as to why they had not acted. Apathy, operating like Freud's 'death instinct', is a gradual letting go of involvement until one finds that life itself has gone by.

Viewing the society freshly, students often have a clearer insight into this than older adults – though they tend, in oversimplified fashion, to blame it on the institutions. 'We have just not been given any passionate sense of the excitement of intellectual life around here,' said the editor of the Columbia *Spectator*. A student columnist in *The Michigan Daily* wrote, 'This institution has dismally failed to inculcate, in most of its undergraduates at least, anything approaching an intellectual appetite.' He spoke of the drift 'towards something worse than mediocrity – and that is absolute indifference. An indifference towards perhaps even life itself.' 'We were all divided up into punches on an IBM card,' a Berkeley student remarked. 'We decided to punch back in the riots of 1964, but the *real* revolution around here will come when we decide to burn computer cards as well as draft cards.'

There is a dialectical relationship between apathy and violence. To live in apathy provokes violence; and, in incidents like those cited above, violence promotes apathy. Violence is the ultimate destructive substitute which surges in to fill the vacuum where there is no relatedness. There are degrees of violence, from the relatively normal shock effect of many forms of modern art, through pornography and obscenity – which achieve their desired reaction through violence to our forms of life – to the extreme pathology of assassinations and the murders of the moors. When inward life dries up, when feeling decreases and apathy increases, when one cannot affect or even genuinely *touch* another person, violence flares up as a daimonic necessity for contact, a mad drive forcing touch in the most direct way possible. This is one aspect of the well-known relationship between sexual feelings and crimes of violence. To inflict pain and torture at least proves that one can affect somebody. In the alienated state of mass communication, the average citizen knows dozens of TV personalities who come smiling into his living room of an evening – but he *himself is never known*. In this state of alienation and anonymity, painful for anyone to bear, the average person may well have fantasies which hover on the edge of real pathology. The mood of the anonymous person is, If I cannot affect or touch anybody, I can at least shock you into some feeling, force you into some passion through wounds and pain; I shall at least make sure we both feel something, and I shall force you to see me and know that I also am here! Many a child or adolescent has forced the group to take cognizance of him by destructive behavior; and though he is condemned, at least the community notices him. To be actively hated is almost as good as to be actively liked; it breaks down the utterly unbearable situation of anonymity and aloneness.

But having seen the serious effects of apathy, we need now to turn to the fact of its necessity; and, in its 'normal schizoid' form, how it can be turned into a constructive function. Our tragic paradox is that in contemporary history, we *have* to protect ourselves by some kind of apathy. 'Apathy is a curious state,' remarks Harry Stack Sullivan; 'It is a way used to survive defeat without material damage, although if it endures too long one is damaged by the passage of time. Apathy seems to me to be a miracle of protection by which a personality in utter fiasco rests until it can do something else.'[11] The longer the situation goes unmet, the more apathy is prolonged and it sooner or later becomes a character state. This affectlessness is a shrinking-up in the winds of continuous demands, a freezing in the face of hyperstimuli, letting the current go by since one fears he would be overwhelmed if he responded to it. No one who has ever ridden the subway at rush hour with a cacophonous din and burden of anonymous humanity will be surprised at this.

It is not difficult to appreciate how people living in a schizoid age have to protect themselves from tremendous overstimulation –

protect themselves from the barrage of words and noise over radio and TV, protect themselves from the assembly line demands of collectivized industry and gigantic factory-modeled multiversities. In a world where numbers inexorably take over as our means of identification, like flowing lava threatening to suffocate and fossilize all breathing life in its path; in a world where 'normality' is defined as keeping your cool; where sex is so available that the only way to preserve any inner center is to learn to have intercourse without committing yourself – in such a schizoid world, which young people experience more directly since they have not had time to build up the defenses which dull the senses of their elders, it is not surprising that will and love have become increasingly problematic and even, as some people believe, impossible of achievement.

But what of the constructive use of this schizoid situation? We have seen how Cézanne could turn his schizoid personality into a way of expressing the most significant forms of modern life, and could stand against the debilitating tendencies in our society by means of his art. We have seen that the schizoid stand is necessary; now we shall inquire how, in its healthy dimensions, it can also be turned to good. The constructive schizoid person stands against the spiritual emptiness of encroaching technology and does not let himself be emptied by it. He lives and works with the machine without becoming a machine. He finds it necessary to remain detached enough to get meaning from the experience, but in doing so to protect his own inner life from impoverishment.

Dr Bruno Bettelheim finds the same supremacy of the aloof person – whom I would call schizoid – in his experiences in the concentration camps during World War II.

According to psychoanalytic convictions then current . . . aloofness from other persons and emotional distance from the world were viewed as weakness of character. My comments . . . on the admirable way in which a group of what I call 'annointed persons' behaved in the concentration camps suggest how struck I was with these very aloof persons. They were very much out of contact with their unconscious but nevertheless retained their old personality structure, stuck to their values in the face of extreme hardships, and as persons were hardly touched by the camp experience. . . . These very persons who, according to existing psychoanalytic theory, should have had weak personalities apt to readily disintegrate, turned out to be heroic leaders, mainly because of the strength of their character.[12]

Indeed, studies have shown that the persons who survive most effectively in space ships, and who can adjust to the sensory deprivation necessary for such a life – our comrades of the twenty-first century – are those who can detach and withdraw into themselves. 'There are reasons to believe,' writes Arthur J. Brodbeck after summarizing the evidence, 'that it may well be the schizoid personality that will be best able to endure the requirements of extended space travel.' They preserve the inner world which the very hyperstimuli of our age would take away. These introverts can continue to exist despite the overpowering stimuli or lack of it, for they have learned to develop a 'constructive' schizoid attitude toward life. Since we must live in the world as we find it, this distinguishing of the constructively schizoid attitude is an important part of our problem.

Apathy is the withdrawal of will and love, a statement that they 'don't matter', a suspension of commitment. It is necessary in times of stress and turmoil; and the present great quantity of stimuli is a form of stress. But apathy, now in contrast to the 'normal' schizoid attitude, leads to emptiness and makes one less able to defend oneself, less able to survive. However understandable the state we are describing by the term apathy is, it is also essential that we seek to find a new basis for the love and will which have been its chief casualties.

1 See David Shapiro, *Neurotic Styles*, Basic Books, 1965.
2 See Pamela Hansford Johnson, *On Iniquity*, Scribners.
3 *Man's Search for Himself*, W. W. Norton, 1953.
4 *Ibid.*
5 *Ibid.*
6 *Ibid.*
7 *Ibid.*
8 *New York Times*, March 27, 1969.
9 *New York Times*, April 16, 1964.
10 *New York Times*, May 6, 1964.
11 *The Psychiatric Interview*, W. W. Norton, p. 184.
12 *The Informed Heart*, The Free Press of Glencoe, 1960, p. 20.

F

PSEUDO-SEXUALITY AND THE SEXUAL REVOLUTION

David Boadella, B.A., M.Ed.

[*Author's Note:* The chapter that follows originated as a review of a book by Reimut Reiche, 'Sexuality and class consciousness', the German edition of which came out in 1968 (published by NBL in English in November 1970). Reiche studied sociology in West Berlin and Frankfurt, and joined the German Socialist movement, the SDS, becoming not only its President in 1966–7, but one of its leading theoreticians, developing many of his views in its journal *Neue Kritik*. Reiche is one of the few people who, whilst learning much from Wilhelm Reich's sex-political work, has had the ability and the insight to move beyond it, in the way that Reich himself saw the need, towards a critique of contemporary 'sexualism'.

Whilst my debt to Reimut Reiche in this chapter is clear, the 'review' turned into a fuller elaboration of my own views, and the responsibility for the ideas expressed in it is mine alone, except where otherwise indicated. In addition to potential confusion between the names of Reich and Reiche, the reader should be warned to distinguish between Herbert Marcuse and Steven Marcus, both of whom are referred to in the text.]

WILHELM REICH'S psychiatric work led him to formulate a fundamental distinction between *primary* and *secondary* drives. He rejected on clinical ground the pessimistic view that there was a fundamental rift between nature and culture, and that the child required 'civilizing' by a process of education aimed at controlling and disciplining the primitive animal needs. Reich found his experience both in therapy and in upbringing revealed that the destructive anti-social impulses arise as secondary disturbances when the primary needs had been frustrated or repressed.

This led to a radical divergence between the goals of character-analysis and later vegetotherapy, and those of orthodox psycho-

144

analysis. Whereas the goals of traditional analysis were to strengthen the ego in its defences against the repressed unconscious, in the belief that 'an adequate degree of repression is necessary for a healthy mind' (Pearson, 1954), Reich's approach was to provide an outlet in the therapeutic session for the discharge of all the destructive and hostile impulses; after which it became possible for the deeper feelings of spontaneous warmth and open-heartedness to be liberated. In terms of therapy this meant in practice that it was possible to work through a layer of murderous rage, or of sadistic sexual feelings, and to reach a layer of emotion which was wholesome, integrating, and 'naturally moral'. 'Beneath the neurotic mechanism Reich wrote, 'behind all these dangerous, grotesque, irrational phantasies and impulses, I found a bit of simple, matter-of-fact decent nature. I found this in every single patient in whom it was possible to penetrate sufficiently deeply.'[1]

In *The Mass Psychology of Fascism* Reich related these successive layers of personality to social structures and attitudes. The top, repressive layer he connected with compulsory moralism; the secondary layer with the break-out of fascist destructiveness, and the primary layer with sex-economic and work-democratic social forms. In my article on 'Social structure and character structure'[2] some of these distinctions were elaborated as they apply to modern political attitudes. It was pointed out there how Reich's formulations introduce much greater subtlety into the way one looks at social developments, in place of the traditional *dualism* of traditionalist v. revolutionary and avante-garde movements.

In the realm of the sweeping changes in sexual behaviour and attitudes that have been taking place during the last quarter of a century, there is need for similar careful distinctions if one is to avoid falling into the trap of equating all challenges to traditional moralistic and repressive sexual attitudes, with progress. When Reich spoke of the 'sexual revolution' he envisaged and worked for the replacement of the authoritarian family, the sex-negative upbringing, and the emotional conflicts of puberty, with a much freer climate of opinion where relationships were formed on the basis of mutual love, instead of on the basis of neurotic compulsiveness or the requirements of social taboos. When Reich built up the Sexpol movement in Germany he hoped to help build such a climate of opinion amongst the young, and to challenge politically many of the oppressive practices that worked against it – such as the ban on contraceptive information, the absence of a decent sexual education, the inculcation of feelings of shame and guilt about the body, during upbringing, and so forth.

145

His experiences taught him that to encourage such a mass movement had many grave hazards. He found for example that people's character structures could not adapt to such changes easily. There was great confusion centered round the concept of 'sexual freedom', between the loosening of the tight grip that society had on healthy sexuality and its expressions, and the loosening of the grip it had on the living out of sick and sadistic drives. Reich finally abandoned his efforts to reform sexual attitudes by political means, and threw all his efforts into the realm of infant development, which was so decisive for the later emotional and sexual life of the individual. He warned that one of the most disastrous things that could happen to the cause of the sexual revolution that he had worked for, was the same message in the hands of heavily armoured people who might champion it chiefly as an opportunity for living out their secondary drives on the social scene. He wrote that the development of a 'brothel religion' out of his sex-economic concepts of the genital embrace would be a disaster. The natural desire to liberate the deep bodily streamings, and with them the urge to flow out, and to express oneself in sexual love with another person, was totally confused with the desire to liberate the distorted and split sexual impulses. 'Natural love pouring into dead genitals turns into hatred and stale murder of social living.'³ (p. 96).

An analogy may help to clarify Reich's fear of a massive unleashing of perverse drives and fantasies on the social scene. Few people have been as critical of Reich of the police state as he met it in Nazi Germany, and in Austria. But his work-democratic writings led him to a careful discrimination between the life-positive and the life-negative roles of the power agents in society. The policeman is life-negative when he works for a state which threatens the fundamental liberties of the individual. He has a life-positive effect when he works to defend those liberties. The campaign for 'freedom from the police' is meaningless unless one distinguishes between these two functions, since otherwise complete freedom from the police would leave people no defence against for example, robbery or murder. It is possible to visualize the 'complete freedom' of having no police force, only in a society which has no criminals.

In the realm of 'sexual freedom' the repeal of the laws against homosexuality is an example of progressive legislation designed to eradicate police persecution of private sexual behaviour which was the concern of no-one but the people concerned. The retention of the laws against rape, or child-seduction, is an example of necessary protection of the individual from the invasion of others (however

146

much the concept of punishment for such acts needs rethinking). It is undeniable that in the course of the increasing slackening of repressive controls that characterizes the 'permissive society', there has been greater freedom from authoritarian regression, for people to lead their own emotional lives, and to remove sexual ignorance. But the very freedom that has been won is being rapidly eroded by the emergence of what Marcuse has called 'repressive desublimation.'[4]

'De-sublimation', because the gates are now open for a free-flow of pornographic, but socially-permitted sexual expressions which are championed by liberals as an advance, but which are no nearer to health than the moralistic standards that preceded them. 'Repressive', because any social conditioning that reinforces and imprints a sick and distorted concept of sexuality, must block and impede the development of mature feelings and genuine sexual expression.

Of course, nothing angers the champions of an indiscriminate sexual freedom more than the concept of 'healthy sexuality', with its built-in value structures, and its emphasis on the qualitative, on the emotional tone of a person, and the contactfulness of a relationship. The hallmark of the 'freedom-pedlars' in sexual matters is that they are *against* the previous norms, taboos, restrictions, etc., but they are not *for* anything specific, except the release of whatever was held in check previously. Reich's concept of a healthy sex-economy offered, however, a precise, definable and discriminating goal for the sexual freedom movement, and it is just this goal which is threatened as the exploiters of commercial or sadistic sexuality enjoy their field day. In the struggle against anti-sexual and anti-life measures and attitudes, those who champion and uphold the natural stream of life, and those who defend the cause of the pornographic flood-tide, make strange bedfellows.

Reich recognized that compulsive moralism and pornography were two sides of the same penny. The obverse of the obsessional refusal to face sexual realities on the part of the repressive moralist, is the obsessional fascination that sexual material holds in the permissive era. From the vantage point of the moralist, desperately trying to stem the flood and to batten down the hatches, *every* release of the repressed is indistinguishable from the pornographic. This was why Reich was always dogged throughout his life by the 'specific emotional plague reaction', that is by personal smears against his character and reputation, such as when he was prominently referred to in the Scandinavian campaign as a 'Jewish pornographer'. But from

147

the point of view of the freedom pedlar rejoicing in each new escalation of the offences he can offer against the 'bourgeois morality' of the square society, it is Reich who appears in the guise of a moralist, since with his clear vision of sexual health, and his sharp division of primary and secondary drives, he was as harsh a critic of pornography as he was of authoritarian moralism.

The prime enemy that sex-economy has to face is no longer the repressive antisexual social system, but the repressive pro-pornographic culture pattern that is beginning to emerge as the old control systems break down, and a new system of emotional conditioning on a mass scale takes over. It is time we looked at these cultural manifestations in more detail.

False Sexualization and the Technology of Arousal

The hall mark of the traditionally repressive cultural system was the use of an anti-sexual ideology to deaden the body, and split off the mind. The cold head was turned against the warmth of the body and its desires. In the desublimating repression of the permissive society, a pseudo-sexual ideology is used to try and re-awaken the deadened body. The cold head tries to re-evoke the warmth it had once turned against. There are specific social reasons, which Marcuse has described at some length, why desublimation should be a characteristic of late capitalist technological society. As the conditions of life in large cities deteriorate, and the explosive tensions of an increasingly dehumanized affluent society magnify, there is political advantage to be gained both by channelling rebellion into personal forms that can be manipulated commercially, and by increasing social provision of various forms of 'sexual relaxation therapy' of the type once limited to the night club, or the pornographic book shop, but now available increasingly in West End theatres, country cinemas, and on any bookstall. As the technologizing of society steps up, pollution levels rise, and the environment becomes bleaker, so the attempt to raise the level of sexual arousal escalates. Of course there is no real 'relaxation' in the desperate attempt to use sexuality as a diversive form of 'fun' to offset the compulsive rigours of work.[5] Whilst levels of *stimulation* need to be constantly shifting, so as to create their effect, the degree of *gratification* does not improve. But this is disguised by the fact that there is the illusion of gratification : one can read about gratification, one can witness it simulated on the cinema screen, study manuals about it, all of which may be very stimulating, but does not help any individual to cope with the real problems he has in personal relationships. It is a characteristic of

148

the high-level arousal promoted by the swinging scene, that it gets trapped at the stage of fore-pleasure. The hallmark of the pseudo-genital type of individual who becomes almost a culture here, is that he has difficulty in moving 'beyond fore-pleasure to achieve sexual satisfaction in end-pleasure. Quite often without being aware of it, they are doomed to remain in a state of permanent sexual tension.'[6] (p. 94). In this respect the latent pornographic attitude becomes clear, for as Steven Marcus pointed out, the obsession with infinite pleasure does not permit the counter idea of genuine gratification, and of an end to pleasure to develop. 'The idea of fulfilment inevitably carried in its train the idea of completion, of gratification, of an ending, and the pornographic fantasy resists such notions. The ideal pornographic novel as everyone knows would go on forever – it would have no ending.'[7] (p. 198).

Reimut Reiche, who has published a very detailed and perceptive study of contemporary cultural trends, has pointed out how manipulative fashion exemplifies the influences which prevent this type of person from getting beyond fore-pleasure:

'Not content with prescribing what modern man and his girl friend should wear, which part of their body should be partially eroticized by the way they wear it (mini or maxi skirt) and suggesting that if they do not comply they will not be attractive, advertising also dictates complexion colour, hair colour, hair style (transforming the natural shape of the head) and a multitude of other special practices, ranging from the way in which one holds a whisky glass and the way one smokes a cigar or cigarette, to how one dances, how one walks if attractiveness is to be kept at full market value. All these accessories simultaneously reduce and fetishize personal attributes.'[8] (p. 97).

The misconception which underlies the whole concept of 'false sexualization' (a term introduced, incidentally, by Rudi Dutschke) is that sexual feeling is proportionate to the intensity of the stimulus designed to arouse it. A naturally alive body has its own rhythms of excitation and tends to follow a pattern that Paul Ritter described as 'attraction, fusion, liberation'.[12] The feeling of attraction between two people leads them to closer and closer contact, which leads after a process of gradually getting to know one another, to a sexual embrace where the energy systems of the two people can fuse, and a sense of renewal and re-integration follows. A deadened body on the other hand, is dependent upon the outer stimulus to kick some life into it. Sexuality instead of being a genuine contact-function between individuals, becomes a 'talisman against depres-

149

sion',[8] a way of trying to re-assure oneself that one is still alive, of injecting a bit of colour into a body that is grey to start with.

If one theme tends to dominate the wide range of phenomena which appear in the pseudo-sexual revolution, it is the theme of 'servicing'. Reich satirized this tendency in contemporary sexology, when he wrote:

'They will give advice to the ignorant and the impotent as to how to be "successful" (mark the word "successful") in "performing" (mark the word "performing") the sexual act. They will teach love "techniques" (mark the word "techniques"), how to play with each other's genitals, how to excite each other, what to do and what not to do, what positions to take in the sexual embrace. They will rightly try hard to reduce the great guilt feeling that drowns out all genital activity, from the self-satisfaction of the maturing adolescent to the first embrace after the marriage ceremony. But they will not touch or permit anyone to touch the streaming of love in the body of the children, of the maturing young ones and in the natural full embrace.'[8] (p. 97).

Alexander Lowen took up this theme when he wrote that the 'good lover' is generally a poor male. 'Unfortunately it seems to be part of the homosexual trend in our culture to equate masculine sexuality with the ability to satisfy a woman. But the woman is never truly satisfied with such a performance by the male, whether in the course of coital sex relations or in any other way. The so-called sex techniques end with the man losing more than he gains, with the woman losing what she truly wants – a man.'[9] The same is equally true of the woman, but whereas the woman was formerly the passive object of the man's desire, the feminine counterpart of the pseudo-sexual male is active in her participation in the mutual-servicing.

The stress on technique leads as in other spheres, to a depersonalizing of sex. The person becomes reduced to a sexual object. The marriage manual comes to resemble more and more the scenario for a blue movie. One has only to mentally interpolate the clinical Latin terms of the marriage manual for the Anglo-Saxon of the pornographic novel, to realize that in both cases it is not persons that one is really concerned with, but organs. Marcus describes how one of the key characteristics of pornography is 'the belief that one's sexuality, one's potency, comes not from within oneself, but depends upon some outside agent, some energizer, which can be taken at will and mechanically. As a result, human sexuality is again regarded mechanically, and human sexuality is again ideally represented as the func-

150

tioning of machines.... The mechanical view of the universe ... undertakes to control sexuality by mentally splitting off the sexual apparatus from the sexual emotions."[7] (p. 254).

Reimut Reiche describes at least four different areas where the pseudo-sexual attitudes are prevalent.

1. *Within marriage.* It is only an extension of the 'service' concept and the depersonalization implied in it to consider the involvement of new partners as 'objects' of and for sexual arousal. The practice of 'swinging', or 'wife-swapping', is a socially approved way of acting out previously taboo pornographic fantasies. The fact that husband and wife normally take part in swinging activities together, gives a collusive support for it, which minimizes guilt that might be present otherwise. 'The people concerned generally claim that love and sex are quite different things, that they love each other, and that in order to love each other properly they need the widest possible sexual variety and experience.... The individuals in question work off the discontentment that they feel with their lives by indulging in what is virtually a sport. Even when they get addicted, as is nearly always the case, they do not see it as a sign that their way of life is not fulfilling their needs, but as an increased attachment to their sport. The reigning form of sexual relationship, the compulsorily monogamous and permanent partnership, or better still the compulsory use of a single partner, is not genuinely superseded when people compulsorily abolish all rules and all selectiveness from their sexual lives.'[6]

The facade of pleasure and fun disguises a latent need to attack and destroy the real love-needs which are repressed by this kind of narcissistic behaviour. 'They are acting on a need to repeat an injury done to them at a pre-oedipal stage. They seem to be saying: if I can't be happy with one beloved person, then love is not worth anything, and I will at least have my revenge on the person who refused me by having sex with everyone and everything. These people put up an extraordinarily convincing genital facade only to hide their pre-genital wounds. Sexuality becomes radically similar to capitalist forms of consumption, in which goods have no intrinsic worth outside the value attributed to them by advertising and the rising scale on which they are consumed. Translated into sexual terms, the principle is: I get no satisfaction from any individual thing I buy because I only wear it out, not really use it. Therefore I might as well wear it out thoroughly, give it the highest possible market value, and persuade other people of its merits, photograph it, collect it, treat it sadistically, etc.'[6] (p. 106).

2. *Dating behaviour in adolescence.* The American pattern of dating, which Reiche studied, may be as he says one that is unique in industrialized countries, but many of its features can be found if in less extreme forms, in other Western cultures. Defining dating as an 'as if' form of sexuality, Reiche points out that 'the real object of the exercise is the gratification of narcissism. Dating belongs firmly in the category of narcissitic object choice (to be loved, not love). Love is in fact the most complete expression of defeat, and puts an end to the 'game'.[6] (p. 110).

The modern pseudo-sexual image is summed up in the word 'cool' : the ability to enter sexual situations without having one's deeper feelings involved, indeed the ability to use sexual behaviour as a way of avoiding deeper feelings. 'The victor is the one who makes the other lose self-control without losing it him or herself. An example of this would be a girl making a boy have an orgasm without "losing her head", or a boy managing to get a girl to have intercourse with him' (ibid) this signifying a successful conquest for the boy, which justifies his moving on to a fresh partner.

3. *'Revolutionary' life-styles.* Reiche's third example is taken from the First Commune which came into being at the end of 1966 in West Berlin. It traced its ideological roots to the youth-communes of Russia after the revolution, but was also heavily influenced by Reich's critique of bourgeois morality under capitalism, and by Marcuse. In the name of challenging and over-throwing the repressive sexual morality, they developed the notion that liberation could only be won through a form of deliberately and consciously cultivated promiscuity :

'It is like breaking in a horse. One person has to break it in, and then anyone can ride it. First of all, it's love or something like that, then afterwards it's only pleasure. The secret is terribly simple : you make a girl fall in love with you, sleep with her, and then after a time appear to be disappointed or lose interest. Then you leave her to the attention of the others, and it's done. She's a full member.' (ibid, p. 151).

Very many revolutionary-minded groups have adopted some kind of promiscuity-ideology and attempted to defend it in terms of Reich's concepts, even though Reich himself made it perfectly clear that he regarded promiscuity as arising on the basis of a disturbed sex-economy. In 1932 in his book for adolescents, in describing the possibilities for better human relationships between young people, be warned that 'thorough experience teaches that the more the outward appearances of sexuality push themselves forward, so much more disturbed, torn and unsatisfied in every way is the actual inner sex life of these individuals.'[11] In other words the more obtrusive and blatant the pseudo-genitality, the further removed from real sexual maturity one is. Reimut Reiche concludes that the communards he studied had replaced the conventional repression with a repression of their own of an even more horrific form.

It is not a great step from the attitude described above to the use of depersonalized sex by groups such as the 'Hell's Angels' as a form of initiation rite, or to the use of sexual stimuli and situations in the Underground press as a kind of mailed fist with which the better to destroy the enemy. From here one is well on the way to what Leo Abse, himself a pioneer in progressive sexual reform, called 'sexual fascism' (*Observer*, 2 May 1971).

4. *Welfare pornography*. Reiche's main target of criticism here is that particular variant of bourgeois sexual reform that is found in Sweden, which he calls a 'capitalist welfare state par excellence'. 'Nowhere else do sexual taboos and repressions carry so little weight in social norms and the law, nowhere else has individual sexual education become so much a matter for the community, no other place has a greater traditional concern for the bourgeois freedom of the individual and for the protection of political, racial and sexual minorities.'[6] But what is offered in place of the previous taboos and repressions? Reiche quotes as typical a book by Lars Ullerstam called *The Sexual Minorities* which is hailed as a progressive and radical breakthrough. The tendency the book shows is to regard all sexual manifestations as equal and as equally permissible, and to encourage their occurrence, even down to acts involving physical cruelty to people and to animals. Reiche describes his approach in these words:

'Ullerstam starts from the empirically and theoretically sound assumption that no sexual behaviour should be illegal, except rape, incest, and in some cases intercourse with minors. So far his suggestions for reform are acceptable and right. But this is not the core of the book. His basic proposition is that everyone possessed by a manifestly perverted, neurotic, infantile or regressive instinct should be allowed – without regard to what his particular deviation is – to "work it off" and gain as much enjoyment in the process as possible. To this purpose a whole network of arrangements should be set up to gratify the various needs. In his view every division in sexual matters between "normal" and "abnormal" or "unhealthy" is only a matter of definition, the defining agencies being at present the state, the church and popular morality. If this could be done away with an optimum of individual happiness would almost automatically come into being.'⁶ (p. 138).

Sten and Inge Hegeler had argued, in the preface to their book the *ABZ of Love*¹⁰ that the only answer to bad pornography, was to supply good pornography. It is an appropriate occasion to seek for a definition of pornography which is adequate to the point of view being developed here. I would offer the definition that pornography is an attitude of mind aimed at degrading and doing contempt to the body, sexually. It is essential, in my view, to put the stress on the attitude of mind, otherwise one gets into the trap of passing judgement on particular sexual activities. One and the same sexual activity, could be a celebration of the body, in one case, and a degradation of it in another. The only sense in which I can understand the Hegeler's statement above, is that they would like to see art-forms, literature, etc., which celebrated the body, in place of forms that 'did dirt upon it' in Lawrence's sense. *Lady Chatterley's Lover*, the photography of Jean Straker and the dance sequences in *Oh! Calcutta!* would all qualify as 'celebrations', tending to lead to a wholesome and non-exploitative attitude to sexuality; while the novels of De Sade (that modern culture-hero), blue movies, and the Victorian smut in Kenneth Tynan's production, would exemplify the opposite direction.

What Ullerstam is recommending is an all-out kind of sexual open-house where all such distinctions are obliterated. He is advocating a kind of welfare pornography service, with all types of sexual possibilities offered to suit all kinds of tastes. 'Let us improve the pornographic service,' he writes. 'There ought to be films showing masturbation, heterosexual intercourse, lesbian activities, sodomy, group sex, and so on, to cater for all different tastes. It would be a good idea if some cinemas were so arranged that people could masturbate in the auditorium.'⁶ (p. 138). The argument is one that deceives many liberals and progressives: if nothing is taboo, the old repressions will lose their force, people will get bored, the interest will exhaust itself. It takes a deeper insight to realize that a programme such as Ullerstam's is something other than a helpful therapy service to encourage disturbed people to work off their repressions and improve their health, and so lead to greater happiness.

The abolition of qualitative distinctions carries with it the implication that we are all healthy already, we have just been conditioned to see ourselves as sick. All that is needed is a reverse conditioning, on a mass scale, which teaches us that split-off, depersonalized, compulsively obtrusive sexuality is perfectly normal, natural, and healthy, and that we need look for nothing better. Such a mass-conditioning amounts to a progressive prostitution of culture, and involves a hidden and subtle control over people's feelings that is more insidious than the old repressive system, because that was fought as an enemy, while the new threat is welcomed as a friend. The answer is not to restore the heavy hand of censorship and repression but to improve and extend sexual education. What is needed is not further manuals on technique, but clear sex-economic teaching on the relation between sexual energy, character structure and social structure.

'This model of a multi-form system of gratification,' writes Reiche, 'is an example of economic efficiency via pseudo-gratification: social regulation of conflicts and sexual manipulation, combined in one. . . . It is actually the last most radical example which demonstrates most clearly that the gratification being offered is only an institutionalization of sexual pseudo-gratification. In point of fact it is a characteristic of the voyeur's perversion that it cannot do without permanent sexual tensions.'[6] (p. 139).

Two of the most perceptive critics of the defence-function latent in all forms of pseudo-sexual activity, are William and Claire Russell who devoted a section of their book on *Human Behaviour* to a description of what they call simply 'Pseudo-sex'. They contrast genuine communication and relationship between people where, sexuality heightens awareness and the capacity for all-round enjoyment and vitality, with 'pseudo-sexual exploitation and seduction', which is used as a means of combating anxiety and alleviating depression. 'The simplest way to cramp another person's sexual enjoyment is to arouse their masturbation fantasies,' or in the fashion of the pornographic service model, to provide them with mass-produced dreams. If people can be brain-washed by political propaganda and have their freedom of choice narrowed by sublimal advertising, they are not likely to achieve liberation of much that is worth liberating through a pseudo-sexual conditioning where, in Alexander Lowen's telling phrase, 'anything goes, but nothing comes off'.[5]

Steven Marcus is hopeful that the open and legal encouragement of pornography is a step in the direction of social health, that it shows a society in the process of maturation. 'Pornography is, after all, nothing more than a representation of the fantasies of infantile sexual life, as these fantasies are edited and re-organized in the masturbatory daydreams of adolescence. Every man who grows up must pass through such a phase in his existence, and I can see no reason for supposing that our society, in the history of its own life, should not have to pass through such a phase as well." (p. 289). I wish it were as simple as he sees it, but there is little evidence that the social living out of the perverse secondary layer in the human structure can lead to health or happiness, least of all when the living out is proclaimed in itself as the essence of health. The patient in therapy can only exhaust his secondary drives when he has withdrawn them from socially approved and heavily rationalized expression, and has come to face their essentially infantile and pathological nature; and as he experiences them more sharply in the deeply personal context of therapy, he begins to experience their irrelevance in his adult life.

The welfare pornography solution, on the other hand, leads to a situation where 'increased freedom can be used to justify increased compulsion' (Reiche) and where a schizo-hysterical attitude to life is reinforced and championed as a happy alternative to the old anal-compulsive system of patriarchy.

We have had long periods of time when love was encouraged and socially valued, but sex was taboo. The current scene tries to reverse this by valuing sex but making love and commitment taboo. But sex split off from love becomes pseudo-sex, the posturings of a body which has lost its deep feelings and is desperately trying to recover them by stimulation from without. The distinctions are clear, and must be looked for in all areas where celebration of the body, and exploitation of it are in danger of confusion. *Either* one believes that sexual feelings are proportionate to the intensity of the stimulus, in which case one follows the road that leads to the leather shop, the vibrator, and the titillation manuals; *or* one believes that sexuality arises from deep feelings for another person, in which case one follows the therapeutic paths that encourage people to relate better to themselves and to others, to their own bodies, and to the bodies of others. The two revolutions lead in opposite directions.

1 Reich, Wilhelm, *The Function of the Orgasm*, New York, 1948.
2 Boadella, David, "Social structure and character structure", *Energy and Character*, Vol. 2, No. 2, May 1972.
3 Reich, Wilhelm, *The Murder of Christ*, New York, 1952.
4 Marcuse, Herbert, *One Dimensional Man*, London, 1968.
5 Lowen, Alexander, *Pleasure*, New York, 1970.
6 Reiche, Reimut, *Sexuality and Class Struggle*, London, 1970.
7 Marcus, Steven, *The Other Victorians*, London, 1969.
8 Russell, W. M. S. and Claire, *Human Behaviour*, London, 1961.
9 Lowen, Alexander, *Sex and Personality*, New York, 1963.
10 Reich, Wilhelm, *Der Sexuelle Kampf der Jugend*, Berlin 1932.
11 Ritter, Paul, *Educreation*, London, 1966.

THE ECONOMIC STEAM BEHIND PORNOGRAPHY

E. J. Mishan

ALTHOUGH drawing support from writers and liberals, the steam behind the movement for the abolition of all forms of censorship, and more specifically in favour of complete freedom of erotic subjects, is predominantly commercial. So-called men's magazines and post-war cinema have accustomed the public to tolerate new forms of bowdlerized pornography. The only question now is should the public succumb to the pressure of interested groups – well-meaning liberals as well as Peeping Toms and enterprising publishers – for the removal of all legal restraints.

The arguments for extending licence are not new. Indeed, they are more of historic than of current interest. The popular liberal arguments turn on thin-edge-of-the-wedge themes and on the social or aesthetic consequences of subjecting artistic and literary inspiration to the veto of the authorities. The good liberal will readily admit the possibility of abuses but, he insists, an open society must run such risks in order that artistic expression may flourish and enrich the imaginative experience and thus the lives of its citizens. To the argument that literature is invariably impoverished by any restraint, legal or social, that prohibits the treatment of any aspect of life – a proposition that compels us to ponder on the unrealized potential of a Dickens, a Hardy or a Conrad – we may add the hedonistic view that pure pornography be recognized as an art form that affords pleasure and excitement to some people, and also the therapeutic view (currently, however, in ill odour among psychiatrists) that depiction of sexual extravagances, perversions and cruelties, either in literature or on the stage or screen, tends to air our repressed fantasies, purge us of our tensions, and so improve our emotional health.

These arguments for an extension of licence are somewhat removed from the realities of the interests involved. None the less, those who accept them ought to recognize the difficulties they lead to. Inasmuch as one or other of such arguments is believed to justify

157

the removal of any particular kind of censorship it justifies also the removal al *all* kinds of censorship. If, in the defence of freedom of expression, it is affirmed that anything done by men or women, or anything thought by men or women, is a part of life, and, *therefore*, a potential art form, we have excluded nothing. If James Joyce is permitted to follow his hero into the toilet so as to reveal certain aspects of his character, what obscene or brutal incidents cannot be absolved on the grounds of character revelation? If any controversial book or play is to be vindicated by its capacity to stir thought or feeling in a man, then again there can be no objection to sexual intimacies performed on the stage if the drama 'calls for it'. Neither can there be any objection to any stage presentation of homosexual, incestuous or other perverse sexual practices, performed in all circumstance and detail. For such a performance would undoubtedly reveal something of the character of the participants and could be counted upon to excite some feelings among the spectators. And what of performances of physical sadism, the exquisite torture of naked bodies, the crucifixion of squealing infants, or any other such inspired scene designed to pluck sharply at the raw ends of our nerves? After all, the resultant excitement, the shock or horror, or savage relish, are all deeply-felt experiences – though we must allow for the possibility over time of our appetites becoming jaded for lack of yet stronger fare.

Whatever the answer, the fact remains that until recently private interests were condemned to scavenging odd nuggets of alloyed pornography found lying about the banned entrance to a mine of apparently unlimited commercial potential. It may be a brave gesture to open up the entrance, another challenge maybe. But the result of the experiment, even if not disastrous, is hardly likely to promote the happiness of mankind.

It is idle to pretend that after passing through a dark period of confused counsels, a more mature society is now attempting no more than to restore to health and freedom natural instincts erroneously repressed. For we no longer live in a stable society, much less a mature one, but a society being rent apart by the torrential forces of modern technology and commerce, and one already torn wide open by modern communications, a society in a state of rapid dissolution. This is not the time to search for lost innocence. It is not as if we are, or could ever be made like, the primitive Tahitian islanders discovered by Captain Cook, who openly enjoyed their sexual activities and found every prospect pleasing. And if we could be, the medium of transfiguration is not likely to have much affinity with those employed by commercial interests. Is it possible for sophisti-cated people to believe that 'erotic' picture magazines displaying white and black starkness of thighs and wombs, of breasts and buttocks in mammoth proportions, provide nothing but aesthetic and sensuous pleasure to their beholders? Or that the highly spiced sadistic sexual fiction which, even under the present dispensation, finds its way into pulp magazines and paperbacks, offers to its readers no more than natural enjoyment. The sad truth is that the vast market for this proliferating pornographica is one of the clearest symptoms of the sickness of society. For complex reasons, associated with the pace and pressure of modern life, all too many adults who find themselves unable to attain ordinary sexual fulfilment are tempted by the new supercarnal erotic art to withdraw further from the potential reality of experience, set by biological limitations into the gaping jaws of fantasy, so isolating themselves further from affectionate communication with others.

The movement to legalize pornography is one with the movement to legalize the sale of drugs – and for motives that have little in common with John Stuart Mill's eloquent plea for liberty. In a civili-zation, where sexual frustrations are magnified by a rising tide of commercially inspired and quite unrealizable expectations, such movements gather their force from a desperate search for some magic potion to spark off buried instincts, or some catalyst to cleave open the kernels of sensation.

Alcoholics who cannot resist a drink would be wise to vote for the closing of public bars. In a civilization as vulnerable as ours is to the many corrupting influences of commercial enterprise, we should have the prudence to resist the invitation to 'crash through the sex barrier'.[1]

The last word must be with Plato, a man who was more fearful of corruption through freedom than through tyranny. The good life is the whole life, a harmony, each attribute present in just propor-tion. Each part of a man's nature can be likened to a musical instru-ment that has its place in an orchestra. If all play in harmony the tone is rich and musical. If some instruments play too loudly and other instruments are neglected, the resultant sound is harsh, per-haps unbearable.

The rapid economic growth of the West over the last half century and especially the last two decades, has not yet been accomplished without traumatic effects on their populations. Tension is every-where more evident than harmony, disproportion more evident than proportion. The gross overdevelopment of the acquisitive instinct has its genesis in the industrial free enterprise system of the Classical economists. The increasing obsession with sex, and with sexual display masquerading as fashion; the technique of distilling the carnality of sex, as though it were an essence to be poured lavishly into all forms of modern entertainment, these too owe much to private enterprise and advertising. The result, today, with commerce eagerly reacting to the expectations of excitement it has done so much to create, is the gross displacement of a social libido. And there are no countervailing forces at work today to coax it back into a proper scheme of things. Since there is no road back there is, alas, the undeniable inclination to move 'forward'. Indeed, with the Church in disarray, with the 'experts' divided and the public perplexed, it is not to be expected that the law will hold out much longer against the mounting commercial pressure, backed by naïve writers and liberals, to abolish all forms of censorship leaving a morally fragile and edgy society to cope with the flood as best it can.

1 A time when the study by Johnson and Masters, *Human Sexual Response* (May 1966), is arousing interest among the critics provides an opportunity of expressing doubts also about this approach to the mid-century obsession with sex. If there were no other choice, the recent and engagingly pathetic 'refreshingly frank discussion' phase is to be preferred to the yet more futile phase that would disseminate among the general public the findings of prolonged and detached studies of the physiology of sex. Though it is generally conceded that there may be more in the human sex relation than can be satisfactorily explained in physical terms, and that there are nuances of pleasure and intimacy incompletely revealed by indices of performance and measure of orgasm, the ingenuous liberal will persist in his quest for truth. Why not measure all that can be measured today, and tomorrow we shall measure more? Why not let the light of day into dark places, and so combat error and superstition? Why not, indeed, in this heroic age of barrier-crashing? Yet one does wonder just what extra dimension people hope to discover on emerging. After all, their manifest impatience to break through each new 'barrier' itself arises from the growing frustrations of a way of life that is a by-product of so many other much-heralded breakthroughs.

Already we have touched on some of the consequences on our lives of being deprived of the warmth of myth and mystery by the advance of knowledge. In so far as knowledge supplants spontaneity it also reduces the intensity of a man's experience. Detailed contemplation of the particular ways in which our reflexes function is more apt to hinder than to help them. If we think too closely about the process of absorbing information from, say, the act of reading a book, we will find it harder to continue the process. By trying to watch ourselves thinking, the thinking itself falters to a halt. An inescapable consciousness of the phases and chemistry of the sexual act must serve also to weaken its spontaneity and to qualify that surrender to the upsurge of feeling necessary for its fulfilment.

IS PORNOGRAPHY A CAUSE OF CRIME?

Ernest van den Haag

WHETHER pornography should be treated as a crime is largely a moral question. In her book *On Iniquity*, Pamela Hansford Johnson was more concerned with a factual and logical question: Is pornography a cause of crime? She became inclined to think so as she reported (scantily) and reflected (impressionistically) on the 'Moors' trial in which Ian Brady and Myra Hindley were found guilty of having murdered an adolescent boy (Evans) and of having abused, tortured and murdered a little girl aged ten and a boy twelve years old. The bodies of the child victims were found in the moors nearby. The motive was sexual gratification: the pair compelled the children to pose for obscene pictures and made a recording of the terrified screams, the sobs and pitiful pleas for mercy of ten-year-old Lesley Ann Downey as they tortured her to death. In 1966, a court in Chester sentenced the couple to life imprisonment, the severest penalty available.

Although continuing her longstanding opposition to the death penalty, Lady Snow felt uneasy: the outcome of the trial was 'aesthetically' disappointing – it did not produce a catharsis. The parents of the dead children (and possibly the community generally) probably were not relieved either by learning that English law now compels them to feed, house and protect the murderers as long as they live. (The death penalty may have drawbacks but life imprisonment has no fewer.)

Miss Johnson briefly asks whether the murderers might be insane but finds no reason to think so. Neither did the defence. (Both defendants testified rationally, if not very credibly.) In the U.S. insanity might have been pleaded more easily: many American judges and psychiatrists are convinced that people are born good and that wicked acts are sufficient proof that the perpetrators were sick (preferably driven into sickness by society). These psychiatrists and judges transform 'sickness' from an independently testable clinical category into the morally necessary cause of all wicked acts. Therefore, the perpetrators of outrageous acts are made sick by definition. Thus, a factual category is transformed into a (rather dubious) moral category unfalsifiable by evidence, yet withdrawn from philosophical scrutiny by being disguised as a scientific (clinical) finding. Psychiatry becomes a normative pseudo-science; and the administration of justice an odd way of providing therapy.

Unfortunately Miss Johnson's reporting tells us more about her reactions to the proceedings, and to the defendants, than about their personalities. Perhaps it is because she is so honestly puzzled about behaviour so alien to her that she wonders whether it was Brady's reading which transformed the benevolent utilitarianism so familiar to her – it does not occur to her to question it – into the malevolent utilitarianism which Brady used to rationalize his actions.

Brady had a library almost exclusively concerned with sex and sadism. The works of the Marquis de Sade were prominent and Brady thought of himself as a disciple of his philosophy.

It is here that the issue is joined. Did Brady read what he read because he was what he was? (Might he even have gratified his pre-existing disposition more often by action without the vicarious satisfaction yielded by his reading?) Or, conversely, did Brady become what he became because of his reading? In short, was the reading the effect of the cause?[1] Posed in this way, the question can be (and has been) endlessly debated. But if it is formulated more reasonably, a tentative answer can be given.

Obviously not all readers of de Sade become sadists; nor do all non-readers lead blameless lives. It follows that reading de Sade is not sufficient to become a sadist, nor necessary. It does not follow that reading him has no effect, or that the effect cannot be, at times, decisive either in initiating an inclination leading to acts, or in precipitating acts when the inclination exists.[2] The possibility of sadism is in all of us. Various external conditions may lead us to sadistic actions, or to mere fantasies, or to repudiation of either. Reading of the fantasies of others may lead to actions no less than other external stimuli. From the fact that not all readers of the Bible become Christians or act as such, and that some non-readers do, few people would conclude that the Bible has no influence. Or (to avoid the issue of 'grace'): not all readers of Marx become Marxists, but some do; some non-readers might have become socialists anyway. Are we to say that Marx has no influence?

How can literate persons accept Jimmy Walker's famous dictum,

'No girl was ever seduced by a book'? Dante's view expressed by Francesca, that she and Paolo were seduced by a book (*galeotto fu il libro e chi lo scrisse*) is certainly more realistic. Actions are influenced by ideas; even emotions – such as love or hate – are often shaped by ideas and ideal models. Else why write about them, or about anything? The desire for sex may inhere in us. But when and how to gratify it, what actions are morally permissible and what actions are not, whether and when to seduce (or be seduced) and how, whether and when to rape, or torture, or kill – these decisions are influenced by culture and milieu, in turn certainly influenced by literature – quite apart from its direct influence on individuals.

Of course it is hard to trace the direct causes of any individual act, and to say whether it would have occurred without the book that, however indirectly, suggested it. The possible causes cannot be isolated from each other and their role in any action is difficult to assess. But this hardly argues that books have no influence. It is odd (as well as wrong) to defend the freedom of literature by pretending that it has no influence. The influence of books varies from case to case; it can contribute to the formation of dispositions (given the individual potential for the disposition) or can precipitate the action, once the disposition has been formed for whatever reasons – just as LSD may precipitate a psychotic episode when there is a disposition. Since a book hardly ever can be the only influence, or be influential in isolation – it is always a person with previous experiences and pre-existing disposition who is being influenced – its precise quantitative role in causation is hard to trace. But the conclusion that it has *no role* is logically unwarranted and empirically implausible. Nor can one argue reasonably that something else would necessarily have taken the place of books among the causes of action. The drug addict might have become an alcoholic – but not necessarily.

It is strange that the criminal rampage of, say, a deprived Negro in the U.S.A. is easily ascribed to his deprivation. We are told that we are guilty of failing to remedy it, and thus of his acts (and that he is not). But why are we not guilty then of failing to restrict literature, no less logically connected with the rampage of the sadist who reads it? In neither case can a direct causal connection be established, or such matters as disposition discounted. In both cases, a causal connection of some sort seems quite likely.

Unless one objects to pornography *per se*, these reflections apply only to sadistic pornography, or to literature that invites non-consensual sexual acts. However, I believe that pornography nearly always leads to sadistic pornography. By definition, pornography de-individualizes and dehumanizes sexual acts; by eliminating all the contexts it reduces people simply to bearers of impersonal sensations of pleasure and pain. This de-humanization eliminates the empathy that restrains us ultimately from sadism and non-consensual acts. The cliché-language and the stereotyped situations, the characters not characterized except sexually, are defining characteristics of pornography: the pornographer avoids distraction from the masturbatory fantasy by avoiding art and humanity. Art may 'cancel lust' (as Santayana thought) or sublimate it. The pornographer wants to desublimate it. Those who resort to such fantasies habitually are people who are ungratified by others (for endogenous or external reasons). They seek gratification in using others, in inflicting pain (sometimes in suffering it) at least in their fantasy. In this respect, *The Story of O*, which, itself pornographic, also depicts the (rather self-defeating) outcome of pornographic fantasy, is paradigmatic.

In a sense, pornographic and finally sadistic literature is anti-human. Were it directed against a specific human group – e.g. Jews or Negroes – the same libertarian ideologues who now oppose censorship might advocate it. Should we find a little Negro or Jewish girl tortured to death and her death agony taped by her murderers, and should we find the murderers imbued with sadistic anti-Semitic or anti-Negro literature – certainly most liberals would advocate that the circulation of such literature be prohibited. But why should humanity as such be less protected than any of the specific groups that compose it? That the hate articulated is directed against people in general rather than against only Jews or Negroes makes it no less dangerous; on the contrary: it makes it as dangerous to more people.

I do not foresee a social organization which can avoid resentments in individuals or sadistic wishes and fantasies. But we could do better in controlling them by, among other things, censoring the literature that, by offering models and rationalizations fosters their growth and precipitates them into action.

But shouldn't an adult be able to control himself and read without enacting what he knows to be wrong or, at least, illegal? Perhaps he should. But we are not dealing with a homogeneous group called grown-ups (nor is it possible in the American modern environment to limit anything to adults; children and adolescents are not supervised enough – and the authority of the supervisors has been absent far too long – to make that possible). Too many grown-ups are far from the self-restrained healthy type envisaged by democratic theory. They may easily be given a last, or first, push by the literature I would like to see restricted.

Now, if that literature had literary value, we would have to weigh its loss against the importance of avoiding the deleterious influence it may have. We may even be ready to sacrifice some probable victims for the sake of this literary value. But pornographic 'literature' is without literary value. It is printed but it is not literature. Hence there is nothing to be lost by restricting it, and there possibly is something to be gained – the lives of the victims who are spared.

There remains the problem of distinguishing pornography from literature. I am convinced that our presumed inability to do so is largely a pretended inability and often pretended in bad faith. But how do you determine what is to be censored? 'Lewdness' and 'prurience' are matters of opinion; so, therefore, is censorship. Because the power of the censor cannot but be used arbitrarily, by relying on one opinion or another, it endangers the freedom of literature, ultimately of all expression, no less than the license of pornography. Isn't this too high a price to pay?

I don't think we have to pay this price. And, I know of no historical instance where censorship of pornography has endangered freedom in other areas. (The converse does occur, but is irrelevant. Communism or Nazism restricts freedom and *thereupon* censors pornography.) Anyway, a definition of pornography which distinguishes it from literature is neither so nearly impossible a task as some lawyers make it, nor as different from other legal distinctions as they presume. And if we can distinguish pornography from literature we can censor one without restricting the other.

Several extrinsic and intrinsic qualities set pornography apart. The extrinsic qualities are: (1) the intention of the author (or painter, comedian, actor, photographer, editor – or anyone who communicates); (2) the use made of his work – the means used to advertise and sell it, the context created for it; (3) the actual effect on the consumer.

1. If pornographic intention is admitted or proved by testimony and circumstances, there is no problem. If doubtful, intention must be tested by the intrinsic qualities of the work.

2. Regardless of the author's intent his work may be advertised or sold by stressing its (actual or putative) prurient appeal. By itself this justifies action against the seller only. Yet, although sales tactics are neither sufficient nor necessary to establish the prurient appeal of

what is sold, they can be relevant: the image created by the seller may well fuse with the object of which it is an image and have effects on the consumer. Advertisers often claim they achieve this fusion. Sometimes they can – when the object lends itself to it.

3. The actual effect on the consumer – whether 'prurient interest' is, or is not, aroused – depends on the work, its presentation, and the character of the consumer. A work not intended to be pornographic may nonetheless awaken lust, or have lewd effects; and one intended to do so may fail. Censors must consult not only their own reactions but rely on testimony about probable and prevailing reactions and standards. Pornography, to be such, must be likely to have a prurient or lewd effect. But this effect alone, though necessary, is not sufficient. However, together the three extrinsic qualities certainly are. Any two of them seem quite enough.

These qualities suffice to characterize 'hard-core' pornography, which is 'hard-core' precisely because it has at least two of these extrinsic qualities – and not much else to confuse matters. But what about works which cannot be classified by means of their extrinsic qualities alone – where effect or intention are mixed, or doubtful? Such works can be dealt with only by exploring the intrinsic qualities which make pornography pornographic.

Characteristically, pornography, while dreary and repulsive to one part of the normal (most usual) personality, is also seductive to another: it severs sex from its human context (the Id from Ego and Super-ego), reduces the world to orifices and organs, the action to their combinations.

The pornographic reduction of life to varieties of sex is but the spinning out of pre-adolescent fantasies which reject the burdens of reality and individualization, of conflict, commitment, thought, consideration and love, of regarding others as more than objects – a burden which becomes heavier and less avoidable in adolescence. Thus in fantasy a return to the pure libidinal pleasure principle is achieved – and fantasy may regress to even more infantile fears and wishes: people are literally devoured, tortured, mutilated and altogether dehumanized. (Such fantasies are acted out – e.g. in concentration camps – whenever authority fails to control, or supports, the impulses it usually helps to repress.)

So much for the content of pornography. It has one aim only: to arouse the reader's lust so that, by sharing the fantasy manufactured for him, he may attain a vicarious sexual experience. Pornography is intended to produce this experience, unlike literature, which aims at the contemplation of experience, at the revelation of its significance. Revelation too is an experience – but one which helps understand and enlarge the possibilities and complexities of the human career – whereas pornography narrows and simplifies them till they are reduced to a series of more or less sophisticated but anonymous (therefore monotonous) sensations.

It is impossible, of course, to serve pornography pure. The vicarious experience must occur through the medium of words, and be depicted in a setting that permits the suspension of disbelief. Yet aesthetic merit would be distracting. To avoid this, pornographers use well-worn and inconspicuous clichés and conventions which do not encumber the libidinous purpose. These qualities are intrinsic to pornography and distinguish it from literature.

Some lawyers argue that the perception of the intrinsic qualities of pornography in any work depends on literary criticism and is, therefore, a matter of opinion. It seems odd, though, that, in a legal context, serious critics themselves often behave as though they believed criticism to be a matter of opinion. Why be a critic – and teach in universities – if it involves no more than uttering capricious and arbitrary opinions? And if criticism cannot tell pornography from literature what can it tell us? Of course critics may disagree; so do other witnesses, including psychiatrists and handwriting experts. The decision is up to the court; the literary witnesses only have the obligation to testify truthfully as to what is or is not pornography.

Some of the critics who claim that they cannot make the distinction do not wish to because they regard pornography as legitimate; others fear that censorship of pornography may be extended to literature. Whatever the merits of such views, they do not justify testifying that the distinction cannot be made. A witness is not entitled to deny that he saw what he did see, simply to save the accused from a punishment he dislikes. A critic who is really incapable of distinguishing pornography from literature certainly has no business being one; a critic who is capable of making the distinction has no business testifying that he is not.

Impulsively, I am against both censors and pornographers – but even more am I against one without the other; if you are for either you should be for both. On reflection, I am: both are wanted and they call for each other, as toreros and bulls do, or hunters and game.

167

[Censorship is no less possible nor less needed than pornography. If we indulge pornography, and do not allow censorship to restrict it, our society at best will become ever more coarse, brutal, anxious, indifferent, de-individualized, hedonistic; at worst its ethos will disintegrate altogether.]

[The self-restrained and controlled individual may exist and function in an environment which fosters reasonable conduct – but few such individuals will be created, and they will function less well in an environment where they receive little social support, where sadistic acts are openly held up as models and sadistic fantasies are sold to any purchaser. To be sure, a virtuous man will not commit adultery. But a wise wife will avoid situations where the possibility is alluring and the opportunity available. Why must society leads its members into temptation and then punish them when they do what they were tempted to do?

1 Mr J. W. Lambert knows that 'the appetites of people like Brady are formed long before any books . . . can have influenced them. Their appetites will lead them to literature not *vice versa*.' Unfortunately Mr Lambert does not disclose the source of his knowledge. If he has evidence why not disclose it? Or is he pronouncing a dogma? That the opposite case has not been proven is, he surely knows, not proof of his contention. At any rate the issue is not so much 'appetites' – these are common enough although usually unconscious – but their translation into action. This translation can plausibly be fostered by literary, moral, or social support. I think it has been.

2 Certainly Mr Kenneth Allsop's argument that 'vile deeds originated' with non-readers of sadistic books as well, is irrelevant as an argument against eliminating *one* of the possible causes of 'vile deeds'. So is his remarkable argument that 'a far greater number of children are killed by the motor car each year', or 'by aerial bombardment'. I am against traffic accidents and wars but I do not see why their occurrence argues for not controlling homicidal literature (or for it not being homicidal). Oddly enough, the fact that we have not found expedient means of preventing traffic accidents or wars has not persuaded Messrs Lambert and Allsop to come out in favour of either; nor do they favour giving up attempts to control them. Yet they both argue as though their belief that no reasonable way of distinguishing and controlling sadistic literature can be found – quite unrealistic in my opinion – shows the undesirability or unnecessariness of attempting to control it. Of course it merely shows the difficulties facing (possibly the inexpediency of) an enterprise that remains desirable. It is surely easier to get rid of, and as a first step to prohibit, sadistic literature, than to abolish wars and traffic accidents. Although prohibition will not prevent all distribution it will reduce it and deprive it of social approval. The advantage of this must be weighed against likely disadvantages. I find no such pondering in the intemperate, fustian *ex cathedra* rhetoric of Messrs Lambert and Allsop.

CULTURAL
PORNO(

Pornography is now a political w‹
tical nihilist, who has taken advan
freedoms brought to the Arts by 'pe
destroy not only the values of 'bourg‹
civilization, and human values into the
liberal-minded individuals who believe t
the liberation of man, and the release o
wondering whether this is quite what she
a decade or so ago, for more freedom. F̶ ̶ ̶ ̶ ̶ ̶ ̶ ̶ ̶ ̶ ̶ ̶ ̶ ̶ ̶om
itself threatened, while new movements ̶ ̶ ̶ ̶ ̶ ̶ ̶ ̶ ̶y ̶to spring up,
armed with such philosophies as the Behaviourism of B. F. Skinner,
to 'control' man 'for his own good', with a new ruthlessness. In the
face of this, it must needs be admitted that ethical values apply in
the realm of culture as elsewhere, and that here, too, the essential
privacy and inward life of human beings needs protection, by democratic assent, from violation.

PORNOGRAPHY

Ian Robinson

Hate stronger, under shew of Love well feign'd

IT is an obvious fact that there is a great deal more pornographic
material about now than there was ten years ago, at least by the
standards of ten years ago. To get to the scantier store of books in
the local W. H. Smith's you have to pick your way past an array of
paperbacks which, unless their covers are designed to deceive, exist
only to titillate. The majority of new films in the West End depend
for their appeal – again, unless their posters are lies – on photographed sex and, often enough, on the depiction of some hitherto
undreamed of perversion; while on the B.B.C. things are performed
before the cameras which used to be done, if at all, only in bedrooms.
The newspaper founded as a successor to that bastion of Labour respectability, *The Daily Herald*, is rescued from financial collapse by

... of an unprecedented quantity of what (according to
... its proprietor refers to as 'tit'. We shall be adding to
... ome things that are not ordinarily thought to belong to it,
... x education and polemical works such as Miss Germaine Greer's
... ent *Female Eunuch*. What we want to consider is whether this
new state of affairs threatens anybody, and if so, in what ways. If
we can show that pornography *is* a threat we shall have got further
than the predominant enlightenment which insists that pornography
is harmless; and if we can say what kind of threat we shall have
gone further than the opposition to pornography, which is not very
good at offering reasons for a response which seems largely instinctive and irrational.

The Arts Council working party based its view of the harmlessness
of pornography on the undeniable proposition that there is no causal
connection between erotica and sexual offences, and the debate is
always conducted in these terms: pornography is always thought of
as causing (or not causing) some future action. This, as *The Times*
explained, is the way the law treats the question.

Judges in charging juries in obscenity cases are always at pains to
explain that they are not being asked whether the thing in front of
them is shocking, disgusting, outrageous, or offensive to decent feeling or anything like that, but strictly whether it has a tendency to
deprave or corrupt – although it is significant that evidence of this
process having actually occurred is never adduced. (October 30, 1970)

The reason that evidence can never be adduced is that it is always
assumed that 'evidence' must be the future conduct of the hypothetically depraved or corrupted. And when no causal connection is ob-
servable between the reading of pornography and the committing
of depraved and corrupt actions, pornography is found not guilty by
the enlightened, and its attackers feel hard put to it to maintain the
attack.

It might at least have occurred both to the people who think
pornography is a threat and to the liberal experts, that the failure of
all efforts to catch pornography in the act of tampering with our
moral actions does not itself establish the harmlessness of pornography, any more than does the lawyers' inability to adduce factual
evidence of a work's tendency to deprave and corrupt. This persistent
attempt to treat the matter in a consistently frustrated way could
well mean that to consider pornography within some scheme of
cause and effect is to place it in the wrong category. The cause-and-
effect talk is perhaps yet another sign of the utilitarian mania for

judging everything by practical effects and denying that anything without a practical effect can be judged at all. So it was that when Cardinal Heenan denounced pornography (on 17 November 1970) his wish was to show that unbridled pornography will lead to anarchy.[1] We are living in odd times when a cardinal is against sin not because it is sinful but because it may do social damage. And *The Times*, the leader, one supposes, of the opposition to pornography – on those pages, at least, where it is not offering pornography of its own – is similarly caught by the prudential. In one leader the paper tried to show that the function of censorship should not be simply to protect us from 'the threat of tumult and violence', but it still went on, 'If it is the case that a sufficiently shared morality, a sufficiently accepted set of common assumptions, is a necessary condition if society is not to disintegrate or lapse into tyranny, then the law has a function to perform in defence of that morality.' (6 August 1970). This is still looking for the criteria of judgment for pornography in events that follow or do not follow upon the 'disintegration'.

If we begin by agreeing that there are no causes and effects in the places they are searched for, that is not to deny all connections between pornography and the rest of life. There are obvious connections, visible to all but the liberal vanguard (and this blind-nesse too much light breeds) between the flood of pornography, the contemporary legalization of abortion, the increase in venereal diseases, and the achievement by fornication and promiscuity of the high modern status of a fashion. It is not difficult to see that the popularity of 'pop' and 'pot' is more than accidentally contemporary with the popularity of pornography; and it is no objection to this view of the way things belong together in an age to say that pornography and the pox are not to one another as cause to effect. It is all too possible to make very unhappy sense of them together.[2] If, therefore, we can remove the discussion from the factual plane that doesn't mean we shall be disconnecting the discussion from questions of conduct and action. It does mean that pornography will have to be judged in the way proper to its mode of existence.

The cause-and-effect talk commits the basic mistake of trying to judge what happens in the imagination by some factual yardstick or other.

What happens in the imagination will certainly have very important bearings on conduct, but the connections will not be causal or demonstrable in a court of law. Lawyers called upon to judge questions about depravity and corruption will naturally want to keep to tangible proofs of judgment, but that should not force us into the absurdity of admitting that what happens in the imagination is of no importance. There is, with due respect to the Bible, a great difference between looking on a woman to lust after her and committing adultery, but yet it can certainly matter (and could conceivably matter more than adultery) when a man commits adultery 'in his heart'. (Matthew 5, 28)

Our most obvious remark – so obvious that were it not for the assumptions of the contemporary 'debate' about pornography we would not trouble to make it – is therefore that any judgment of pornography involves questions about values. For even if pornography could be caught causing events, the question whether the events are instances of depravity or corruption could not be answered by the events themselves *qua* events. What is and what is not depravity depends not on events but on a scheme of values. If we say that Brady and Hindley were depraved and corrupted, we are judging them within a set of values which makes us believe that it is wicked to take pleasure in murder. Within that set of values, but only within it, the murders are seen as proofs of depravity. What to a physiologist may be different instances of the same action may be adultery, fornication or married bliss, depending on circumstances. What counts as depraving a human being is not to be determined by measurements of any sort. It is the central questions of value that defenders of pornography, and liberalizing sex-talk in general, tend to ignore – which is itself, we shall argue, a tendency to deprave and corrupt. (The complementary fault of the opposition is to suppose that values are to be taken for granted and relied on mechanically as moral rules of thumb.)

'For couples, orgasm instigated by manual stimulation may lead to better coition . . . It is easy to make fun of the researchers . . . but such research has led to the demolition of a lot of old beliefs and the discovery of simple procedures that can lead many people who think themselves sexual cripples into full enjoyment' – as the *TLS* informed us, 16 July 1970. Or, as Miss Mary Breasted writes, in a book called *Oh! Sex Education!* of the deprived poor, 'their women are not frequently treated to the long foreplay that is helping middle-class women achieve more and better orgasms' (p. 293). But what are the criteria of success here? In these quotations they are purely and simply biological: the degree of sexual success is the intensity or extent of orgasm. (And we are here, of course, within whiffing distance of the ambition to *measure* orgasm, which some American sexologists have been fatuous enough to attempt.) The *TLS* writer's

172

way of treating the matter is itself an example of sexual crippling. It is a brutal way of begging the questions of value which must be at the centre of all thought about human sex. Another way of putting that is to say that such trust in orgasm as the final good is very untrue to life. It is obviously possible that the most thoroughgoing orgasms can occur more or less by chance, in a dull dream, or in the course of an insignificant masturbation. Conversely it is possible for there to be a deep and important sexual relationship between two people who never touch each other.

Challenged by this question Pierre raised his head and felt a need to express the thoughts that filled his mind. He began to explain that he understood love for a woman somewhat differently. He said that in all his life he had loved and still loved only one woman, and that she could never be his.

'*Tiens!*' said the captain.

— *War and Peace*, Book XI, Chapter XXIX

Further, we shall not remove the necessity to consider questions of value by saying that sex is natural. Sex is a necessary condition of human life; but for us, in our own experience, humanity is a necessary condition of sex.

Our experience of sex — the events bodily and social, the dreams, the memories, the talk, the thought — if it *is* our experience, occurs in our lives. Whatever significance sex has, it can have only in our lives. If sex matters (and God help us if it doesn't) it matters to us in our lives as a whole. We don't mean by that that life is like a long *Radio Times* with places for sex as if for the weather forecast, but that it is only in connection with our humanity, with life as a whole, that sex might be significant to us. Even when some profound significance for one's whole life is expressed by the sexual experience itself — or perhaps particularly in that case — we can still say that the significance is expressed in the man's life, the woman's life as a whole. Without the whole life it could not be the same experience.

What sex can mean to us will depend upon what life it can take us into: but what is new can only have significance within whatever organizes our life into a whole. And our lives are, of course, unimaginably complex and individual. We create strange meanings by the commonest perceptions; we tell ourselves truths in dreams (and then, perhaps, forget them); things dawn on us and are modified as we think about them. Any value that belongs to any experience of sex comes, inexplicably and as a gift of grace, into the individual

173

life. And it is unlikely that anybody will seek psychiatric help with his sex-life because he thinks it is happening to someone else.

Nevertheless, the web of the individual's significances, where alone human sex belongs, cannot be a merely private-and-personal creation: it cannot be made without the rest of the world. Our values are our own; but they are also what our circumstances permit.

'Our circumstances' include everything from the individual's heredity and the people he knows in his family and friends, to the cultural tradition, in the widest sense, into which he grows – the growing into a man or a woman being here the re-creation and modification of the values of others. The possibilities of sex do vary coherently with time and place, as well as with individuality, and to establish that, there is no need to go round, electrode in hand, collecting the kind of statistics provided by those self-righteous peeping-tomes, the works of American sexology. How could sex be the same as our sex in any human community without something or other corresponding to our word 'love'? And a society in which homosexual behaviour is respectable *ipso facto* makes homosexual experience different from 'the same' activities in a society where they are frowned on: pederasty is the same in classical Athens and in a modern English public school only if one is talking of biology.

'Circumstances' in this wide sense do not, of course, compel anybody into anything. They do make certain significances possible and certain other significances impossible: they set bounds for whatever individuals and the gods may create. In this way, what we call 'circumstances' are language-like. A language may be thought of by those who like to do so as a restriction (though one should remember that all restrictions are also permissions): but within the restriction of the language new creation takes place. As Professor Chomsky keeps insisting, most of the sentences of a language are quite new, and the grammarian's puzzle is to say how something that has never been heard before obeys rules and is intelligible as part of a language.

Sex has its unpredictable significance within what we will call 'a language of sex' in the individual's life – meaning by that phrase everything that can make sex part of humanity: images, dreams, memories, ideals, moralities, pictures, words. The last item ranges from love poetry to the tones of tenderness, the names of the sex organs, and pornography.

We have sufficiently emphasized, we hope, that by 'a language of sex' we do not mean a predetermined place for sex in the individual life or the life of society. But it is still true that the individual re-creates the value of sex from the language of sex of those around

174

him. (Could there be a society which contained just one married couple?) It is also true that language in the narrower sense of verbal expression is a very important part of the circumstances of sex: the language of sex spoken and written in a society expresses the commonly understood significance of sex there, and a change in the language of sex *is* a change in the experience and evaluation of sex in the lives of the speakers of the language.

If pornography is a threat it is not because any man reading Mr David Storey's novel *Radcliffe* is likely to develop a taste for being orally homosexually assaulted – though he might – and not because any woman reading Mr Adrian Mitchell's latest, *The Bodyguard*, is likely to make for the nearest bar, there to enjoy fellatio – though that might happen too – but because pornography works on, affects and changes the common language of sex, and because it tends to deprave and corrupt that language.

Straightforward pornography – the ordinarily titillating novel or poem – works in the same mode as any other novel or poem.

It is possible to distinguish between understanding a work of art – or a sentence – and responding to it: one may respond inappropriately for a variety of personal reasons. But it is also true that a kind of response is part of understanding. Works of art (and sentences heard) exist only in the individual's re-creation and response, and individual involvement is part of the re-creation. In that sense there is no reading a poem without being implicated by it: we cannot read a poem neutrally, objectively or disinterestedly. While we are reading, we are understanding in the language of the poem; it is, for the duration, our language. (Hence the characteristic response to a work of art, 'Good God, the world can be like *that* . . . !') Then perhaps we feel one of the vast variety of inner protests or admirations that is the beginning of criticism of what we read: but that can only follow from participation in the poem.

To read and understand pornography is to understand sex in the language of pornography. To do so habitually and with enjoyment is to demonstrate that one's mind is fully at home in the language of pornography. Without the depraved, participating understanding (whatever we are to mean by that) pornography is not properly itself. It is not, for instance, possible for a child to read pornography if it knows nothing of sex: what it reads is not pornography.

Pornography doesn't *cause* depravity and corruption, it *is* depravity and corruption. In this way it is possible to see a tendency to corrupt and deprave connected with pornography not in a cause-and-effect

G

way but as an internal relationship: the corruption occurs in whatever reading allows pornography to be itself.

If this is so, the question what is and what is not pornography falls within literary criticism, and so is unlikely to be dealt with well in courts of law.

This clears up the old confusion about a writer's intentions. Many an honest legal penny has been earned by counsel demonstrating that a writer's intention was innocent though his work may look guilty. But having transferred the discussion to literary criticism we can say that a writer's intention is to be dealt with here in the same way as elsewhere in literary criticism. The question is again resolved into consideration of the work in our inner possession: the real intention is the one that gets expressed, and intention is the same as expression. Unless an author is incompetent his work intends to say what it does say.

If, however, the definition of pornography must be left to a court of law, the important dialogues ought at least to go differently. At present the ordinary thing is for the defence to discomfit prosecution witnesses by asking them whether they personally have been depraved or corrupted by the work in question. Usually a witness will refuse to admit he has been, and the case against the book is weakened. Or perhaps he will say very bravely (as Sir Basil Blackwell did) that he *has* been corrupted – but then the following question *how?* will still be unanswerable except in embarrassingly personal terms. Instead the dialogue should go:

Question: Has it corrupted *you*?
Answer: Yes.
Question: How?
Answer: Look how it works *here* and *here*. This is depraved isn't it?

– the discussion is now to be continued of the book, not of the witness's possibly abnormal psychology: the discussion is resolved into literary criticism; and if *The Times* want to find 'disintegration' the place to look is in the pornography itself. (Similarly the general answer to the questions: 'Have you personally benefited from reading Dickens? How?' should take the form of Captain Brown's exclamation in *Cranford*, 'Don't you think it is famously good?') But this will hardly do in court, where neither criticism nor the language of sex are much at home. The questions we have to ask, though not quite the ones that are forbidden, are too much like them, 'Is the thing in front of us shocking, outrageous or offensive to decent feeling?' From the point of view of the lawyer the trouble is that really 'the thing' is not in front of us, it is within us.

Because we have to do here with a language of sex, and with corruption as part of understanding, all readers are corrupted to the degree of their reading, and non-readers are corrupted to the degree of the impact of pornography on the common language. This last is why the matter affects everybody: the language of sex is everyone's concern, celibates and all, because we all have to make sense or nonsense of sex within it.

So all those elegantly uninvolved essays by mildly disapproving liberals (e.g. Robert Craft, *The Sex Explosion*, *The New York Review of Books*, 6 June 1969, Gore Vidal, *Straight Sex*, *ibid.*, 4 June 1970) are off the point. Even if one accepts these writers' imperviousness to pornographical stimulation, which we ourselves envy and make no claim to possess, they cannot escape the involvement of both the particular and general kind we have discussed. Anyone who re-creates in his imagination something depraved and corrupt is to that extent depraved and corrupted, and he does general damage to the extent that his language of sex is affected.

How, though, to decide what is and what is not pornographic? The identification of a pornographic work will depend, like any other judgement in literature, on the agreement of competent judges (not 'experts') discussing the tendencies expressed in the work; and competence here will depend, as in any other branch of literary criticism, on things like experience of reading and thinking about the kinds of work in question and better kinds, and disciplined involvement in language and life.

That sounds vague, and we hope to make a few of the possibly sharper distinctions. But it is very important to see the need for vagueness here. All literary talk is vague when put beside anything as demonstrable as causes and effects, but 'the same accuracy or finish is not to be looked for in all discussions.'[3] To say so is not, however, to say that judgements of pornography are either impossible or merely 'subjective', but to reiterate that they are the kind of questions of value which are central to language and life. It is, indeed, easier to recognize a pornographic poem than a great poem, yet there is pretty general agreement – necessarily based in individual experience and commitment – about who the great poets are. If there is no corresponding agreement about who are the pornographers, that says more about the state of our language of sex and about the complementary feebleness of criticism in our time, than about the difficulty of judgement.

He showed a group of children, aged between 11 and 18, films depicting violence and sex, including one called *491* which showed a girl being raped by a group of intoxicated louts and forced to have intercourse with a dog. None of the children were frightened either during or after the film. . . . Curiously enough two adults, who saw the experiment, one a grandmother and the other a mother, were so upset that they needed psychological treatment for a month afterwards! In thirty years' experience of treating patients I have never seen anyone who proved to have been corrupted by pornography.

– Letter in New Statesman, 10 July 1970

The writer has 'never seen' because he doesn't know corruption when he sees it; the shock to the women suggests they were far better judges than he was.

We can, however, on the strength of the foregoing discussion, make some general distinctions between what is and what is not pornographic.

A work whose sexual content is left deliberately uncontrolled by the artist is pornographic. Nude love-making on stage or screen is always necessarily pornographic because the expression – the understanding of the audience – cannot be controlled as part of the work. Nude love-making immediately breaks the art of the play and instead thrusts real voyeurism upon the audience. It is possible to imagine times and places where an audience would not be un-artistically engaged by stage sex, but that time and place cannot be Christendom at the end of its second millennium. We are used to modesty and privacy, and in our language of sex the response to nude love-making is not to the play but to the real (or not) actions. We want to know how far they're really going and what they feel like doing it. And are they really doing IT? (How, by the way, can a fully frontal male nude *simulate* an erection?) Do not retort that any erotic gesture or pose of an actor or actress's *might* provoke similar unseemly questions. There will be doubt in some cases whether some gestures or poses point what a play says, but there are many cases where there is no doubt. The bare-bottomed bouncings, grapplings, wide-eyed oohings and aaahings, the long-drawn gasps and sudden grabs now almost *de riguer* in plays on B.B.C. television are no more art than a brothel's exibeesh is. It is appropriate that the groups who specialize in stage copulation – reintroduced for the first time since the days of Heliogabalus[4] – should also wish to do away with the proscenium arch, the final development of the 'circumstances' of drama, when they cross it in order to lay the audience. This is a straightforward attack on the language of the art, a determination to destroy the art in favour of 'real life' – the real life in question being, again, strictly that of a brothel.

To emphasize that works of art control and judge the events they depict is one way of defending many great stories and plays against charges of pornography. It certainly doesn't follow that if a work makes fun of sex it is pornographic; on the contrary it is arguable that part of our present plight results from the determination of the Christian tradition to suppress anything like satyr plays or Aristophanic comedy. The feeling that if sex is serious it cannot be 'the olde daunce' is itself an impoverishment of the language of sex, for is it not obviously a necessary condition of sex, and therefore of any significance we find in it, that sex in many of its aspects is a pretty funny business? But a real work of literature will provide a context – even for obscenity – which will allow us to take the old dance seriously. Hence one can distinguish between pornography and obscenity. Chaucer's Miller is obscene enough, but the obscenity is recognized as such both within the tale and by its context in *The Canterbury Tales* which as a whole give so many other ways of looking at sex. Perhaps the extreme case is Chaucer's *Merchant's Tale*, a malign attack on all significance in sex. But even there one can distinguish between an attack on significance defined as such by the rich significance of the rest of Chaucer's tales, and the true, the unblushful reductiveness of the real thing.

The 'hard core pornography' than which, according to a Q.C. and member of the Arts Council, there can be nothing more innocent, works, at its simplest, by trying to disconnect sexual response from whatever significance it has in our lives. The ideal pornography would work directly upon the sex organs, using eyes and mind only as untouched intermediaries. The ideal is quite unattainable; and it is because pornography has to work through, in and on language that it can be seen as a threat to that language. The attempt to ignore values is itself an attack upon them and upon the belief that other works can create values. Even President Nixon sees this: it takes the Arts Council, or a Cambridge professor of Moral Science,[5] to be so confident of the utter powerlessness of imaginative literature. Pornographic novels and poems offer images and their language as much as any other work of literature: the defining characteristic of pornography is its determination to set off the strength of our sexuality without engaging whatever it is that makes it ours.

179

So we say that the bearings and possible consequences of pornography are serious enough, but the worst thing about it is the thing as in itself it really is, an attack on the significance of sex. Pornography is identifiable as that which uses imaginative language for purposes of low stimulation (whereas literature might use stimulation for its imaginative purpose). It is because pornography speaks the imaginative language of real poetry, real novels, that one can see it as an indecent assault upon the kind of seriousness which real literature makes possible.

If one offers something like 'hatred of significance in sex' as the mark of true pornography, that takes care of the absurdity of the present British law which allows pornographic works to be published if they are of sufficient literary merit. Without arguing in favour of censorship one can say that a hatred of significance is the extreme opposite of merit in a work of literature, and that therefore, simply enough, a work of pornography, a work whose tendency is to deprive sex of significance, can have no literary merit. (The word 'literary' is in any case bound to confuse the issue: if an imaginative work has merit nothing is added by calling the merit literary.) It is one of the more fantastic signs of the times that attempts should be made to treat the fashionable higher pornography specialized in by a few publishers as literary art.

Pornography is not the comic, the obscene or even the malign treatment of sex, it is the unserious treatment – 'unserious' in the sense that it tries to deny that sex is a concern of humanity and human language and values. And in this way much of the liberalizing drive in sex education has so much in common with such pro-pornography demonstrations as *Oh! Calcutta!* that both might convincingly be seen as branches of the same thing. We may have been unfortunate in the examples we know: but the sex education we have come across seems to be an attempt in the primary schools to talk about sex without using a language of sex, the result of which can only be to bewilder and frighten children. What is sex education supposed to teach? Not what used to be called 'the facts of life': it is not offered as a lesson in human biology. Sex education gives the child insignificant, factual and functional images as a language of sex it will store up to misuse at the right moment. To inflict value-less sex upon little children is a particularly revolting kind of obscenity. The Institute for Sex Education and Research, surely the University of Birmingham's answer to the ambition of the late Labour Government to allow each university to develop a few areas of special academic devotion, has for instance produced under the direction of

Dr Martin Cole a film called *Growing Up*, described by the *Daily Mail* as 'a film of a naked couple making love' which is 'to be offered to schools throughout Britain in a drive for better sex education.' Its 'intercourse shots' are a '15-second sequence, most unerotic'. Children will thus be shown what in the course of a normal sexual life they may hope never to see. Another sex educator, according to *The Times*, 'went further and said he was in favour of some sort of sexual adventure playgrounds, where young people could make love in comfort, privacy and hygienic conditions'. (13 November 1970) The period touch here is surely the word 'hygienic': and it goes with the way that both examples use 'making love' as a euphemism for 'copulation'. The ambition is to make sex safe, clean hygienic – and insignificant and inhuman, to reduce it to the unique technique which has no point beyond itself. (The opposite extreme here is the women's magazine morality which survived into the 'sixties as a coarse *fixing* of values.)

Then there is the other, more humane pain-killer of a sex education which tries to *tell* children about the value of interpersonal relationships and such mouthfilling things. This is a misunderstanding of how language is learned. (By a strange coincidence we have never heard, either, of a programme of sex education which explains to children that one normal state of marriage is as living hell.) Real 'sex education', which could hardly be so called, is the interaction of individual experience and a language of sex: it consists of growing up in a community, learning its words and ways and trying – perhaps desperately and with agony – to see how they mean the strange things that befall one. School sex education makes that process of becoming fully human more difficult, because it tends to make the common language of sex coldly trivial.

The popular manuals of sexual techniques which also offer, in their way, an education in a sort of sexual acrobatics, do so with a rather similar fraudulence. They too offer to teach what cannot be taught, and masquerade as practical advice though really, like all pornography, they are works of debased imagination.

Advice, information and new ideas are needed to create interest and stimulate one's own imagination ... America, bless her, has been the first to walk on the moon. But Europe has always and probably will always lead the world in sexual knowledge and enlightenment ... [This book] will be another weapon at your disposal in the battle for happiness and the war against sexual boredom and frustration ... If after reading this book, you and your partner are not enjoying new heights of sexual enjoyment and pleasure, simply return the book.[6]

The reader is given a synthetic fantasy which he may later, if he can find anyone to play with, play out with his 'partner': but the book itself exists as the fantasy not the results. One again objects that the language is debased – that the debasement is within the language, in the mind of the reader as part of understanding, not in any later consequences with the 'partner'.

The language of the liberal debate about pornography, and about sexual 'freedom' in general, itself tends to deprave and corrupt in just the same way, because it is a language in which sex can have no significance. One cannot *discuss* with, e.g., Mr John Calder,[7] whether commonplace stage copulation might perhaps do harm to our common language of sex – he has progressed well beyond the point where such a question means anything. There is no common language: each side feels the other is making mere pointless noises. (And alas! there is far more income in his noises than ours.)

'Masturbation is not just something we can make less fuss about: it is a necessary exploration for the ultimate discovery of full adult sexuality.' (*TLS*, 16 July 1970) That is itself verging on pornography: it is talking of sex in a low, meaningless way. We could make the objection by saying that the writer gives no grounds for thinking 'full adult sexuality' more valuable than adolescent masturbation. Both sound deadly dull. Miss Breasted commends somebody for dealing 'with masturbation in a matter-of-fact fashion'. (*op. cit.*, p. 293.) That is only appropriate if masturbation is a matter of fact. If on the other hand it is a matter of human sexuality, to treat it as a matter of fact is to debase human sexuality. Put beside those quotations the words of a great English writer:

Is masturbation so harmless, though? Is it even comparatively pure and harmless? Not to my thinking. In the young, a certain amount of masturbation is inevitable, but not therefore natural. I think, there is no boy or girl who masturbates without feeling a sense of shame, anger, and futility. Following the excitement comes the shame, anger, humiliation, and the sense of futility. This sense of futility and humiliation deepens as the years go on, into a suppressed rage, because of the impossibility of escape.
– D. H. Lawrence, 'Pornography and Obscenity', *Phoenix*, p. 179.

Our concern is not to offer opinions about masturbation, or about 'nature' (which in Lawrence's work is no more attempted science

182

than his 'no boy or girl' is attempted statistics). We do think, though, that Lawrence is truer to life, because he is using with conviction a real language of sex. In that way he finds a responsive echo in the reader even if the reader wants to argue. And generally speaking we think that Lawrence, in his unmatchedly pure and direct way, says all that needs to be said to define pornography:

Pornography is the attempt to insult sex, to do dirt on it. This is unpardonable. Take the very lowest instance,[8] picture post-card sold ...in most cities. What I have seen of them have been of an ugliness to make you cry. The insult to the human body, the insult to a vital human relationship! Ugly and cheap they make the human nudity, ugly and degraded they make the sexual act, trivial and cheap and nasty. (ibid., p. 175)

– but any uglier, any more degraded, any more cheap and nasty than a hundred west-end films, every other new fashionable play, and a large proportion of what the B.B.C. offers as family entertainment? No uglier, cheaper and nastier, at any rate, than the TLS writer on masturbation.

In our first quotation from D. H. Lawrence the word 'guilty' is in the background, not stated. It is at least a sign of coherence on the part of the enlightened that they should wish to do away with guilt. 'Solid research such as supports the writing of this book can do much to mitigate the guilt and shame often associated with divorce.'[9] Similarly Miss Germaine Greer exhorts one group of her disciples to 'choose lesbianism in an honourable, clear-eyed fashion, rejecting shame and inferiority feelings as a matter of principle, whether such feelings exist or not.' (The Female Eunuch, p. 294.) The aim of the aforementioned film of Dr Cole's was – like his earlier classes in hard-core pornography for Birmingham undergraduates – 'to dispel the sense of guilt and shame that surrounds the subject'.

Anything rather than face the fact that sex belongs to human life, that we *must* do our best to judge ourselves, and that the removal of the possibility of guilt is the removal of the possibility of significance.

In the end much modern pornography, whether of the 'creative' or polemical or educative sort, seems inexplicable in terms of an innocent breakdown: it makes more sense as hatred of human life, a wilful and controlled effort to destroy whatever makes us human. The nag-nag-nag of ugliness and triviality in so many new novels and films is very like what Lawrence saw in the picture postcards.

The possibility of guilt is one great guarantee of the existence of a language of sex; and that implies some conventional standards perhaps even of a kind as simple as 'Thou shalt not commit adultery'. Whether one is right to feel guilty in any situation is a question that concerns self-knowledge – a question, so to speak, between a human being and God. And yet without some conventions it is hard to see how there could be an idea of guilt to start from. To say, for example, 'fellatio is wrong' might be to fall into just the trap of judging by rule-of-thumb standards that we are protesting against. But unless there are things like marriage and the family, and unless there are some agreements (e.g., that incestuous necrophily is not quite the thing) there can hardly be the finer distinctions and judgements that we mean by a common language of sex. Perhaps this is to say that in very crude cases pornography might be judged in courts of law. Conversely the central convention, marriage, would hardly be worth defending unless it permitted a certain splendour as well as the ghastly muddles we see around us: marriage is defensible not as likely to lead to happiness, but as one guarantee of the possibility of significance.

Another guarantee is the opposite end from pornography of the range of the imaginative language of sex – the great love-poems and novels, The Song of Songs,[10] *Troilus and Criseyde*, *Antony and Cleopatra*, *Macbeth* [sic], *Le Rouge et le Noir*, *Anna Karenina*, *Women in Love*. How they can be a guarantee must be the subject of a future article: all we would say at present is that the judgement that *Anna Karenina* is a great novel about love implies the judgement that *Oh! Calcutta!* is a contemptible debasement of the language of love. (Our change from 'the language of sex' to 'the language of love' is also something to be explored later.)

If the question then arises: what to do about pornography and how to prevent the corruption of our language of sex, we would say that the main answer is: recognize pornography. The recognition is the best thing that could happen. Perhaps when recognized it will slink away – pornography ought to die of contempt – but that is not the reason for recognizing it. The recognition is itself the maintenance of a language of sex, and that is what we ought to hope for.

But we also observe that insofar as recent pornography is a demonstration, it is vulnerable to counter-demonstration. Why should people go running to law when they could have more fun elsewhere? English life might be a little more eventful and the news a little less dully confined to money matters if it dawned on people that *Oh! Calcutta!* could be made impossible to perform by a well-organized claque, that the B.B.C. switchboard could be put out of action by phone calls on the frequent occasions of its broadcasting sexual ath-

184

letics, and that, assistants in bookshops being human, it would have some effect on the people in W. H. Smith's if the contempt of many customers for their pornographic stock-in-trade were plainly expressed. Perhaps even Mr Rupert Murdoch is not beyond the reach of reproach. Schools that perpetrate sex-education could be inundated by angry parents. We do not particularly advocate any of these activities; although we confess to a certain curiosity to know whether Dr Martin Cole's freedom from embarrassment would survive a really loud shout of foul-mouthed four-letter-worded abuse from his lecture-audience, that experiment would not be justified – the punishment would be too like the crime.

Our own objective is less exciting : it is merely to show that there is no need to treat liberalizing intellectuals with a respect they have done nothing to deserve when they try to speak a language they palpably fail to understand.

> What art of prose or verse
> Should bring their like to book?
> What consecrated curse
> And pious rhetoric?
> Not one: we need but look.
> For these have come too far:
> They stand here, coarse and lined,
> And permanent as stone,
> In the final light of mind.[11]

---

1 For instance the Cardinal is reported to have said more generally of sexual morality, 'It was true that the church had often reserved its most severe denunciation for sexual sins. They had often been singled out for especially trenchant condemnation because they so often led to the breakdown of the social order.'
2 Cf. this letter to *The New Statesman* : 'I recently brought back from Denmark *Ekstra Bladet*, the afternoon tabloid. On two pages of classified ads there were 18 different live-show clubs, offering such attractions as Topless or Nude Go-Go, Strip-Tease, Masturbation ("Young, lovely Girl"), Lesbian Intercourse, Copulation ("Visible Orgasm"), relaxing Intimate Massage (of customers), One Extra: Woman and Dog, one Triangle, and one offer of Sadism. NS readers may like to consider whether all this constitutes the harmless and legitimate ... requirements of deprived people'. (July 24, 1970) The advertisements obviously work in the first place as pornography, by titillating the imagination; but unless they are unsuccessful they have a close connection with 'real' events.

3 Aristotle, *Nicomachean Ethics*, I, iii.
4 When that other Roman refinement, real death onstage, is brought back, we hope to make a few suggestions about casting.
5 Professor Bernard Williams on BBC television, November 1, 1970.
6 Advertisement for *The Pictorial Guide to Sexual Intercourse* in *The New York Review of Books*, June 18, 1970. This British dollar-earner promises 'Over 100 full colour—full page photographs/ For educational purposes, of a live man and a live woman,/ together engaged in sexual intercourse/ positions with descriptive text.'
7 We heard him give a talk to a university literary society a few years ago in which he pretended to advocate complete 'permissiveness' in sexual matters. This is not, of course, a very permissive country. A freeborn Briton may not copulate with his daughter, with a schoolboy or with a goat; he is not allowed to bathe without a costume or to masturbate in the street—all of which have been permissible at sundry times and places. An English teacher will be more frowned on if he seduces his pupils of either sex even than if he beats them. Even Mr Calder, we couldn't help observing, happened as he delivered his lecture to be wearing trousers.
8 Lawrence was writing many years before the modern development which allows an official of the national theatre to turn himself into a pornographic impressario.
9 *Publishers' Weekly*, quoted in an advertisement in *The New York Review of Books*, October 22, 1970.
10 Is it not sinister that at the present day *The Encyclopaedia of Adult Relationships* sounds much more like a book about sex than The Song of Songs?
11 Yvor Winters, 'An Ode on the Despoilers of Learning in an American University 1947.'

IS THIS WHAT WE WANTED?

Irving Kristol

BEING frustrated is disagreeable, but the real disasters in life begin when you get what you want. For almost a century now, a great many intelligent, well-meaning and articulate people – of a kind generally called liberal or intellectual, or both – have argued eloquently against any kind of censorship of art and/or entertainment.

Within the past ten years, the courts and the legislatures of most western nations have found these arguments persuasive – so persuasive that hardly a man is now alive who clearly remembers what the answers to these arguments were. Today, in the United States and other democracies, censorship has to all intents and purposes ceased to exist.

Is there a sense of triumphant exhilaration in the land? Hardly. There is, on the contrary, a rapidly growing unease and disquiet. Somehow, things have not worked out as they were supposed to, and many notable civil libertarians have gone on record as saying this was not what they meant at all.

They wanted a world in which *Desire Under the Elms* could be produced, or *Ulysses* published, without interference by philistine busybodies holding public office. They have got that, of course, but they have also got a world in which homosexual rape takes place on the stage, in which the public flocks during lunch hours to witness varieties of professional fornication, in which Times Square in New York City has become little more than a hideous market for the sale and distribution of printed filth that panders to all known (and some fanciful) sexual perversions.

But disagreeable as this may be, does it really matter? Might not our unease and disquiet be merely a cultural hangover – a 'hangup', as they say? What reason is there to think that anyone was ever corrupted by a book?

This last question, oddly enough, is asked by the very same people who seem convinced that advertisements in magazines or displays of violence on television do indeed have the power to corrupt. It is

187

also asked, incredibly enough and in all sincerity, by people – e.g., university professors and school teachers – whose very lives provide all the answers one could want.

After all, if you believe that no one was ever corrupted by a book, you have also to believe that no one was ever improved by a book (or a play or a movie). You have to believe, in other words, that all art is morally trivial and that, consequently, all education is morally irrelevant. No one, not even a university professor, really believes that.[1]

To be sure, it is extremely difficult to trace the effects of any single book (or play or movie) on an individual reader or any class of readers. But we all know, and social scientists know it too, that the ways in which we use our minds and imaginations do shape our characters and help define us as persons. That those who certainly know this are nevertheless moved to deny it merely indicates how a dogmatic resistance to the idea of censorship can – like most dogmatism – result in a mindless insistence on the absurd.

I have used these harsh terms – 'dogmatism' and 'mindless' – advisedly. I might also have added 'hypocritical'. For the plain fact is that none of us is a complete civil libertarian. We all believe that there is some point at which the public authorities ought to step in to limit the 'self-expression' of an individual or a group, even where this might be seriously intended as a form of artistic expression, and even where the artistic transaction is between consenting adults.

A playwright or theatrical director might, in this crazy world of ours, find someone willing to commit suicide on the stage, as called for by the script. We would not allow that any more than we would permit scenes of real physical torture on the stage, even if the victim were a willing masochist.[2]

The basic point that emerges is one that Professor Walter Berns has powerfully argued in his superb essay, 'pornography v. democracy': no society can be utterly indifferent to the ways its citizens publicly entertain themselves.

Bearbaiting and cockfighting are prohibited only in part out of compassion for the suffering animals; the main reason they were abolished was that it was felt they debased and brutalized the citizenry who flocked to witness such spectacles. The question we face with regard to pornography and obscenity is whether, now that they have such strong legal protection from the supreme court, (in the U.S.) they can or will brutalize and debase our citizenry.

We are, after all, not dealing with one passing incident – one book, or one play, or one movie. We are dealing with a general tendency that is suffusing our entire culture.

I say pornography and obscenity because, though they have different dictionary definitions and are frequently distinguishable as 'artistic' genres, they are nevertheless in the end identical in effect. Pornography is not objectionable simply because it arouses sexual desire or lust or prurience in the mind of the reader or spectator; this is a silly Victorian notion.

A great many non-pornographic works – including some parts of the bible – excite sexual desire very successfully. What is distinctive about pornography is that, in the words of D. H. Lawrence, it attempts 'to do dirt on (sex) . . . (it is an) insult to a vital human relationship'.

In other words, pornography differs from erotic art in that its whole purpose is to treat human beings obscenely, to deprive human beings of their specifically human dimension. That is what obscenity is all about. It is light years removed from any kind of carefree sensuality – there is no continuum between Fielding's 'Tom Jones' and the Marquis de Sade's 'Justine'.

These words have quite opposite intentions, to quote Susan Sontag: 'what pornographic literature does is precisely to drive a wedge between one's existence as a full human being and one's existence as a sexual being – while in ordinary life a healthy person is one who prevents such a gap from opening up.'

This definition occurs in an essay defending pornography – Miss Sontag is a candid as well as gifted critic – so the definition, which I accept, is neither tendentious nor censorious.

Along these same lines, one can point out – as C. S. Lewis pointed out some years back – that it is no accident that in the history of all literatures obscene words – the so-called 'four-letter words' – have always been the vocabulary of farce or vituperation. The reason is clear; they reduce men and women to some of their mere bodily functions – they reduce man to his animal component, and such a reduction is an essential purpose of farce or vituperation.

It may well be that western society, in the latter half of the 20th century, is experiencing a drastic change in sexual mores and sexual relationships. We have had many such 'sexual revolutions' in the past – and the bourgeois family and bourgeois ideas of sexual propriety were themselves established in the course of a revolution against 18th century 'licentiousness' – and we shall doubtless have others in the future.

It is, however, highly improbable (to put it mildly) that what we are witnessing is the final revolution which will make sexual relations utterly unproblematic, permit us to dispense with any kind of ordered relationships between the sexes, and allow us to freely redefine the human condition. So long as humanity has not reached that Utopia, obscenity will remain a problem.

One of the reasons it will remain a problem is that obscenity is not merely about sex, any more than science fiction is about science. Science fiction, as every student of the genre knows, is a peculiar vision of power: what it is really about is politics. Obscenity is a peculiar vision of humanity: what it is really about is ethics and metaphysics.

Sex, like death, is an activity that is both animal and human. There are human sentiments and human ideals involved in this animal activity. But when sex is public, the viewer does not see – cannot see – the sentiments and the ideals. He can only see the animal coupling, and that is why, when men and women make love, as we say, they prefer to be alone – because it is only when you are alone that you can make love, as distinct from merely copulating in an animal and casual way.

The basic psychological fact about pornography and obscenity is that it appeals to and provides a kind of sexual regression. The sexual pleasure one gets from pornography and obscenity is auto-erotic and infantile; put bluntly, it is a masturbatory exercise of the imagination, when it is not masturbation pure and simple. Now, people who masturbate do not get bored with masturbation, just as sadists don't get bored with sadism, and voyeurs don't get bored with voyeurism.

In other words, infantile sexuality is not only a permanent temptation for the adolescent or even the adult, it can quite easily become a permanent, self-reinforcing neurosis.

This is the true meaning of Portnoy's complaint. Portnoy (in the book, 'Portnoy's complaint') grows up to be a man who is incapable of having an adult sexual relationship with a woman; his sexuality remains fixed in an infantile mode, the prison of his auto-erotic fantasies. Inevitably, Portnoy comes to think, in a perfectly infantile way, that it was all his mother's fault.

It is true that, in our time, some quite brilliant minds have come to the conclusion that a reversion to infantile sexuality is the ultimate mission and secret destiny of the human race. I am thinking in particular of Norman O. Brown, for whose writings I have the deepest respect. One of the reasons I respect them so deeply is that Mr Brown is a serious thinker who is unafraid to face up to the radical consequences of his radical theories. Thus, Mr Brown knows and says that for his kind of salvation to be achieved, humanity must annul the civilization it has created – not merely the civilization we have today, but all civilization – so as to be able to make the long descent backwards into animal innocence.

What is at stake is civilization and humanity, nothing less. The idea that 'everything is permitted', as Nietzsche put it, rests on the premise of nihilism and his nihilistic implications. I will not pretend that the case against nihilism and for civilization is an easy one to make. We are here confronting the most fundamental of philosophical questions, on the deepest levels. But that is precisely my point, that the matter of pornography and obscenity is not a trivial one, and that only superficial minds can take a bland and untroubled view of it.

In this connection, I might also point out those who are primarily against censorship on liberal grounds tell us not to take pornography or obscenity seriously, while those who are for pornography and obscenity, on radical grounds, take it very seriously indeed.

I believe the radicals, writers like Susan Sontag, Herbert Marcuse, Norman O. Brown, and even Jerry Rubin are right, and the liberals are wrong. I also believe that those young radicals at Berkeley, some five years ago, who provoked a major confrontation over the public use of obscene words, showed a brilliant political instinct.

Once the faculty and administration had capitulated on this issue saying: 'Oh, for God's sake, let's be adult: what difference does it make anyway?' – once they said that, they were bound to lose on every other issue. Once Mark Rudd could publicly ascribe to the President of Columbia University a notoriously obscene relationship to his mother, without provoking any kind of reaction, the S.D.S. had already won the day. The occupation of Columbia's buildings merely ratified their victory.

Men who show themselves unwilling to defend civilization against nihilism are not going to be either resolute or effective in defending the university against anything.

Though the phrase, 'the quality of life', trips easily from so many lips these days, it tends to be one of these clichés with many trivial meanings and no large serious one. Rarely does it have anything to do with the way the citizen in a democracy views himself – his obligations, his intentions, his ultimate self-definition.

Instead, what I would call the 'managerial' conception of democracy is the predominant opinion among political scientists, sociologists and economists, and has, through the untiring efforts of these scholars, become the conventional journalistic opinion as well.

The root idea behind this 'managerial' conception is that democracy is a 'political system' (as they say) which can be adequately defined in terms of – can be fully reduced to – its mechanical arrangements. Democracy is then seen as and nothing but a set of rules and procedures, whereby majority rule and minority rights are reconciled into a state of equilibrium.

If everyone follows these rules and procedures, then a democracy is in working order. I think this is a fair description of the democratic idea that currently prevails in academia. One can also fairly say that it is now the liberal idea of democracy par excellence.

I cannot help but feel that there is something ridiculous about being this kind of democrat, and I must further confess to having a sneaking sympathy for those of our young radicals who also find it ridiculous. The absurdity is the absurdity of idolatry, of taking the symbolic for the real, the means for the end. The purpose of democracy cannot possibly be the endless functioning of its own political machinery. The purpose of any political regime is to achieve some version of the good life and the good society.

There is an older idea of democracy – one which was fairly common until about the beginning of this century – for which the conception of the quality of public life is absolutely crucial. This idea starts from the proposition that democracy is a form of self-government, and that if you want it to be a meritorious polity, you have to care about what kind of people govern it. Indeed, it puts the matter more strongly and declares that, if you want self-government, you are only entitled to it if that 'self' is worthy of governing.

Because the desirability of self-government depends on the character of the people who govern, the older idea of democracy was very solicitous of the condition of this character. It was solicitous of that collective self which we call public opinion and which, in a democracy, governs us collectively. Perhaps in some respects it was nervously oversolicitous – that would not be surprising. The main thing is that it cared, not merely about the machinery of democracy but about the quality of life that this machinery might generate. Because it cared, this older idea of democracy had no problem in principle with pornography and/or obscenity. It censored them – and it did so with a perfect clarity of mind and a perfectly clear conscience. It was not about to permit people capriciously to corrupt themselves. Or, to put it more precisely: in this version of democracy, the people took some care not to let themselves be governed by the more infantile and irrational parts of themselves.

I have, it may be noticed, uttered that dreadful word, 'censorship'. I am not about to back away from it. If you think pornography and/or obscenity is a serious problem, you have to be for censorship. I'll go even further and say that if you want to prevent pornography and/or obscenity from becoming a problem, you have to be for censorship. And lest there be any misunderstanding as to what I am saying, I'll put it as bluntly as possible: if you care for the quality of life in our American democracy, then you have to be for censorship.

But can a liberal be for censorship? Unless one assumes that being a liberal *must* mean being indifferent to the quality of life, then the answer has to be: yes, a liberal can be for censorship – but he ought to favor a liberal form of censorship.

Is that a contradiction in terms? I don't think so. In the U.S. we have no problem in contrasting *repressive* laws governing alcohol and drugs and tobacco with laws *regulating* (i.e., discouraging the sale of) alcohol and drugs and tobacco. Laws encouraging temperance are not the same thing as laws that have as their goal prohibition or abolition. We have not made the smoking of cigarettes a criminal offence. We have, however, and with good liberal conscience, prohibited cigarette advertising on television, and may yet, again with good liberal conscience, prohibit it in newspapers and magazines. The idea of restricting individual freedom, in a liberal way, is not at all unfamiliar to us.

I therefore see no reason why we should not be able to distinguish repressive censorship from liberal censorship of the written and spoken word.

This possibility, of course, occasions much distress among artists and academics. It is a fact, one that cannot and should not be denied, that any system of censorship is bound, upon occasion, to treat unjustly a particular work of art – to find pornography where there is only gentle eroticism, to find obscenity where none really exists, or to find both where its existence ought to be tolerated because it serves a larger moral purpose.

It is such works of art that are likely to suffer at the hands of the censor. That is the price one has to be prepared to pay for censorship even liberal censorship.

But just how high is this price? If you believe, as so many artists seem to believe today, that art is the only sacrosanct activity in our profane and vulgar world – that any man who designates himself an artist thereby acquires a sacred office – then obviously censorship is an intolerable form of sacrilege. But for those of us who do not subscribe to this religion of art, the costs of censorship do not seem so high at all.

But I must repeat and emphasize: what kind of laws we pass governing pornography and obscenity, what kind of censorship – or, since we are still a federal nation – what kinds of censorship we institute in our various localities may indeed be difficult matters to cope with – nevertheless the real issue is one of principle.

I subscribe to a liberal view of the enforcement problem: I think that pornography should be illegal *and* available to anyone who wants it so badly as to make a pretty strenuous effort to get it. We have lived with under-the-counter pornography for centuries now, in a fairly comfortable way. But the issue of principle, of whether it should be over or under the counter, has to be settled before we can reflect on the advantages of alternative modes of censorship.

I think the settlement we are living under now, in which obscenity and democracy are regarded as equals, is wrong; I believe it is inherently unstable; I think it will, in the long run, be incompatible with any authentic concern for the quality of life in our democracy.

1 Except, presumably, Professor Bernard Williams, quoted in the previous chapter. See also Lord Annan, below, p. 199. (Editor).
2 An American film producer has, however, announced his intention of having actors really stabbed – a development recently discussed by Equity in its *Journal*, Spring 1972. See also a programme note on *Tar Babies* by Alexandro Jodorowshy: 'The actors were stripped naked, tortured and beaten. Artificial blood was never used.' *Brighton Film Theatre*, 1971. (Editor).

PEDDLING THE PORNOGRAPHY OF VIOLENCE

FURTHER THOUGHTS ON 'INIQUITY'

Pamela Hansford Johnson

THE public has been exposed, through the mass media, to scenes of violence or sadistic sex for quite a long time, time enough, in fact, to begin to draw some tentative conclusions. Is there an effect? If so, what is it? When I wrote my book *On Iniquity*, designed to ask social questions which seemed to me to arise out of the Moors Murder trial, it was in the hope that it would provoke serious discussion with all participants keeping their voices down. I should not have been so sanguine.

My postbag was remarkable for its size and distribution of views: about 97 per cent were with me, and of this figure only about 3 per cent displayed the symptoms of the blue-nosed. Of the remaining 3 per cent in opposition, 2 per cent were obscene, unsigned, and usually both. It is obvious that the whole debate arouses the most furious emotions. As Dr Fredric Wertham wrote (it was he who stemmed the worst horror comics in the United States), he found himself, when *A Sign for Cain* (1966) came out, accused of being 'intemperate', 'impassioned', 'infuriated', and 'vehement'. This was the response I had myself from many 'liberal intellectuals' (a poor phrase, since I am a fairly liberal intellectual myself, but I can't find a better one). On sound radio, I was bully-ragged by two people who should not have joined in the discussion at all, and who seemed incapable of understanding, such was their wrath, what I was trying to say. As someone else said, there are certain states of fury which make reading an impossibility. Certainly my pretty mild, question-asking book produced that effect upon some.

On the matter of censorship, I repeat now what I said then – and, moreover, put in italics, so that even the most hostile might actually read the words: *I did not want to see any more censorship, or any less, until the effect of violence and sadistic sex, via television, the cinema screen and (to a lesser extent) books, had been thoroughly investigated.*

That was all. Not being ethically dead, of course I had my own opinion, which is that the 'catharsis theory' doesn't work, and that the constant display of violence (I was not much interested in the display of unsadistic sexuality) on the two most important of the mass-media, was likely to corrupt.

Indeed, I now see less and less how it could be otherwise. If such publications have no effect upon the viewer, why on earth are business firms spending, on both sides of the Atlantic, millions upon advertising? So far as books go, the moment you state that they can do no harm, then you must also state that they can do no good: which is to put them absurdly into neutral gear. Books do have an effect, of course: leaving aside that unfinished one which sent Paolo and Francesca off to bed, there was a book called *Das Kapital* and another called *Mein Kampf*. Which will do to be going along with.

Now we have two reports to consider: one, the report by the Working Party set up by a Conference on the Obscenity Laws, under the chairmanship of the Arts Council in Britain:[1] and two, an American document entitled *Commission Statement on Violence in Television Entertainment Programmes* (under the chairmanship of Dr Milton S. Eisenhower).

The second makes the first, in my opinion, look a flaccid document, Panglossian in its beaming optimism. Files of witnesses appeared before the Arts Council Committee, doctors, psychiatrists, lawyers, etc., each bringing with him a cornucopia of largely unsupported judgments. The Eisenhower report did not ask for opinions, but stated facts obtained from mass surveys, and is indeed far too factual to be accused of the 'catharsis theory' bias so noticeable in the report of the Arts Council.[2]

One piece of bias stuck out like a sore thumb. It has always been stated that nobody ever complained of having been corrupted by a book – to quote the report,

. . . it becomes less mysterious that nobody appears to find *in himself* an example of a person actually depraved by erotica. Nobody seems to have met such a person. Far more people claim to have seen a ghost.

But the Reverend David Sheppard, now Bishop of Woolwich, said that he 'had not been unscathed by reading the book' (*Last Exit to Brooklyn*). This was a brave statement on his part. At last, the ghost had been seen! But what, then, did the Committee do?

In the event he impressed us deeply, but not as an awful example of depravity. On the contrary he left us with the feeling that, if this was a depraved man, this society had little to fear and much to gain from his multiplication.

These two quotations from the Report are characteristic of its prevailing flippancy. A nice young man, you see, but an awkward one. In fact, we don't believe what he was saying. Sweep him under the carpet. More *Last Exits*, more David Sheppards. What could be more desirable?

Then, there is the thoughtless comment. Of the Moors murderers —

Analysis of their early life history shows that Brady had a typical background, in that he was illegitimate, had a reputation for cruelty before he was ten, and 'always carried a flick knife'.

So far, so good: at least, passable. But we read on:

Hindley was brought up by her grandmother where she could stay out late and truant frequently from school.

Thus giving her an acceptable background for murder? Tush! In fact, the grandmother's home was only 200 yards from the mother's, the separation was made for reasons of space, and the girl was always in and out of both houses, being devoted to her infant sister. There was some mild record of truancy, but, so far as I know, none that she was persistently out late. And even if she had been? Truants who return home at 3 a.m. do not necessarily take to murdering small children. It would be far nearer the truth to say that she was corrupted by Brady, with whom she was wildly and masochistically in love. If she had never met him, she certainly would not have committed the crimes she did, in such a manner, and might have been a different woman. Not, perhaps, an agreeable one: but different.

This statement is by Dr G. S. Barker who, while admitting Dr Wertham's figures ('in one week, one station on American television showed 334 completed or attempted killings and the total channels in one city showed in one week 7,887 acts of violence and 1,087 threats of violence') goes on to proclaim: 'Children should not be subject to saturation of violence as at present,' but – 'I personally would allow both so-called pornographic and sadistic literature in prisons. I believe it would relieve and not provoke tension.' Belief, but no evidence, here. The suspicion is obvious: that such saturation may harm children, by no means relieving tension. It is logical to pass from that suspicion to the concept that prisoners also, if offered sadistic literature, may not, after all, find tensions not relieved but worsened?

On violence, the British report runs as follows:

We had some sympathy when Mr Trevelyan, who agreed in regarding erotica as socially harmless, confessed to feeling 'not quite so sure' about the depiction of violence. This could well be due simply to the fact that most people ... don't like violence and do like sex. But a majority must resist the temptation to prohibit whatever it happens to dislike and be guided instead by social consequences if they are calculable.

It sounds all right, until it is realized that the Working Party did *not* find the social consequences of violence 'calculable', so were not prepared to do anything about such hard evidence as was later produced by the Eisenhower report. Mr Halloran, whose views are not so committed as those of others, does believe that the constant exposure to violence may have a 'desensitizing effect', although he made it clear that this was 'no more than speculation'. Now, as Dr Wertham points out, you cannot prove moral harm as you prove a proposition in physics or biology: therefore it is necessary to 'speculate' on some kind of informed basis.

In my own debates with many people on the subject of violence or sadistic sex, I have inevitably found that though I am accused of making assumptions, they have already made theirs and are not really prepared to listen to argument which discounts the 'catharsis theory' at all. Yet, in *On Iniquity*, my own assumptions were few, though I asked a good many questions and did not attempt to conceal my partial bias in doing so.

A man can at least know in his heart whether he is guilty of embezzling; he cannot possibly know whether he is guilty of depraving and corrupting. *Arts Council Report.*

Oh, yes, he can. What about the combine of New York journalists who wrote (as a hoax) a novel deliberately to out-pornograph the pornographers? What about the contributors to, say, the pre-war *London Life*?

Then, there is some pretty wild confusion of double-thinking.

Custom and acceptance are the great anti-aphrodisiacs. Nothing could be more antiseptic sexually than a nudist colony.

I gasp and stretch my eyes. So that is what the permissive society has been up to all along – to provide anti-aphrodisiacs! Could any project be duller?

The Report itself concludes:

We would leave intact the Children and Young Persons (Harmful Publications) Act, 1955.

Good. But this must lead, surely, to the proposition that children can be harmed but adults cannot, whatever the mental age of the latter.

In the Reports on Discussions, Lord Annan writes:

In any case it was difficult to argue that the author's 'intention' had any direct bearing on the excellence or worthlessness of a work of art. The criteria of 'art' or 'good taste' were equally difficult to apply.

But surely not impossible. I am myself in full agreement with Professor Harry S. Levin who thinks that it is not, and that we are perfectly used to sorting out the rubbish from the rest. If we were not, a good deal of the purpose would have departed from the practice of criticism.

Dr Anthony Storr makes reference to the active investigation into violence on television then in progress in the United States and to a forthcoming visit from Professor Berkowitz to this country. He himself cannot be convinced that even the literature of drug-taking – say, the encouragement to take heroin – would play a major part in causing addiction: 'though it might certainly play a minor contributory role.' Would that minor role, then, be nothing? The risks people are prepared to take because they cannot get mathematically exact answers to their questions scare me stiff. Further, does Dr Storr really believe that a combined effort by propagandist writers couldn't have a major effect? Or that a TV programme advertising heroin would be pointless? Why should heroin, in this case, be different from Quaker Oats?

As Dr Wertham has written:

To use the term *catharsis* as a justification for media mayhem is at best a misunderstanding. Neither Aristotle nor Frantz Fanon meant it that way. . . . Do we give a child an erector set so that he will get rid of his interest in real construction, or a chemistry set so that he gets out of his system his natural bent for science?

He has observed, furthermore, that if approached by teenagers on a

199

dark night he would prefer that they had not seen *Bonnie and Clyde*. On this point, the Eisenhower Report backs him.

The vast majority of experimental studies on this question [i.e., the 'drain-off', or catharsis theory] have found that observed violence stimulates aggressive behaviour rather than the opposite. Moreover, the stimulation of aggression responses from exposure to filmed aggression is more likely to occur when the witnessed aggression occurs in a justified, rather than an unjustified, context.

Which means, the goodies killing the baddies.

But, let us work through this report, making clear its salient findings.

Unlike the British Arts Council report, the American Commission's statement is serious throughout in tone and is quite unrelieved by little jokes.

1. 'Some of these studies' (testimony presented in hearings before the Senate Subcommittee to Investigate Juvenile Delinquency in 1955, 1961, and 1964) 'counted the number and kinds of violent acts on television, finding, for example, in a week of television watching in New York City in 1953, an average of 6·2 acts or threats of violence per one-hour programme. Another study in 1962 compared the occurrence of "aggressive episodes" to the occurrence of "protective and affectionate behaviour", finding a four to one ratio of assault to affection.'

No, it hasn't happened here yet – not quite, though we have our moments. I complained to a young woman of my acquaintance about an episode in *Wojeck*, where a man slaps a girl about the face till she falls down bleeding, squirts a soda-siphon at her to bring her round and then, if my memory serves me, starts again. The young woman pooh-poohed my concern. 'You see,' she said, '*it was all right in the context.*'

2. 'Cartoon programmes comprises only about 10 per cent of the total hours of dramatic programmes, but they were almost entirely concentrated in the children's programmes on Saturday morning. Almost all the cartoon programmes contained violence, and the rate of violent episodes was quite high in both years – more than twenty per hour.'

It is a good many years since I wrote to *The Times* on the subject of a Tom and Jerry cartoon, in which a dog, strapped in a chair, had all his teeth deliberately smashed to pieces. Tom and Jerry cartoons

200

seem to have improved a little with time, at least, those we are shown on television here.

3. 'Violent encounters on televised drama, unlike violent encounters in real life, are rarely between intimates. They generally occur at close range between young to middle-aged single males who, half the time, are strangers to each other. Six times out of ten, the violent acts involve the use of weapons: equally often, the act evokes no counter-violence from the victim.'

It is well known that crime itself is imitative: 'three laws' on the Imitation of Crime were first propounded by Gabriel Tarde in 1847. If we can judge by the rising figures of crimes of violence against the person, both in America and in this country, it would seem fairly obvious that simulated crime is imitative also – especially when (as the Eisenhower Report remarks) television crime serials are often believed by people of low intelligence to be 'real': these people make no distinction between fictional and actual violence.

4. 'Those who commit acts of violence more often perceive them to be in their self-interest than in the service of some other cause. Nearly half of all the leading characters who kill . . . achieve a clearly happy ending in the programme. To this extent, violence is portrayed as a successful means of attaining a desired end.'

The report goes on to point out how this violence is romanticized, since 'physical pain – details of injury and death – is shown to be a consequence of violence in only one out of every four violent acts. In television drama violence does not hurt too much, nor are its consequences very bloody or messy, even though it may lead to injury or death.'

Therefore the act of violence may be imitated in real life, without the perpetrators having any very clear idea of what it really means in terms of pain, messiness, murder or manslaughter. At this point the report turns to the effect of television violence, starting the section by asking why advertisers should every year spend $2½ billion in the belief that television can affect human behaviour, if in fact it does not. I have raised this point earlier. It seems to me incontrovertible.

5. 'Some defenders of violence on television, however, contend that viewers "drain off" aggressive tendencies by their vicarious participation in violent media programmes. . . . Laboratory experiments on the reactions of adults and teenagers to violent film content provides a little support for this theory. In fact, the vast majority of experimental studies on this question have found that observed violence stimulates aggressive behaviour, rather than the opposite. . . .

Violence on television encourages violent forms of behaviour, and fosters moral and social attitudes about violence in daily life which are unacceptable in civilized society. We do not suggest that television is a principal cause of violence in society. We do suggest that it is a contributing factor.'

Well, this is temperate enough. The writers of the report are not unduly discouraged: they can point already to a recent favourable trend towards less violent programmes which is already showing itself in the U.S.A.: and about time too.

We may pass from the two reports now to more general considerations. A question was asked by Professor Samuel Hynes, of North-Western University, Illinois (*Evening Standard*, 28 July 1969) which has not been asked before. *Cui bono?* If we totally abolish the censorship laws in general, to whose good will it be? Surely we cannot seriously believe that by doing so we should embark upon a therapeutic enterprise, beneficial to all. Simply because we do not know enough yet about cause and effect, we should be doubly careful what changes we introduce. The 'success' of the Danish experiment – it is claimed that with free-for-all pornography the sales of such material has dropped (though quite why ultimately permissive persons regard this as 'success' is mysterious to me) – needs some looking at in the light of October's Pornographic Fair. This appears to have attracted gigantic crowds of young Danes, exactly as we would expect.

Again, Professor Hynes writes:

Another possible consequence of repeal is even less cheering. One of the witnesses, a psychiatrist, testified that 'saturation' of television with scenes of violence must condition children to take life cheaply. He did not offer what seems a reasonable correlative, that saturation with sex might condition children to take physical love cheaply.

Quite so. And when we look around us, at the enormous pressures to be sexy, trendy, naked, joyously promiscuous, it is obvious that many of our children can and do take physical love cheaply. They see quite clearly that their elders, the publicists, regard it as a cheap thing. Though the display of violence is my main preoccupation, I am in agreement with Dr George Steiner[3] when he inveighs against the invasion of our sexual privacy.

The craze for nudity, for making love in public on the screen and now, I suppose, on the stage, is of course puerile. *Dr Faustus* at Stratford was thrown quite out of balance by the obvious interest in the audience to see a naked Helen toddle across the stage. Neither the body nor its sexual activities should be held cheaply, and this kind of display is only too often a cheapening thing. I have said in blither moments that I should like to see all plays in all theatres performed in stark nakedness for a month, so that we might get this particular silliness out of our systems. *The Mousetrap* might even increase its bookings.

Dr Fredric Wertham claims that we do know far more about the effects of violence than we are claiming to, and in the light of rising crime figures I am sure now that he is right.

Actually we are confronted in the mass media with a display to *children* of brutality, sadism and violence such as the world has never seen before. At the same time there is such a rise of violence among our youth that no peace corps abroad can make up for the violence corps at home.

But are we, then – an old cry – to tailor our display for the benefit of childen? I would suggest that it is not realized how many adults *are* children, especially the illiterate and the poorly-read. Not that I am naïve enough to believe that all literate and well-read persons are incorruptible. The person who says, 'It doesn't hurt *me*, therefore it can't hurt you,' is a kind of intellectual snob.

The test [Dr Wertham continues] of science is prediction. On the basis of my studies I predicted *fifteen years ago* that more and more brutal violence would be committed by younger and younger age groups. This was met then with disbelief. Now it is common know-ledge. We are raising a generation of violence-worshippers.

Yes, and raising ugliness all round us. No beauty, terrible or other-wise, is being born. Soho is a nightmare of ugliness, and so is the façade of many a cinema. We are offering the spectacle of a great number of perversions to people for whom it is all new and *shocking* – witness the use of the word 'shocking' in film and book advertise-ments, to attract the customer. There are those who claim that being 'shocked' is good for us, startling us out of our complacency. What impudence! Again, intellectual impudence and snobbery, the cult of 'we' and 'they'. What nonsense it is to regard an entire theatre-audience as 'complacent'! What have most of us to be complacent about, in this rocking world of wars and starvation? I deplore the tendency for actors to go around insulting, or literally prodding, audiences; this is mere, mindless cheek. It is the apogee of the absurd mass-assumption which has come to us along with our new and doubtful freedoms.

As I have said, the figures in this country as well as in the U.S.A. of crimes of violence against the person are rising. To ignore these figures is crass, as crass as to glance at them and say that they don't mean anything. Of course they mean *something*: any noticeable trend in statistics always does. Therefore it is foolish to campaign for more and more new 'liberties' until we begin to see what the effects are of those we have, and all that needs is a little patience. Like greedy children, we are clamouring that what we want we must have *at once*.

I have said in *On Iniquity* that there is nothing especially 'left wing' about the demand for more violence and pornography. One has only to observe the social mores of Russia and China to see that. They may be, to our eyes, detestably restrictive: but the fact that they do have restrictions is not in any doubt at all. And they are left-wing countries, are they not?

I also implied that the Theatre of Cruelty was one of the nastiest ideas that man has come up with. It implies, of course, violence: psychological or actual. Can anyone tell me (I read the mass-circulation Sundays papers) when a baby was rolled in its own excreta and stoned to death by yobs in a park? Or is this pure fantasy? If it is fantasy, it is an ugly one for public display. And if it is not fantasy – *cui bono*? Not that I take the theatre as seriously as I take television or cinema as a social force: it is very far from being a mass medium. Still, that's the way the wind blows. The old excuse comes up – it is all to help us to face up to life. But suppose it isn't – as yet – life? I am aware that Mr Edward Bond, to whom I have been referring, could have taken plenty of tales from the *faits divers* of our own newspapers. Yet to the best of my knowledge he has not: so he is presumably playing out a fantasy and trying to rub our noses into fantasticized horror. We have horrors enough of our own.

A word on 'clean-up campaigns'. They may at times be roughly on the right lines, but are too prone to use their sledgehammers to crack nuts. I remember them coming into action over one of those weepy TV plays about a hapless homosexual who went about crying in the back garden. It wasn't a very good play, but it was really quite inoffensive. No, I want to see a tighter hand, on television and cinema, upon orgies of violence and cruelty. I am not so interested in sexual display, unless it is sexually-sadistic, though I have suggested that in excess its effect is cheapening: and I cannot for the life of me see that orgiastic violence would be beneficial to anyone. To whose benefit could it possibly be?

What we are asking for is the backlash, which, if it comes, may be as ugly as anything we have created for our own delectation. It is that which I want, by the general exercise of self-control, to avoid. We saw a hint of it in the street scenes outside 144 Piccadilly, and we don't want to see it again; but we shall, if we don't watch out.

The 'general public' always lags behind the generous action, and if it had been taken into account we should not have had the short-term repeal of capital punishment, nor the laws which have softened life for the homosexual. But the 'general public' has never been so constantly blared at, on either issue, as it is being blared at now on a multiplicity of others. The wind of change is inescapable, and if it smells like exploding excrement, some people may think of trying to alter the direction of the weather-vane.

I have not kept my voice down, and I regret it. But I am sure we are going too fast and too far, in our demand for total liberty of com-munication. Society insists on its own safeguards: upon the drug laws, for instance, whether these cover pot or heroin. It does not guarantee freedom to the burglar, or to the embezzler, or to the murderer. And we do not doubt that it is right for society to be in control, unless we have an anarchic vision that without the law all men would be good and sweet.

What is to be done? It seems to me that we now have enough evidence, statistical and clinical, to know that we are doing wrong. So far as sex is concerned, we have let sexual pornography go so far that it would be hard to stop it continuing its seedy exercise. But where the pornography of violence is concerned, we should back-pedal. The doing of this must, of course, be left to the B.B.C., I.T.A., the producers of plays and films, the publishers of books. Easier said than done? Certainly. Violence has a ravishing attraction for many people unlikely to be on the receiving end of the reality. It is easily equated with virility, where it is not an actual substitute for it. Still, if we start thinking in the right way, we may start doing the right thing for our rickety society. As a beginning, we ought at least to stop acting upon optimistic assumptions for which there is no basis whatsoever. In any case, we need again to look seriously at the 'Catharsis Theory', and see whether it is not merely an optimistic metaphor.

1 *The Obscenity Laws.* (André Deutsch, 1969), 30s.
2 It is fair to state at this point that Lord Goodman was hoping for the reform of the Obscenity Laws, and not the demand for total repeal.
3 'Night Words: High Pornography and Human Privacy,' *Encounter*, October 1965.

THE RETREAT FROM THE PLEASURE PRINCIPLE

Storm Jameson

IN the millennial debate between critics persuaded that imaginative literature is created to please and those who think it should serve manners or morals, the hedonists had the best of it. The death of Hector, the lamentations of the Trojan women, the cruelties of the sagas, the agony of Lear, were meant to give pleasure by the manner of their telling, by what it reveals of the human spirit. Their writers' purpose was not to civilize the tribe – nor indeed have they had very much success in that field – but to enrich the senses and engage the mind. In the long history of criticism, few of the great critics considered that it could or should be otherwise. Neither did the writers. Even a writer whose aim was to exhort and purify knew or feared that he must first or also please.

We have changed all that.

That voguish American writer, Miss Susan Sontag, notes the change, but not, I think, correctly. 'Another way of characterizing the present cultural situation, in its most creative aspects, would be to speak of a new attitude towards pleasure. In one sense, the new art and the new sensibility take a rather dim view of pleasure . . . If hedonism means sustaining the old ways in which we have found pleasure in art (the old sensory and psychic modalities) then the new art is anti-hedonistic. Having one's sensorium challenged or stretched hurts. The new serious music hurts one's ears, the new films and the few interesting new prose works do not go down easily . . . But the purpose of art is, always, ultimately, to give pleasure – though our sensibilities may take time to catch up with the forms of pleasure that art in a given time may offer.'

To think only of literature, nothing in the contemporary field stretches the whole range of our senses as they are stretched by *Medea* or the *Duchess of Malfi* or *The Possessed*. Were great novels ever intended to go down easily? Did they? *Middlemarch? War and Peace? A la recherche du temps perdu? Der Mann ohne Eigenschaften?* What is more, her assertion that the purpose of art is always, ultimately, to give pleasure fails to take account of an obvious change in the attitude of some modern novelists. Call it a retreat from the pleasure principle. That sounds reassuringly Freudian – but is not at once enlightening.

What is happening is the rise to the surface of a new cold current in the novel. It is difficult to say at what point it emerged. At what moment in the evolution of the novel did the impulse to tell the awful truth about the horror and absurdity of life, to strip human life of meaning and the human being of dignity, take precedence in the minds of some writers over the older impulse to present as steadily observed a vision of reality as possible, with no more intention *to show life up* – as senseless and ugly – than Homer when he described a young man's death at Achilles' pitiless hands – *So friend, you die also* ...?

No absolute reason why a writer should not, if he is so moved, use his talents to instruct, or denounce, or reduce man to his status as a poor forked radish. *Nous avons tous notre gibier*. The point at issue is the change in sensibility and purpose.

Perhaps it started effectively with the Goncourts, with their solemn rather naïve belief that their born task as writers was to shock out of his complacency the bourgeois philistine whose tastes and social assumptions they despised. 'Aujourd'hui que le Roman ... commence à être le grande forme sérieuse, passionnée, vivante, de l'étude littéraire et l'enquête social ... [et] s'est imposé les études et les devoirs de la science ...' Which being interpreted meant something less than it said.

The first great realists of the nineteenth century, including Stendhal, extending the boundaries of fiction to take in political, social, and economic developments, had not made a manifesto of it. Nor were the Goncourts – in this unlike Zola – interested in these developments for their own sake; they were interested primarily in tearing the rags off the putrefying body of bourgeois society and its commercial ethos, and the pleasure they chiefly sought was the pleasure it gave them to express themselves and their distaste and curiosity by telling the unpleasant or repulsive truth. Not only must the novel be truthful, but if the truth is ugly so much the more meritorious the novelist's effort.

I am being much less than just to the Goncourts. They would find crudely unaesthetic those living novelists who exploit the confusion and indignities of a society in which not only all is permitted, but abuse of the self and of others obligatory. As indeed would the founder of the abbey of Thélème, intended for 'men that

207

are free, well-born, well-bred, and conversant in honest companies.' He would hold his nose at the stench rising from some well-praised modern novels, a very curious stench, compounded of hostility not merely to a condemned society but to such civilization as exists, delight in mocking the humble necessary virtues of gentleness and self-sacrifice, and an impulse, conscious or involuntary, to show up human nature in its more brutal, more addle-pated forms. Not to speak of their barbarous way with language, a habit at the opposite pole from Rabelais' pleasure in teaching it new steps.

Ankle deep in this new current, we are a long way from the idea of pleasure as a Good, in life or literature. Some simplicity has been lost. The classic Greeks knew everything about ugliness and cruelty, but they kept their heads, their capacity for reverence and wonder, their capacity for delight. So did most writers of every century until the last. No doubt the decline was inevitable. The intellect devours its children.

Is it possible that the instinct involved really is that dark instinct Freud thought he had detected? The turning of the face away from life towards extinction. A refusal to look for pleasure in literature wherever it used to be found, wherever the free mind could discover gaiety, sensual warmth, dignity in the madness of Quixote, light in Oedipus' eyeless sockets, a kernel of joy in defeat. What is most noticeable about the description of acts of cruelty so common in novels now is the minute laboured detail, like the fingers of a child carefully vivisecting an insect.

A fissure has opened in the imagination: the aggressive instinct we honour in war and make secret use of in civic torture is showing its face in places where it used to be cold-shouldered, in films, plays, novels, and receiving the applause of lettered critics.

I have a shrewd notion that when Miss Sontag spoke of 'the few interesting new prose writers', she was thinking of Mr William Burroughs, whose borborygmus style has the same effect on me as thinking about Grenoble had on Stendhal, *comme le souvenir d'une abominable indigestion*. Has she not somewhere described him as 'the most serious, urgent, and original voice in American letters to be heard for many years'?

(Original? Well, perhaps, yes, in the sense of my Yorkshire childhood, when it was said by indulgent adults of a child not naturally defective, but deliberately behaving like a clown, 'Eeh, he's an original'.)

The eruption into common daylight of more or less literate

pornographic fiction is the only wholly new direction taken since the second war: it has received nearly as much critical attention and respect as electronic music and M. Marcel Duchamp's urinal.

Only its sudden rise to the surface is new; bawdry is as old as writing, and no doubt as old as story-telling. To class it, obsessed as it is with one form of pleasure, as a retreat from the pleasure principle is not perverse. Simply, it is irrational to try to make the same term cover the pleasure given by Stendhal and that given by a meticulous description of coitus and sodomy. Irrational? Well, of course. Only reflect that the pleasures to be expected from literature have always included intellectual delight, and that the intellect, which plays as eagerly with passions as with ideas, cannot find a great deal to amuse it in a novel concerned to repeat, in a necessarily limited and repetitive vocabulary, variants of the same familiar act, the same set of reflexes. The two pleasures are so monstrously unlike that so confound them under one head is absurd and slovenly.

Reading contemporary criticism, you might suppose that the terms *erotic novel* and *pornography* are interchangeable. That they are used as though they were is part of the slovenliness.

Hunger, ambition, parenthood, the controlled ferocities of the artist and the scientist, can at any moment, in any individual, elbow the sexual impulse aside; none of them equals it in complexity and range of energy. It is the underlying note of existence, an intricate web of pleasure and anguish spread through life. It interferes with these other powerful impulses at all levels: the sexual aspect of ambition or intellectual research is detached from the need itself but not from its procreative energy. It penetrates literature on all levels. An ignorant child below the age of puberty can eroticize a story of the Indian Mutiny by transferring sensations of excitement to organs he does know the use of. The 'infernal world' invented and described in so many thousands of lines of microscopic writing by the young Brontës was fed from deeply erotic sources. Calling up the image of the Duke of Zamorna leaning against an obelisk, Charlotte almost fainted – 'I was quite gone ... I felt myself breathing quick and short.' Many imaginative children indulge in such daydreams, dubiously innocent, mental games played on a level some distance below the cross-roads turning off in later life towards pornography or genuine erotic art.

To celebrate sensual and sexual love, show it as the subtlest form of kindness between bodies, show it blazing, absorbing, possibly destroying – *Vénus toute entière à sa proie attachée* – an involvement of the whole nervous system, an ecstasy not only of the sexual

209

parts, but of every other organ, including the brain, stretches the novelist's inventive subtlety and force, his capacity for experience and its re-creation in words, to their limit. Should he be moved to portray physical details, the degree of his success is measurable by his readers' sense of their point and moment as part of the bodily and spiritual disturbance touched off by the erotic impulse, going far beyond the act.

The use in erotic literature of sexual terms and gestures is neither here nor there. The intensely erotic writing of the early Mauriac, of Proust, Thomas Mann, Montherlant, Malraux, John Cowper Powys, has no need of either. Nor, on the other hand, is their use what makes a novel a pornographic work. The detailed descriptions of the sexual act in *Les deux étendards*, by that unhappy novelist, now after his escape from execution as a collaborator, living obscurely in Paris, Lucien Rebatet, are splendidly, at times savagely erotic; they are not pornographic, since at every moment the reader is aware of other emotions and sensations than the narrowly sexual. The supplest and most complex sympathies of the imagination are involved.

Literature is concerned to explore and illumine the infinite possibilities of the whole man. Your simple-minded professional pornographer, playing over his few notes on the genital organ, is anything you like to call him, a humble worker for a pittance, an exciter of solitary lusts, a wretch, a benefactor of the lonely, anything but a writer of erotic novels. The mass-produced pornography which used to be secluded in small seedy shops had, has, only one aim : to excite its readers sexually. Like the writing of a party hack or a professional advertiser, it is committed writing, intended to stimulate or coerce its readers to an action. It has a strictly non-literary end in view. Boring to the adult mind, exciting to the adolescent or sexually immature, pornography of this plain lewd sort probably does neither harm nor good to its users.

Literary pornography also intends to excite, but it is a much odder quirk of the mind. It is an ill-charted continent, running away at one pole to sadism (not invariably as laboured and piteously boring as the Marquis de Sade's *One Hundred and Twenty Days of Sodom*), and at the opposite pole to a crop of novels which flirt genteelly with indecency, and in which the characters 'have sex' – surely the most nauseating coy phrase ever invented? – between bouts of gossipy foreign travel or flaccid mysticism or talk of Baudelaire and Catullus.

The pornography of a serious writer, a Swinburne, a Verlaine, an

Apollinaire, an Aragon (if so be he wrote *Le con d'Irène*, which he vigorously denies) will bear the thumb-mark of its author. Why a genuinely imaginative writer is moved to write a pornographic novel is a mildly interesting speculation. A regressive defiance, the impulse of an adolescent to shock, to amuse himself by shocking? A species of verbal voyeurism, the revival of the sensations roused in an inquisitive child or an impotent or sexually deprived man or woman by watching a coupling? A semi-adult form of the pleasure a child takes in fantasies confusedly connected with the orifices and organs of his own body? The impulse at a more nearly adult level to show what splendidly fearless animals we are, or would be if we had the courage of our needs? But the sex even in serious pornography has less singularity than the mating of squirrels. By cutting the sexual act out of the complex web of human relationships, to expose it in the form of a naïve recital of bodily gestures and sensations, its authors make everything much too easy for themselves. Nothing, but nothing, is so easy to describe as physical postures. What Romeo may have done with the parts of his body, or what he said in the act, his creator did not think worth recording. Since what he wanted was to give a sense of overwhelming erotic delight, its intensity would have been lowered and dulled by insisting on attention to the animal gestures.

Pornography is essentially reductive, an exercise in the nothing-but mode, a depersonalizing of the human beings involved, a showing-up of human lust as nothing but an affair of the genitals. Reduced to a conjunction of bodies, a display of faintly ridiculous sexual athletics, it becomes tedious or as almost inconceivably silly as the masturbating housemaid in *An American Dream*, noisy misbirth of an immensely talented writer and rude moralist. It needs an effort to take the incontinent authors of these things seriously, not to dismiss them as what in my barbarous northern childhood we spoke of as 'fond apes'.

Or is it possible that the stressing, by writers lacking neither intelligence nor moral energy, of the details of coitus, crudely, clumsily, sometimes with a clear trace of disgust, is a form of exhibitionism, a nervous tic rather than a creative impulse of a writer in control of his energies? A sort of self-voyeurism – as in persons who enjoy making love in front of a looking-glass? Or in effect confessional, as on a psychoanalyst's couch, of aberrations, autoerotic fantasies, or normal impulses which do not get an airing in everyday intelligent conversation?

211

If the solemn portrayal, by formally adult writers, of two persons engaged in sexual activity makes me yawn or starts in me that jeering ironic Yorkshire laughter I dislike and try to silence in myself, I don't yawn and cannot laugh at sadistic pornography, at its account of sexual torture, flagellation, onanism, enforced bestiality. I think coolly that its authors need the attention of a psychiatrist or should be encouraged to write and tear up, that its publishers are sordid fellows who would sell their grandmothers to make soup, and that critics who praise it on whatever grounds – verbal skill, the virtues of free speech, what you will – are either charlatans or pedantic followers of any new fashion.

All pornography is to a degree sadistic – inevitably. Not only is there an element of aggression in all physical attraction, but the insistence that there is nothing more in sexual passion than the pursuit of an orgasm (blessed word) strips the characters of their humanity, and sex itself of that friendship between bodies which, we are told, the gods themselves envy us. The least bearable quality of such novels as *The Naked Lunch* and *An American Dream* – apart from the appalling monotony of the minutiae of fornication and sodomy and the rest of it – is the total absence of common gentleness and humility. Silliness, derision, hate, in plenty, and barely a grain of human warmth. For all I know to the contrary, their authors are admirable persons, who would not hang a mouse. And for all I remind myself that there is no fathoming the cess-pool of human cruelty, I don't at all clearly understand why they are moved not to understand but to exploit it. Why, in short, they are moved to join in the progressive dehumanizing of areas of human sensibility. There must be some intellectual and instinctual kinship between the unhappy unshriven persons who seek gratification in inflicting pain (or suffering it) and writers who enjoy writing about it – no serious writer writes what he does not enjoy writing. It eludes me.

Tentatively, I put forward two clues. From so much of this seriously-intended pornography there rises, even when it is lewdly or boisterously comic, the acrid smell, unmistakable, of self-dislike. It is very noticeable in William Burroughs's work, accepted by reputable critics and some of his fellow-writers as 'a great novelist'. His intention runs far past the obligatory obscenity of actions and language, to turn against and castrate the human instincts themselves. I am genuinely puzzled by the eagerness of any intelligent man or woman to accept as erotic literature the efforts of a writer so revolted by his physical humanity that he labours to make it dull and disgusting to readers. They would be more intelligently employed following to its source the inverted prudery and self-hatred, the underlying distaste for sexual energy and delight. Why he hates himself is no concern of mine. He is rebelling, yes. It is possible to guess against what. But for what? If his intention was to cut off at their source the sensual springs of literature, could he have gone about it more ingeniously than in *The Naked Lunch*? Or marked more clearly the point at which an attack on convention, on a society bullied by the machine (including the bureaucratic machine) – an attack in subtler hands life-giving and gay – becomes an attack on our self-respect and decent self-love? The roots joining a litera- ture of self-hatred and self-contempt to the concentration camp world run underground. But they run.

It is agreed, today, that a sense of guilt is a moral flaw, and should be got rid of in themselves by the enlightened. But the smell of guilt is as strong in sadistic pornography as the other smell. Is it conceivable that its begetters, below the level on which they are consciously working, are still afflicted with the notion of sexual pleasure as sinful, to be punished? For the sexual sadist, the other person is degraded to seem an object, a receptacle for the discharge of his energies and fantasies. The sacrificial victim he humiliates and torments may be expiating in his place *his* sin, the unforgivable sin of exercising power at the expense of a fellow-creature. It may be that in one and the same act he satisfies his mania to possess abso- lutely and punishes himself for it.

Inevitably, the flood of literary pornography loosed on us is dulling our reactions of surprise or shock. Its writers are forced to raise the ante, to provide stronger and stronger stimulants. Or try to provide them, since both the manner, the naming of parts and the few in- expressive four-letter words, and the matter, are narrowly limited. The last novel in this kind I read and read seriously, in honest enquiry – and my goodness it is the last, my endurance of boredom and mental nausea is also limited – piles up everything, torture, sodomy, paederasty, a syphilitic poet too poor to afford paper and writing his great poem in charcoal on pages of the *Chicago Tribune*, the details of a peculiarly horrible abortion, homosexuals bawling about their miseries, the odd incest. Its compiler, James Purdy, described by one of the most intelligent of living critics as 'a writer of fantastic talent', not only outdoes every previous labourer in the field known to me, but – surely? – has reached a frontier beyond which

> Thy hand, great Anarch! lets the curtain fall
> And Universal Dulness buries all.

It falls on a soldier, tortured, brutally raped, tied to a tree and beaten, finished off at last by a long iron weapon 'of monstrous design'. All very phallic and symbolic, a crude symbolism – '. . . . the captain without a word began his work, pushing like flame with the instrument into Daniel's groin upward and over, and then when its work was nearing completion he put his face to Daniel's and pressing said something, in bloody accolade, that not even Daniel heard.'

Not only does this rhetoric start up ludicrous echoes of the ejaculations in horror comics, but the effect – of terror and agony – is infinitely feebler than that of a comparable scene in *La condition humaine*, related with a cold intensity and calm that sear to the bone.

The significant point is that – *pace*, the eminent critic – this elaborate effort to outshock the field, by a reputed and far from unintelligent novelist, over-written as it is, has the regressive quality common to all pornographic fiction, commonplace trash or serious. Its characters are blown out like carnival figures, they weep abundantly, they are continually turning pale, they rave about their love in all the clichés of lush romance, or cannot bring themselves to tell it to the loved one. What was surely designed to express the physical brutality of a brutal society exposes little except the hollowness of sentimental fiction standing on its head.

Could it, given the author's talent, have turned out otherwise? I believe not.

The language, too, lapses from rhetoric into silliness – 'Biting his lips like a traitor, he said . . .' Do you know, you, how to make a difference when you bite your lips like a traitor and when you are biting them in annoyance or from habit?

Why is it, do you suppose, that the pornographic novel has so almost suddenly broken cover to become a critical event?

An intelligent novelist does not write, does not handle language, in a literary vacuum, he stands in an only partly self-dictated relation to society, and writes what in some degree is a response to it, a criticism of, a judgement on it. A new attitude to society, a new social myth, must be taking shape behind the dust of argument.

Every myth is janus-faced. It is both an effort to grasp mentally and emotionally what is felt as an obscure and dangerous force in nature and an impulse to mock it. Death is seen as eloquent, just and mighty, and as comic, the last absurd slip on a banana-skin. Sexual passion is an 'object strange and high . . . begotten by despair Upon impossibility', or an affair of bodily needs and postures little less ludicrous than the sexual antics of penguins. Bawdy amusement

214

and wonder, even awe, are twisted together at the roots of the structure of human sexuality. What is of new interest in the pornographic novel is its emergence at this moment as a recognized literary form, or a public menace – depending on your sensibility.

Its wholehearted admirers see it as a great gesture of moral and intellectual liberation: the mind has been set free to explore unhindered an area of sensual experience, vitally, overwhelmingly important, hitherto repressed and degraded by taboos and hypocrisies. With a perhaps less disinterested enthusiasm, its publishers say as much. The eloquence of a pioneer in the business of making pornographic fiction accessible to a hungry multitude, Mr Maurice Girodias, though pitched a little high, is canonical. 'But in a maturing society the rights of the individual gradually regain precedence. The phenomenon is particularly remarkable in England today, probably because Victorian repression was so intolerably priggish. The smouldering fire has suddenly erupted into a beautiful explosion, shattering all the windows of the Establishment. Fire has issued forth from the loins of one Mellors, from Molly Bloom's libido; fire has erupted from Henry Miller's mammoth groin, from William Burroughs' spastic mannikins. This is war, this is revolution.' (*Encounter*: February 1966.)

This is fine whipping-in talk. And do not be too much put out by erupting groins: enthusiasm plays the deuce with metaphors.

The germ of sense in the loose rhetoric is that Victorian prudery and fears – fear of losing self-control and fear of losing control of women and other possessions – did lay a dead hand on attempts to write freely and candidly about sexual passion in all the forms it takes. The violence of the vengeful reaction is thus in part a legacy from a long period of bigotry, patriarchal restraint, compulsory swaddling clothes. It is a great many other things: the pleasure of frightening the sober citizen with the spectre of his own repressed violence; the still more exhilarating pleasure of flaunting your rejection of a bourgeoisie whose standards, manners, and conformism you despise. And a remote, a caricatural, reflection of Rimbaud's image of himself as a deranged outlaw. Perhaps a society gets the pornographers it deserves.

Myself born a rebel against authority, I prefer any naïve declaration of rights to the vulgar farce of commending pornography as sexual hygiene, a form of therapy. Possibly it is, but, merciful heavens, does anyone genuinely expect a sanitary service to give birth to a literary renaissance? Nor has it done so. With a very few exceptions, the energies freed by the eruption have issued in novels, plays, films, of minimal interest. It may be true that when creative energy is allowed to run away in an obsession with sexual details, it loses heat. No doubt, the novelist writes with his loins and groin as well as with his brain, nerves, and the fluid in his veins, but perhaps they should be controlled?

It may seem a little absurd to see the writers of the newest pornographic fiction as part of the confused revolt against a society in which machines in the service of the Great Interests are turning men into cogs. But what is absurd is not, not necessarily, untrue. The pressures of a triumphant technocracy – ever-increasing mechanization and automation not simply of industry but of all aspects of daily living, the ever-increasing intrusion of bureaucratic controls into our private lives and freedom of movement – affect us doubly, in body and spirit. Over against the powerful and immensely intricate machinery of finance, modern politics, electronic media, driving society towards totalitarianism of one or another or no colour, in nearly irresponsible reaction to it, sprawls the anarchic world – anarchic even when harnessed to commerce – of the pop groups and their screaming adolescent audiences, of quick-witted panders who draw their profit from promoting a collapse into mindlessness, of Carnaby Street in all its incarnations, of the poor self-defeated victims of LSD, of cynical knowingness about human relationships. It is not only the very young, not only the lewd, who cannot pass a monument of the past without lifting a leg against it.

The eruption from their fiery loins may be a revolt on the easiest imaginative level, but it is not inconceivable – since writers write in the hope of being read – that its communicants see it also, over and above their mission to bring light to them that sit in darkness and the shadow of conventional pieties, as a chance of making themselves heard above the roar of a thousand million television sets.

Now that so many of the once living nerves between the individual and society are atrophied, and with the virtual disappearance of the old comforting fraternal rituals, the old communions, religious and social, almost the last self-evident link the single human being can forge between himself and what is not himself is through his sex. It is the one wholly inalienable personal experience. Hence the excessive attention paid to it at every turn now, down to the debased art of the advertiser. Hence, too, the latent hostility, the almost hatred, libertines of either sex feel for their collaborators, born of disappointment in the meagre emotional return for so much desperate expense of energy.

The mocking paradox is that pornographic fiction is itself part of the alienated world of abstractions and mechanical living. Its frenzied concern with the technique of achieving sexual satisfaction, hetero-sexual, homosexual, or sadistic, has too narrow an area to move about in, the situations and responses soon begin to seem computer-ized. Even in cunning hands the subject becomes a bore, like the ghastly boredom of listening to a man (or woman) relating his sexual triumphs and miseries, with always the moment when the most attractive suddenly turns under one's eyes into a performing animal.

Poor Lawrence, who supposed that the sexual scenes in *Lady Chatterley's Lover* were a holy work, a high mass of human passion and physical love, would have been chilled by the latter-day cele-brants of the orgasm. It is all to the good that what he called 'the mind's terror of the body' should be exorcized. The more difficult question is how, while liberating the mind, to civilize the body.

Sex, the dedicated pornographer insists – as if we didn't know – permeates life. When he treats it in fiction it permeates only two anatomies. That is why his boldest scenes are often coldly bathetic. They leave out the essential. They ask us to accept repetitions of familiar bodily movements in two anonymous bodies – very much as in those American faculty wives who demonstrated onanism before the researchers' cameras – in place of the wholeness of per-sonal experience.

In the end it is not a question of good or bad, precise or slovenly writing. The lucid and supple prose John Updike has taught himself to use, an instrument capable, you would suppose, of any miracle of communication, fails to communicate anything more than an appalling boredom when in his latest novel he undertakes to give a cannily frank and lively account of the sexual *chasse-croisé* of ten married couples. Beyond a point fixed by the reader's goodwill towards an immensely talented writer, the book becomes strictly unreadable – unless by persons whose curiosity Mr Updike may or may not have wanted to gratify. Even descriptive passages which have nothing to do with the characters' coital doings and dialogue taken on by a sort of verbal osmosis the aspect of an embalmed body, beautiful and lifeless.

In the sensual experience of adult human beings, what is of com-pelling interest is never the movements of bodies but the movements of soul, the complex fluctuating motives that dictate our behaviour against our knowledge and will. Stendhal's agony over a woman he never possessed is charged with erotic sensibility and potency to a degree that makes a fumbling schoolboy of the windy author of *The Naked Lunch*.

Talk of censorship rouses the most farcical passions in persons otherwise more or less rational. There is little to choose in self-righteousness and irrationality between the outraged moralist and the dogmatic liberal. Because he is fighting a losing battle the first is possibly less of a bore, but it is a near thing. The second's blind insistence that there are no evil human beings, if they behave evilly they are sick, and his equally blind refusal to sanction any check on any form of expression, however senselessly destructive or squalid, makes a dialogue with him difficult: he is in the pulpit, his surplice on, before you can say the Marquis de Sade.

The 'Moors' trial, only too naturally, injected acrimony into an argument that was already more emotional than reasoned. Two sane persons, a man and a young woman, before they killed a little girl carried out on her the sexual tortures prescribed by Sade, and recorded on tape her agonized appeals for mercy. On the man's bookshelves were Sade's novels and other sadistically pornographic works; it could not be and was not denied that he had used them as manuals of conduct.

Two things seem fairly clear. A human being who is cruel by nature – crueller, that is, than at moments or in thought, all humans are – will find ways to make others suffer though he never reads a line of a sadistic book. Or even if he reads only the classics: a love of Goethe never deterred a Nazi official from operating the gas chambers. That is one thing. The other: it is sheer humbug – or sheer pedantry or a lie – to say or think that a sadistic novel has no effect on its readers. An honest man cannot say that he was never, if only when he was young, profoundly disturbed and influenced by some book he read. Disturbed for good or ill, but disturbed, his life and thinking changed. We do not read only with our aesthetic awareness; our whole nervous system is involved, to a greater or lesser degree.

It is conceivable, it is arguably likely, that to read about tortures and acts of sexual degradation will, at the least, reinforce in a reader inclined to cruelty a tendency which might otherwise have been repressed or remained latent. Every reader of L'histoire d'O or of Sade's Justine does not take to flagellation or torturing. But what might be their effect on a mind balanced on an edge between cerebral lechery or sadism and active experiment?

The argument – I have used it myself – that the sources of human cruelty do not need books to make them overflow is sound. But no one – except a man surer of his knowledge of human nature than anybody has a right to be – can assert that the 'Moors' sadists would have done what they did without having read a line of sadistic pornography. It is possible. *It is not certain.* Those people, the liberal-minded critics or only the publishers of sadistic novels, who are perfectly sure that the censorship of pornography is unnecessary or unhygienic or an intellectual or aesthetic outrage, may be right. But would it not become them, as normally fallible men and women, to think, with less arrogance, that they just possibly might be mistaken? The theory that repression of natural tendencies is always a bad thing – a theory which runs all the way from sparing children the annoyance of being house-trained to leaving the field wide open to Mr Girodias's undiscriminating labours in the cause of total freedom and erupting groins – may have gone too far? Have been too blindly accepted?

It is open to anyone to condemn censorship. The arguments for not condemning it are rational and cogent. What is irrational, unjustifiable, is to say: The multiplication of these books, and the ease with which they can be got, will not deprave the imagination, will certainly not encourage readers possibly already corrupted, possibly not, to imitate the forms of sexual gratification described for them in exact detail.

To reject censorship after studying the risks involved is very well. To reject it *ex cathedra*, in the tones of Calvin pronouncing a dogma, eyes and mind closed to the possible consequences, the even marginally possible, is to make things too comfortable for oneself.

I have never been able to make up my mind about the censorship of pornography. Or, rather, I make it up one day and unmake it the next. I know the arguments against it rather well. I have used them. I have said: Express yourself as freely as you want, describe exactly how you behave sexually, or would like to – neither I nor anyone is forced to listen. Repression is bad for the soul even when it makes social life pleasanter. The furtive inhibitions of prudes are as nauseating as they always were, heaven forbid that they should ever again be in a position to dictate what we may or may not write or read. The censorship of pornographic literature – or of mass-produced trash – creates more evils than it prevents.

And the rest of it and the rest of it. I am a dogmatic liberal in my hours.

There are other arguments. No one, or no civilized person, wants to see writers hounded by the self-righteous, the hypocritical, the frightened, as Baudelaire, as Flaubert, as Lawrence, were hounded. Rather than let that happen again, should we not accept the risks we run in publishing sadistic literature *à gogo*? What magistrate, what twelve persons, can be trusted to detect that *Lady Chatterley's Lover* is a passionately serious attempt, by a great writer, to describe the act of sex in words as scrupulously honest, as respectful of the complex emotions involved, as possible? (That the attempt is marred by gruesome sentimentality is neither here nor there: the intention was humane.)

Think, too, with smiling pity – since most great enterprises have their farcical side – of the dilemma forced on the literary don, the well-meaning critic, asked to stand up in the witness box and swear that novels of infinite less worth are to be compared with Dickens or some other classic, because failure to testify in uncompromising terms may mean that the work in question, boring and bad as it is, will be banned.

The ethics of such well-intentioned perjury interest me. Do we praise it as undertaken in defence of literature, because it is better to let a thousand worthless or atrocious books through the net rather than risk strangling a work of genius, or because the witness disapproves so passionately of the practice of banning books that he will swear any nonsense to snatch a victim from burning? Or because censorship is degrading in itself, and if the only way to express abhorrence of it is to praise clumsy or preposterously silly or brutal novels, more's the pity?

It is sad to see honest men morally forced to lie. Minor casualties of Mr Girodias's 'great revolution'. I can think of only one thing that in the circumstances would be even sadder. Suppose that intelligent cultivated persons genuinely believe certain novels and plays to be penetrating social criticism, moving, life-giving.

That really would be something for tears.

And again: not only is a banned book, a prosecution, and the spectacle of writer and publisher fighting for the life of their child in a cloud of witnesses swearing their tongues off the finest of advertisements, but to all of us, and more acutely to the immature, what is forbidden will always seem worth looking into. Its defenders agree that the quality of much of what they call sex fiction is low, and blame the pent-up pressure released. In time, they argue, writers and readers will become used to their freedom and more discriminating. It is a romantic notion, but arguable. No sane person wants to forbid for the sake of forbidding. Balancing one thing against another, it may well seem that to let pornographic fiction run free will improve its quality, like the eggs of free-range hens, and let it find its own level in the market.

That this last could happen is supported by the Danish experiment. In June 1967 Denmark abolished all prohibitions against written pornography. The sales dropped at once.[1] Six months before the ban was lifted, a new illegal pornographic book sold anything from 20,000 to 25,000 copies. Today only half that number are printed and of these a large percentage is returned unsold from the news-stands and kiosks.

And yet, and yet . . . I am not sure. The advocates of total freedom are sure they are right, the would-be censors are sure. I find it impossible to feel so sure that novels filled with accounts of tortures, beatings, sexual cruelties and humiliations of every sort, are fit for anything but burning. And as impossible to be better than uneasy about bureaucratic censorship. Who willingly trusts a bureaucrat?

Sadistic literature is not only inhumane. It is anti-human. I can at times believe that the writing of a sadistically pornographic novel is itself a sadistic art, the equivalent in literature of the scientific creation of atrociously cruel devices for killing. Neither novelist nor scientist may recognize in himself his deepest, least avowable motive. Each may see himself engaged in boldly intelligent labours, justifying the inalienable right of intellect and imagination to explore any new territory, push to its limit any creative curiosity, and be encouraged in his (unconscious) arrogance by the admiration of his fellows.

There is no dodging the truth that cruelty, from its meanest to its most revolting aspects, is a rooted human trait. It shows itself everywhere: in the respectable guise of a scientist inventing the napalm bomb, in the civil servant planning the use of gas-ovens to get rid of unwanted fellow-creatures. In the judicial tortures carried out in prisons and on the bodies of enemies, and in the sexual cruelty faithfully depicted by a talented writer or put into practice by two persons who slowly did a child to death.

Does it then follow that sadism is as legitimate a subject for the novelist as any other human habit – courage, self-sacrifice, generosity? Is it not better – since no one is compelled to read what makes him vomit – to let the pus discharge itself?

I feel every sort of doubt. To write *in this way* about atrocious acts, as if photographing them, is to exploit them for their sickening effect. Understandable in a man with designs on our pocket. Unforgivable self-indulgence on the part of a writer.

Today the doctrine consecrating total freedom of expression is used on us as a bludgeon (like so many excellent doctrines). Compromise, concede a point, they say, and we shall be back in the nineteenth century, cowering before the philistines, or driven underground by a police censor. The argument is completely irrational, which makes it harder to question. It implies that the only advance of which we are capable is an uncontrolled putsch. This is as odd and boring an idea as that there is some meaningful connection between freedom of expression and the impulse to expose the working of our bodily organs and orifices, the everyday details of copulation, menstruation, excretion, in the greatest possible detail. No doubt there is a connection, but so trivial.

Is it really beyond our wits to devise some form of censorship which would trap only the crudely sadistic? Perhaps a publishers' council could judge when a member of their profession is overstepping a line drawn, not between pornography and erotic literature, not between good and bad writing, but between two sorts of pornography. Not everybody, and not I would wish to deprive Mr Girodias of the pleasure he has said he feels in having published a novel in which a countess is serviced by a stallion. Reading such highly implausible nonsense probably does no great harm, though it may give children in the throes of puberty bad dreams. Sadistic pornography is acutely another matter. If there is no more than a chance in a hundred thousand that one child, one, may be tortured in ways suggested by the reading of sadistic fiction, that surely is enough to make its publication an error to be committed as seldom as possible?

Censorship by a government official is repugnant. Is it naïve to think that we might be able to rely on the evolution of a habit of moral responsibility among publishers? Even among writers?

All my life before the last twenty years I believed with passion that the enquiring mind and imagination are sacrosanct, that a scientist has the right and duty to cultivate every area of knowledge, that all that can be known should be. In literature, this scientific doctrine of the sacred right of the mind to go anywhere, open any door, let out on us any terror, is paralleled by the artistic doctrine that all forms of experience are worth exploring. All without exception.

With the best will in the world to me amiable and catholic, I find this inexcusably sentimental.

Since Hiroshima I have allowed myself to wonder whether scientists are any more to be trusted with total freedom of action than the rest of us. In the same spirit I am no longer certain that all conceivable subjects are worth a serious writer's energy and time. (What I mean by serious is the exact opposite of solemn. In a sense, comedy is more serious than tragedy, which ends in final defeat or the peace of death, where comedy changes the living. Or it should and can. In good light hands bawdy is gay, and the laughter it provokes a gift from some earthy god.)

Some subjects may simply have become unusable by a self-respecting writer. The theme of seduction, for instance. When Laclos wrote *Les liaisons dangereuses* the seduction of a well-brought-up virgin was a serious affair, might end in appalling misery. The complacent hobbledehoy of Mr Amis's *Take a Girl Like You*, who at the end of the book succeeds in raping the young woman he has been pursuing, runs no risks, and rouses in us no emotion beyond mild contempt for his methods. Now that seduction is of no social or moral importance, it has perhaps become impossible for a novelist to find in it any incitement to handle the situation in depth. Or could a mature writer, profoundly inquisitive and sceptical about motives, a master of precise and subtle language, use even this impoverished theme to tell us something worth hearing about ourselves? I don't know. Possibly.

Some subjects may be intrinsically boring. I am always being reminded that in this new age I am an involuntarily impious spectator. Not long ago, in one of the Sunday newspapers I read in the hope, always mortified, that one of the lowing herd will break away from it, I found: 'The convention that described the cut of a man's beard but never the hairs on his razor, the proposal in the conservatory but never the heaving bed-springs, now strikes us as unreal.'

Can I be the only survivor of a generation, rebellious, irreverent towards all sacred monsters, which did not take itself with this comical seriousness? Those bed-springs heaving through the novels of the last two or three decades lack every dimension of meaning except the most commonplace, add as little to our knowledge of George as the hairs on his razor. I can only see ill-bred silliness in the new habit a few talented women novelists have fallen into of describing in clinical detail how they behave in bed, menstruate, or, like the dim young woman in Miss McCarthys' novel, fit a pessary. It is not difficult to describe these things, far less difficult than to expose the hypocrisy and reticences our minds and feelings practise continually, infinitely less difficult than to find adequate words for the emotions involved, their strength, ambivalence, effects. I can't make up my mind whether these writers can possibly have become intellectually convinced that an account of the method a woman uses to avoid pregnancy will give us a clearer sense of her and her life, a new dimension of its sensual reality. What I am quite certain of is that had Tolstoy shown me Anna Karenina fitting a pessary instead of showing me the slow corrosion of her life by her passion for Vronsky I should have yawned and shut the book.

Novels of this school of neo-naturalism bear the relation to literature that a competent snapshot bears to a portrait by an authentic artist, and remain in the mind little longer than it takes to lay the book aside. We know nothing about the familiar bodily habits of Ulysses or Hamlet or Mr Pickwick – we are reduced to supposing them much like our own – but each lives in us more enduringly than our next-door neighbour. We remember Anna Karenina vividly, steadfastly, long after we have forgotten the name and cannot see the gestures of the young woman in *The Group* who suffered *coitus interruptus* with a layabout in New York (or was it Chicago? No matter). The one is a creation in depth, living the mysterious life of a complex literary character, the other thinner than the paper she is printed on. The one was imagined fully, by a powerful mind (not occupied in admiring its own boldness), the other put together like a jig-saw, with patient ingenuity.

I am bored by accounts of the involuntary aspects of a woman's bodily functions, so far from infinite in their variety, in exactly the same way, for the same reasons, as I am bored by laboured descriptions of normal or eccentric sexual acts. And as I am bored by certain sorts of modern art. I am bored by M. Duchamp's notorious urinal, preserved in eight replicas after the lamented disappearance of the original, and exhibited in art galleries, including the Tate Gallery. When I was younger I might have been shaken by learning that certain art critics and philosophers have solemnly decided that it and the other ready-made objects exhibited since, the hat-rack, the shovel, the tin of beans and the rest, became 'aesthetic objects' when the artist picked them out from all the other identical hat-racks and urinals and canned beans in the shop, as if by this act he conferred on them a value they lacked when they left the factory. Now I am mildly surprised when a hypothetically serious critic asks me to accept as valid a definition which rests on nothing but his intuitive certainty that it must be 'true' or, as he might argue, self-evident. To whom? All his oracular statement does is to make empty nonsense of the word *art* and *artist*. If every object a man named or naming himself as an artist picks up and places on show, with or without his signature and thumb mark, is art then nothing is art. Perhaps we should do better not to try to define art at all. Or leave definition to the neo-Aristotelians. Perhaps we could retreat to the less slippery ground of a negative proposition. Decide, perhaps, that an object which can be mechanically reproduced in mass is not art.

This would cut out the urinals and the chair with a pipe and a packet of tobacco on it manufactured in chromium-plated steel and labelled 'Van Gogh's Chair'. It leaves in the relentlessly boring stone ovoids and effigies, the crushing silliness of action painting, the whimsical silliness of Picasso's handlebar ram (or is it a goat? Again, no matter).

Applied to literature, it leaves in Molly Bloom (*catin sublime*), Mr Updike's strenuously revolving couples, and the pseudo-bucolic Mellors, and cuts out the bulk of Mr Girodias's *Olympia Reader* and Mr Mailer's masturbating housemaid.

I think I have come on the deepest reason why serious pornography bores me. Any writer, any artist, who presents me with an object, whether it is a hat-rack or an anatomical or other physical detail, which has not been worked over and penetrated by his imagination, is cheating, offering as of authentic human worth what is stereotyped. It doesn't amuse me to be cheated: I regret the waste of time I might have given to *la chasse au bonheur*.

That the language of pornography should be impoverished is inevitable. Literature is not an incitement to action, it is a verbal structure designed to capture and press into words as many subtly evasive feelings and ideas as possible. No distinctively human emotion is simple, and to give an account of a sexual passion involves finding words to raise to the surface a tangled mass of half-inarticulate, turbulent, equivocal motives and sensations. Too naïve and indiscriminating a stress on a single act or gesture brings a clumsy fist down on the finally insoluble contradictions in any human being, even the simplest. Not only is it possible to make a faithful and moving analysis of the sexual experience in all its variety and ambiguity without modish violence, without frothing over like a mustard-pot with the conventional four-letter words, but freed from these noisy distractions, the naked truth of the experiences blazes clearer, whether in ecstasy, tragedy, or comedy of the earthiest simplest kind.

Charlus remains one of the most impressive erotic figures in literature precisely because he has not been reduced to a stock figure, we are not shown him going through the unvarying motions of the homosexual act. The exquisite comedy of Charlus and Jupien in the courtyard of the Guermantes house, the tragic farce of Charlus in Jupien's brothel – I shudder when I think of the dreary exercise in the ludicrous or the sickening these scenes would have become in the hands of a contemporary pornographer.

In the end, perhaps there are no unusable subjects, there are only

good, bad, and mediocre writers. A mass-produced urinal is an un-
promising subject for an artist, except in the field of publicity,
though possibly a good sculptor, more likely a good painter, using
his own tools and a modicum of genius could make something of
it. And that a talented or a great writer can set a character on his
stool and elicit from him in that situation what is humanly gay or
interesting, witness Rabelais, Saint-Simon, Joyce.

The rest is a bore, *la blague sérieuse*, or publicity.

1 This does not seem borne out by evidence given to Lord Longford's team
in 1971. The annual production is still 6om$. — Editor.

NIGHT WORDS

George Steiner

IS there any science-fiction pornography? I mean some thing *new*, an invention by the human imagination of new sexual experience? Science-fiction alters at will the co-ordinates of space and time; it can set effect before cause; it works within a logic of total potentiality – 'all that can be imagined can happen'. But has it added a single item to the repertoire of the critic? I understand that in a forthcoming novel the terrestrial hero and explorer indulges in mutual masturbation with a bizarre, interplanetary creature. But there is no real novelty in that. Presumably one can use anything from seaweed to accordions, from meteorites to lunar pumice. A galactic monster would make no essential difference to the act. It would not extend in any real sense the range of our sexual being.

The point is crucial. Despite all the lyric or obsessed cant about the boundless varieties and dynamics of sex, the actual sum of possible gestures, consummations, and imaginings is drastically limited. There are probably more foods, more undiscovered eventualities of gastronomic enjoyment or revulsion than there have been sexual inventions since the Empress Theodora resolved 'to satisfy all amorous orifices of the human body to the full and at the same time'. There just aren't that many orifices. The mechanics of orgasm imply fairly rapid exhaustion and frequent intermission. The nervous system is so organized that responses to simultaneous stimuli at different points of the body tend to yield a single, somewhat blurred sensation. The notion (fundamental to Sade and much pornographic art) that one can double one's ecstasy by engaging in *coitus* while being at the same time deftly sodomized is sheer nonsense. In short: given the physiological and nervous complexion of the human body, the number of ways in which orgasm can be achieved or arrested, the total modes of intercourse, are fundamentally finite. The mathematics of sex stop somewhere in the region of *soixante-neuf*; there are no transcendental series.

This is the logic behind the *120 Days*. With the pedantic frenzy of a man trying to carry *pi* to its final decimal, Sade laboured to imagine and present the sum-total of erotic combinations and variants. He pictured a small group of human bodies and tried to narrate every mode of sexual pleasure and pain to which they could be subject. The variables are surprisingly few. Once all possible positions of the body have been tried – the law of gravity does interfere – once the maximum number of erogenous zones of the maximum number of participants have been brought into contact, abrasive, frictional, or intrusive, there is not much left to do or imagine. One can whip or be whipped; one can eat excrement or quaff urine; mouth and private part can meet in this or that commerce. After which there is the grey of morning and the sour knowledge that things have remained fairly generally the same since man first met goat and woman.

This is the obvious, necessary reason for the inescapable monotony of pornographic writing, for the fact well known to all haunters of Charing Cross Road or pre-Gaullist book-stalls that dirty books are maddeningly the same. The trappings change. Once it was the Victorian nanny in high-button shoes birching the master, or the vicar peering over the edge of the boys' lavatory. The Spanish Civil War brought a plethora of raped nuns, of buttocks on bayonets. At present, specialized dealers report a steady demand for 'WS' (stories of wife-swapping, usually in a suburban or honeymoon resort setting). But the fathomless tide of straight trash has never varied much. It operates within highly conventionalized formulas of low-grade sadism, excremental drollery, and banal fantasies of phallic prowess or feminine responsiveness. In its own way the stuff is as predictable as a Boy Scout manual.

Above the pulp-line – but the exact boundaries are impossible to draw – lies the world of erotica, of sexual writing with literary pretensions or genuine claims. This world is much larger than is commonly realized. It goes back to Egyptian literary papyri. At certain moments in western society, the amount of 'high pornography' being produced may have equalled, if not surpassed, ordinary belles-lettres. I suspect that this was the case in Roman Alexandria, in France during the *Régence*, perhaps in London around the 1890s. Much of this subterranean literature is bound to disappear. But anyone who has been allowed access to the Kinsey library in Bloomington, and has been lucky enough to have Mr John Gagnon as his guide, is made aware of the profoundly revealing, striking fact that there is hardly a major writer of the nineteenth or twentieth centuries who has not, at some point in his career, be it in earnest or in the deeper earnest of jest, produced a pornographic work. Likewise there are remarkably few painters, from the eighteenth century to post-Impressionism, who have not produced at least one set of pornographic plates or sketches. (Would one of the definitions of abstract, non-objective art be that it cannot be pornographic?)

Obviously a certain proportion of this vast body of writing has literary power and significance. Where a Diderot, a Crébillon *fils*, a Verlaine, a Swinburne, or an Apollinaire write erotica, the result will have some of the qualities which distinguish their more public works. Figures such as Beardsley and Pierre Louys are minor, but their lubricities have a period charm. Nevertheless, with very few exceptions, 'high pornography' is *not* of pre-eminent literary importance. It is simply *not* true that the locked cabinets of great libraries or private collections contain masterpieces of poetry or fiction which hypocrisy and censorship banish from the light. (Certain eighteenth-century drawings and certain Japanese prints suggest that the case of graphic art may be different; here there seems to be work of the first quality which is not generally available.) What emerges when one reads some of the classics of erotica is the fact that they too are intensely conventionalized, that their repertoire of fantasy is limited, and that it merges, almost imperceptibly, into the dream-trash of straight, mass-produced pornography.

In other words: the line between, say *Thérèse Philosophe* or *Lesbia Brandon* on the one hand, and *Sweet Lash* or *The Silken Thighs* on the other, is easily blurred. What distinguishes the 'forbidden classic' from under-the-counter delights on Frith Street is, essentially, a matter of semantics, of the level of vocabulary and rhetorical device used to provoke erection. It is not fundamental. Take the masturbating housemaid in a very recent example of the Great American Novel, and the housemaid similarly engaged in *They Called Her Dolly* (n.d., price 30p). From the point of view of erotic stimulus, the difference is one of language, or more exactly – as verbal precisions now appear in high literature as well – the difference is one of narrative sophistication. Neither piece of writing adds anything new to the potential of human emotion; both add to the waste.

Genuine additions are, in fact, very rare. The list of writers who have had the genius to enlarge our actual compass of sexual awareness, who have given the erotic play of the mind a novel focus, an area of recognition previously unknown or fallow, is very small. It would, I think, include Sappho, in whose verse the western ear caught, perhaps for the first time, the shrill, nerve-rending note of sterile sexuality, of a libido necessarily, deliberately, in excess of any assuagement. Catullus seems to have added something, though it is at this historical distance nearly impossible to identify that which startled in his vision, which caused so real a shock of consciousness. The close, delicately plotted concordance between orgasm and death in Baroque and Metaphysical poetry and art clearly enriched our legacy of excitement, as had the earlier focus on virginity. The development in Dostoevsky, Proust, and Mann of the correlations between nervous infirmity, the psychopathology of the organism, and a special erotic vulnerability, is probably new. Sade and Sacher-Masoch codified, found a dramatic syntax for, areas of arousal previously diffuse or less explicitly realized. In *Lolita* there is a genuine enrichment of our common stock of temptations. It is as if Vladimir Nabokov had brought into our field of vision what lay at the far edge (in Balzac's *La Rabouilleuse*, for instance) or what had been kept carefully implausible through disproportion (*Alice in Wonderland*). But such annexations of insight are rare.

The plain truth is that in literary erotica as well as in the great mass of 'dirty books' the same stimuli, the same contortions and fantasies, occur over and over with unutterable monotony. In most erotic writing, as in man's wet dreams, the imagination turns, time and time again, inside the bounded circle of what the body can experience. The actions of the mind when we masturbate are not a dance; they are a treadmill.

Mr Maurice Girodias would riposte that this is not the issue, that the interminable succession of fornications, flagellations, onanisms, masochistic fantasies, and homosexual punch-ups which fill his *Olympia Reader* are inseparable from its literary excellence, from the artistic originality and integrity of the books he published at the Olympia Press in Paris. He would say that several of the books he championed, and from which he has now selected representative passages, stand in the vanguard of modern sensibility, that they are classics of post-war literature. If they are so largely concerned with sexual experience, the reason is that the modern writer has recognized in sexuality the last open frontier, the terrain on which his talent must, if it is to be pertinent and honest, engage the stress of our culture. The pages of the *Reader* are strewn with four-letter words, with detailed accounts of intimate and specialized sexual acts, precisely because the writer has had to complete the campaign of liberation initiated by Freud, because he has had to overcome the verbal taboos, the hypocrisies of imagination in which former generations laboured when alluding to the most vital, complex part of man's being.

'Writing dirty books was a necessary participation in the common fight against the Square World . . . an act of duty.'

Mr Girodias has a case. His reminiscences and polemics make sour reading (he tends to whine); but his actual publishing record shows nerve and brilliance. The writings of Henry Miller matter to the history of American prose and self-definition. Samuel Beckett's *Watt* appeared with Olympia, as did writings of Jean Genet (though not the plays or the best prose). *Fanny Hill* and, to a lesser degree, *Candy*, are mock-epics of orgasm, books in which any sane man will take delight. Lawrence Durrell's *Black Book* seems to me grossly over-rated, but it has its serious defenders. Girodias himself would probably regard *Naked Lunch* as his crowning discernment. I don't see it. The book strikes me as a strident bore, illiterate and self-satisfied right to its heart of pulp. Its repute is important only for what it tells us of the currents of homosexuality, camp, and modish brutality which dominate present 'sophisticated' literacy. Burroughs indicts his readers, but not in the brave, prophetic sense argued by Girodias. Nevertheless, there can be no doubt of the genuineness of Girodias's commitment or of the risks he took.

Moreover, two novels on his list *are* classics, books whose genius he recognized and with which his own name will remain proudly linked : *Lolita* and *The Ginger Man*. It is a piece of bleak irony – beautifully appropriate to the entire 'dirty book' industry – that a subsequent disagreement with Nabokov now prevents Girodias from including anything of *Lolita* in his anthology. To all who first met Humbert Humbert in *The Traveller's Companion Series*, a green cover and the Olympia Press's somewhat mannered typography will remain a part of one of the high moments of contemporary literature. This alone should have spared Mr Girodias the legal and financial harryings by which Gaullist Victorianism hounded him out of business.

But the best of what Olympia published is now available on every drug-store counter – this being the very mark of Girodias's foresight. The *Olympia Reader* must be judged by what it actually contains. And far too much of it is tawdry stuff, 'doing dirt on life', with only the faintest pretensions to literary merit or adult intelligence.

It is almost impossible to get through the book at all. Pick it up at various points and the sense of *déjà-vu* is inescapable. ('This is one stag-movie I've seen before'). Whether a naked woman gets tormented in Sade's dungeons (*Justine*), during Spartacus's revolt (Marcus Van Heller : *Roman Orgy*), in a kinky French château (*L'Histoire d'O*) or in an Arab house (*Kama Houri* by one Ataullah Mordaan) makes damn little difference. *Fellatio* and buggery seem fairly repetitive joys whether enacted between Paris hooligans in Genet's *Thief's Journal*, beween small-time hustlers and ex-prizefighters (*The Gaudy Image*), or between lordly youths by Edwardian gaslight in *Teleny*, a silly piece attributed to Oscar Wilde.

After fifty pages of 'hardening nipples', 'softly opening thighs' and 'hot rivers' flowing in and out of the ecstatic anatomy, the spirit cries out, not in hypocritical outrage, not because I am a poor Square throttling my libido, but in pure, nauseous *boredom*. Even fornication can't be as dull, as hopelessly predictable as all that!

Of course there are moments which excite. *Sin for Breakfast* ends on a subtle, comic note of lewdness. *The Woman Thing* uses all the four-letter words and anatomical exactitudes with real force; it exhibits a fine ear for the way in which sexual heat compresses and erodes our uses of language. Those (and I imagine it includes most men) who use the motif of female onanism in their own fantasy life will find a vivid patch. There may be other nuggets. But who can get through the thing? For my money, there is one sublime moment in the *Reader*. It comes in an extract (possibly spurious?) from Frank Harris's *Life and Loves*. Coiling and uncoiling in diverse postures with two naked Oriental nymphets and their British procuress, Harris is suddenly struck with the revelation that 'there indeed is evidence to prove the weakness of so much of the thought of Karl Marx. It is only the bohemian who can be free, not the proletarian'. The image of Frank Harris, all limbs and propensities ecstatically engaged, suddenly disproving *Das Kapital* is worth the price of admission.

But not really. For that price is much higher than Mr Girodias, Miss Mary McCarthy, Mr Wayland Young, and other advocates of total frankness seem to realize. It is a price which cuts deep not only into the true liberty of the writer, but into the diminishing reserves of feeling and imaginative response in our society.

The preface to the *Olympia Reader* ends in triumph: 'Moral censorship was an inheritance from the past, deriving from centuries of domination by the Christian clergy. Now that it is practically over, we may expect literature to be transformed by the advent of freedom. Not freedom in its negative aspects, but as the means of exploring all the positive aspects of the human mind, which are all more or less related to, or generated by, sex.' This last proposition is almost unbelievably silly. What needs a serious look is the assertion about freedom, about a new and transforming liberation of literature through the abolition of verbal and imaginative taboos.

Since the *Lady Chatterley* case and the defeat of a number of attempts to suppress books by Henry Miller, the sluice gates stand open. Sade, the homosexual elaborations of Genet and Burroughs, *Candy, Sexus, L'Histoire d'O* are freely available. No censorship would chose to make itself ridiculous by challenging the sadistic eroticism, the minutiae of sodomy (smell and all) which grace Mailer's *American Dream*. This is an excellent thing. But let us be perfectly clear why. Censorship is stupid and repugnant for two empirical reasons: censors are men no better than ourselves, their judgments are no less fallible or open to dishonesty. Secondly, the thing won't work: those who really want to get hold of a book will do so somehow. This is an entirely different argument from saying that pornography doesn't in fact deprave the mind of the reader, or incite to wasteful or criminal gestures. *It may, or it may not.* We simply don't have enough evidence either way. The question is far more intricate than many of our literary champions of total freedom would allow. But to say that censorship won't work and should not be asked to, is *not* to say that there has been a liberation of literature, that the writer is, in any genuine sense, freer.

On the contrary. The sensibility of the writer is free where it is most humane, where it seeks to apprehend and re-enact the marvellous variety, complication, and resilience of life by means of words as scrupulous, as personal, as brimful of the mystery of human communication, as the language can yield. The very opposite of freedom is cliché, and nothing is less free, more inert with convention and hollow brutality than a row of four-letter words. Literature is a living dialogue between writer and reader only if the writer shows a twofold respect: for the imaginative maturity of his reader, and in a very complex but central way, for the wholeness, for the independence and quick of life, in the personages he creates.

Respect for the reader signifies that the poet or novelist invites the consciousness of the reader to collaborate with his own in the act of presentment. He does not tell all because his work is not a primer for children or the retarded. He does not exhaust the possible responses of his reader's own imaginings, but delights in the fact that we will fill in from our own lives, from resources of memory and desire proper to ourselves, the contours he has drawn. Tolstoy is infinitely freer, infinitely more exciting than the new eroticists, when he arrests his narrative at the door of the Karenins' bedroom, when he merely initiates, through the simile of a dying flame, of ash cooling in the grate, a perception of sexual defeat which each of us can re-live or detail for himself. George Eliot is free, and treats her readers as free, adult human beings, when she conveys, through inflection of style and mood, the truth about the Casaubon honeymoon in *Middlemarch*, when she makes us imagine for ourselves how Dorothea has been violated by some essential obtuseness. These are profoundly exciting scenes, these enrich and complicate our sexual awareness, far beyond the douche-bag idylls of the contemporary 'free' novel. There is no real freedom whatever in the compulsive physiological exactitudes of present 'high pornography', because there is no respect for the reader whose imaginative means are set at nil.

And there is none for the sanctity of autonomous life in the characters of the novel, for that tenacious integrity of existence which makes a Stendhal, a Tolstoy, a Henry James tread warily around their own creations. The novels being produced under the new code of total statement shout at their personages: strip, fornicate, perform this or that act of sexual perversion. So did the S.S. guards at rows of living men and women. The total attitudes are not, I think, entirely distinct. There may be deeper affinities than we as yet understand between the 'total freedom' of the uncensored erotic imagination and the total freedom of the sadist. That these two freedoms have emerged in close historical proximity may not be coincidence. Both are exercised at the expense of someone else's humanity, of someone else's most precious right – the right to a private life of feeling.

This is the most dangerous aspect of all. Future historians may come to characterize the present era in the West as one of a massive onslaught on human privacy, on the delicate processes by which we seek to become our own singular selves, to hear the echo of our specific being. This onslaught is being pressed by the very conditions of an urban mass-technocracy, by the necessary uniformities of our economic and political choices, by the new electronic media of communication and persuasion, by the ever-increasing exposure of our thoughts and actions to sociological, psychological, and material intrusions and controls. Increasingly, we come to know real privacy, real space in which to experiment with our sensibility, only in extreme guises: nervous breakdown, addiction, economic failure. Hence the appalling monotony and *publicity* – in the full sense of the word – of so many outwardly prosperous lives. Hence also the need for nervous stimuli of an unprecedented brutality and technical authority.

Sexual relations are, or should be, one of the citadels of privacy, the nightplace where we must be allowed to gather the splintered, harried elements of our consciousness to some kind of inviolate order and repose. It is in sexual experience that a human being alone, and two human beings in that attempt at total communication which is also communion, can discover the unique bent of their identity. That we can find for ourselves, through imperfect striving and repeated failure, the words, the gestures, the mental images which set the blood to racing. In that dark and wonder ever-renewed both the fumblings and the light must be our own.

The new pornographers subvert this last, vital privacy; they do our imagining for us. They take away the words that were of the night and shout them over the roof-tops, making them hollow. The images of our love-making, the stammerings we resort to in intimacy, come pre-packed. From the rituals of adolescent petting to the recent university experiment in which faculty wives agreed to practise onanism in front of the researchers' cameras, sexual life, particularly in America, is passing more and more into the public domain. This is a profoundly ugly and demeaning thing whose effects on our identity and resources of feeling we understand as little as we do the impact on our nerves of the perpetual 'sub-eroticism' and sexual suggestion of modern advertisement. Natural selection tells of limbs and functions which atrophy through lack of use; the power to feel, to experience and realize the precarious uniqueness of each other's being, can also wither in a society. And it is no mere accident (as Orwell knew) that the standardization of sexual life, either through controlled licence or compelled puritanism, should accompany totalitarian politics.

Thus the present danger to the freedom of literature and to the inward freedom of our society is not censorship or verbal reticence. The danger lies in the facile contempt which the erotic novelist exhibits for his readers, for his personages, and for the language. Our dreams are marketed wholesale.

Because there were words it did not use, situations it did not represent graphically, because it demanded from the reader not obeisance but live echo, much of western poetry and fiction has been a school to the imagination, an exercise in making one's awareness more exact, more humane. My true quarrel with the *Olympia Reader* and the genre it embodies is not that so much of the stuff should be boring and abjectly written. It is that these books leave a man less free, less himself, than they found him; that they leave language poorer, less endowed with a capacity for fresh discrimina-

tion and excitement. It is not a new freedom that they bring, but a
new servitude. In the name of human privacy, enough!

1 Controversy over this article continued for many months, and is continuing still. My knowledge of and interest in pornography are, I would suppose, no greater than the middle-class average. What I was trying to get
into focus is the notion of the 'stripping naked' of language, of the removal
from private, intensely privileged or adventurous use, of the erotic vocabulary. It does seem to me that we have scarcely begun to understand the
impoverishment of our imaginings, the erosion into generalized banality
of our resources of individual erotic representation and expression. This
erosion is very directly a part of the general reduction of privacy and individual style in a mass consumer civilization. Where everything can be
said with a shout, less and less can be said in a low voice. I was also trying
to raise the question of what relation there *may* be between the dehumanization of the individual in pornography and the making naked and
anonymous of the individual in the totalitarian state (the concentration
camp being the logical epitome of that state). Both pornography and
totalitarianism seem to me to set up power relations which must necessarily
violate privacy.

Though the discussion which followed on publication has been heated,
neither of these two issues has, I feel, been fully understood or engaged.

(Dr. Steiner's points may be studied in the light of Dr. Straus's essay
above, about the intrusion of 'the public' into the private – Editor.)

SEX EDUCATION

Why have a section on 'sex education' in a casebook against pornography? Alas, recent developments have generated approaches to children around this subject which can only be called pornographic. Films, television programmes, and illustrated books offer explicit forms of attention to sexual functions which are based on quite fallacious notions of what is 'real' about sexual love. They are likely to encourage voyeurism, and their sadistic and masochistic elements could do immense harm to children's feelings. The following articles are printed here to emphasize the delicate, personal nature of this question of the necessary enlightenment of the child. As Dr F. G. Lennhoff has said, 'there has been a reaction to the traditional attitudes . . . but this is mostly on a superficial level . . . because this movement seems to have little real concern for the contribution sex (and what surrounds it) makes towards human values, human happiness and the maintenance and improvement of . . . society . . . The "new thinking" seems to have little understanding of what I believe is our human need for security, stability, and satisfactory lasting relationships as the starting point for the whole experience of living . . . .' (*Honesty to Children*, a Shotton Hall Publication, Harmer Hill, Shrewsbury, 1971.)

It is this 'whole' approach that is emphasized here, as against the dehumanized trends of today, not least in the realm of sex education.

LETTER TO THE AUTHOR'S CHILDREN

Tom Stacey

CHILDREN, I wrote this brief guidance on sex in our permissive age with just you in mind, then it struck me that your boy-friends (and in due course, in the case of Sam, girl-friends) might like to read it. And having gone that far – why not offer it for publication?

I do not believe it is wise to place sex, as such, at the centre of one's life – even though perhaps at times, for short periods, this may happen inadvertently. There is no 'ultimate' sensation in the practice of sex; and to pursue the sensation of sex for its own sake can only lead to a feeling of futility and disgust, and quite rapidly to contempt between the partners. It becomes, inevitably, a wholly selfish process

237.

when the sexual urge, the progenitor of love, is reduced to an act of exclusive self-gratification.

Thus it is a sound rule of life that a feeling of love and devotion and respect should accompany sex. And one should love another not in the first place as an extension of oneself, but as herself or himself. Love and sex exist most securely and happily in such a sense of partnership, each partner with his or her own role. 'Man does, woman is,' as Robert Graves has put it.

Immeasurably the greatest sexual delight is to be found in sharing the body of someone you love. In such ecstasy, calculation in the act of loving can scarcely be conscious : such love-making of lovers overrides the imperfections, and all sensation is melded into the overwhelming act of union, one body with another.

I believe I have come across just about all the manuals of love, Eastern and Western. True lovers have little to learn from them. I defy the author of the *Kama Sutra* to show us more than three basic positions of love. Many a life of conjugal bliss has been confined to two. . . .

The point I am making is that sex is for doing – not for studying (beyond a few elementary facts and tips), or for plotting or thinking about. There is a current spate of pornography, and there must be many sorrowful little people shut in their rooms alone with their over-fed imaginations slavering over this or that sexual experience which will never 'come true'. It is a lonely practice which, indulged, makes deeper the loneliness. Men and women are not made for this.

I would also advise you against sexual perversion. I am not speaking of the little tricks that may enhance the act of love between this or that couple. Perverted practices, or the nurturing of perverted desires, can place happy, completing, reciprocal love out of reach. These practices are a cheap form of sensationalism which lead nowhere : at once they degenerate into an auto-eroticism that precludes the ecstasy of completion, one with another. No one is entirely without a degree of self-love in sexual form, however vestigial; but very few are 'natural' perverts. The fashion to exalt perversion, or to place 'homosexual love' alongside 'heterosexual love' as if the former were an acceptable alternative in which the young may seek their pleasure, is to invoke a biological affront and a source of pain and confusion to the innocent.

There is a place for levity and humour concerning sex; but overall it is something a little sacred, to be held in honour, not to be given away lightly. Because it is at the core of loving, and loving other people is at the core of living (I do not say it is not possible to love

238

without sex), to squander or distort it can be to squander or distort life.

Simple observation of oneself or others demonstrates the truth of this. We live in a 'liberated' era in which 'anything goes'. There is little socially-induced guilt. But I have yet to meet a woman who gives herself to men capriciously and who is genuinely happy and fulfilled. And what youth masturbating upon his fancies feels bold enough to conquer the girl of his real-life desire?

A sad commentary on the sexual life of the Western male is the success of the girlie magazines. Men do not have to live in an atmosphere of artificially-induced, miscellaneous lust to perform as men. To a much greater degree than our permissive prophets realize, men and women have always been capable of desiring whom they want to desire. Making love to one's wife with a *Playboy* 'playmate' in the mind's eye is not, I assure you, what lovemaking is about.

One sex act differs from another; and you'll be darned lucky if every time you make love the spheres clash and heaven breaks forth *fortissimo* into chorus. But to humankind certain experiences act upon the spirit as the great universalizers, the sweet and total unravellers, when all creation and one's own part in it resolve into a rightful harmony. Poetry and music are always there for you and in the best of times, shared passion. There is nothing gained in spending time or human essence on bad poetry, bad music, or bad sex.

Soon the time will come when we – and you young ones, in particular – will be less bombarded by cheap temptation and the glorification of loose living. Until then – indeed for always – you must make for yourself your own code. Know what you think, and why you think it. No one can live with all his moral options open. That is the road to misery or madness. The fashionable mentors of our age – Marshall McLuhan, Bishop Robinson, Timothy O'Leary, Roy Jenkins – implicitly characterize the ancient Greek virtues of restraint and reserve as 'inhibition', and imply that they dampen passion and preclude deep-delving experience. I would suggest that those of little acquaintance with self-containment have little acquaintance with rapture. Unlike Tolstoy, our popular mentors have never noticed 'the natural modesty of a woman in love'. In every society in the world, throughout all of history, sex has invoked such 'inhibition' in women.

We live in an age dominated by Freudian or post-Freudian psychology: respect for the whole man is lost among the honour accorded every impulse and instinct lurking within us. The whole man counts for most. It is kept together by a little wisdom, a little discipline – a 'code', such as I have said you must make for yourselves. Do not imagine you can survive happily without one. It may be no more than a consciously directed tilt. But sometimes you will require to be dogmatic; do not be afraid to be so.

By the time you have reached the age of sexual or romantic involvement (as some of you have) we – your mother and I – will have given to you children 90 per cent of what we shall ever give you. That is to say, when anything I have written in this article comes to bear upon you, the ingredients of your character will be more or less settled once and for all. But there will always be a 'best you'. Only on this 'best you' can you base your personal code.

Recognizing and acting on the 'best you' is what is meant by being true to yourself – the fundamental precept of living. There are times when you may feel the compass of identity so great that the 'best self' is obscured. Yet I believe that in practice not much reflection is required to recognize what is most truly you, as you would like to be and are capable of being.

My final word, therefore, is this: that whatever you do sexually is in keeping with what you also believe to be true, generous and to belong to the whole of you.

YOUTH NEEDS PROTECTION

Benjamin Spock

OBSCENITY means sexual material in literature or art, or sexual behaviour in movies, on the stage or in public that is considered offensively lewd (whatever the intention of the creator or seller). Pornography is matter designed with the deliberate purpose of causing sexual excitement.

In recent years the courts have excused more and more of what used to be considered objectionable. British law defines as obscene any writing or article that 'tends to deprave and corrupt'. The United States' Supreme Court now calls a production obscene only if it is clearly designed to 'appeal to prurience' and at the same time is 'utterly without redeeming social value'. A recent film story about delinquency showed scenes of brutality, prostitution, homosexuality and sodomy which 'revolted' the judges who saw it; but they called it not obscene because it could be thought of as having educational value.

From my particular point of view, to judge a work only on these two technical grounds misses the main purpose of obscenity laws, which is to protect people from being revolted or brutalized by crude sexual material – or by brutality without sex for that matter. I think the need for this kind of control is particularly important in a country which has sky-high rates of crime and delinquency and which has been endlessly fascinated with violence on television.

I agree that we overdid prudery and propriety in the Victorian period – we tried to deny our sexuality and our aggression altogether, and the insincerity was corrupting. But I myself think we have swung much too far in the opposite direction. It is revealing that the countries which have recently gone the furthest in legalizing and indulging in pornography are Sweden, Denmark and the United States, all of which were outstandingly puritannical up to a few decades ago. Though it's natural enough for young people of most countries to have their naughty, half-secret fun by allowing sexuality to come partway out of repression, I believe we are now deliberately coarsening and brutalizing sex to prove to ourselves that we are not puritans any more. I feel this is not healthy for our sexual relations or for our idealism or for our civilization in general.

I believe that children in particular should be protected from being shocked by stumbling on crude literature, pictures, films, plays or TV programmes, because they are in the developmental period when character and ideals are in a sensitive and formative state. It is a somewhat different matter when an older adolescent or youth has become curious enough to want to search out very purposefully, for instance, the pornographic literature that is kept out of sight in the public library, or the pictures he can borrow from a friend or buy under the counter. To find these by his own efforts will not be as disillusioning to a sensitive person as having them displayed before him with the approval of the law. Of course all teenagers worth their salt will claim that they are sophisticated enough to be able to take pornography without upset; but this assertion really comes from curiosity and from the ambition to be grown up rather than from a sure knowledge of being unshockable. I do believe that crude or brutal obscenity is disturbing to young people with high ideals, particularly until the age of eighteen or nineteen, when attitudes are better formed. As a matter of fact it is at least slightly shocking to older people too (including myself) unless they are quite coarse to start with.

From *A Young Person's Guide to Life and Love.*

THE LITTLE READ SCHOOLBOOK
An attempt to abolish childhood?

Ronald Butt

IMMEDIATELY after the magistrate's finding last week that the *Little Red Schoolbook* was obscene within the appropriate section of the act, the National Council for Civil Liberties and the Defence of Literature and the Arts Society issued a joint statement of outrage. 'If a publication as harmless and informative as the *Little Red Schoolbook* can be seized, tried and banned in this brutal way,' they asserted, 'no publisher of unorthodox opinion can feel free from censorship. The judgment is an attack on freedom of expression and a victory for those who seek to impose their bigoted views on the rest of the community.'

Reading this sonorous protest, and taking the expression 'civil liberties' at face value, the ordinary citizen without knowledge of the book's contents, might be pardoned for supposing that some vital human freedom had been eroded, or that the heritage of Magna Carta was being undermined. He might even have supposed, from the name of the second organization, that the *Little Red Schoolbook* had something to do with literature or the arts.

During the court case itself, moreover, the ordinary citizen's knowledge of the book's contents was, inevitably, limited to newspaper reports of the opinions on it given by witnesses. Even if it had been legally possible to quote relevant passages from the book in newspapers, without incurring a charge of obscenity or contempt, it is difficult to imagine that any editor would have been prepared to propagate the material in this book into the homes of his readers.

As a result, it may be that many people's view of what they suppose the book to be like may well have been chiefly conditioned by the testimonies they have read in its favour by witnesses whose opinions are assumed to have some special weight, either because of their various occupations or because they have achieved a certain prominence as publicists in one field or another.

Since the end of the case in court, there have also been letters to newspapers from sympathizers with the book avowing that they

243

I

find this manual positively desirable reading for their own children. It is now difficult to doubt that the object of these no doubt unsolicited testimonials and protests is to create a climate in which the public will assume that so much indignation must be in a good cause. In other words, the object is presumably to create public assumptions about the nature of the case and of the book that might pave the way for seeking to have the finding of the magistrate's court overturned.

It is, however, important that public opinions should not be formed simply on the say-so of the vociferous sympathizers of the book and, in particular, that they should not be allowed to get away with the argument, put forward by Mr Mortimer, the defence counsel in the case, that the issue was part of 'the continuing argument between those who believe that young children should not be told and those who believe that children should be encouraged to find out for themselves.'

The idea that this book leaves children any scope to find out anything for themselves would be laughable if the social implications of its sophistry were not so tragic. The issue has nothing to do with whether children should be told facts but what they should be told *about* them and how. No parent or anybody else is in a position to judge the rationality of the argument about this book until he or she is aware of at least one central passage in the section which was the subject of the court case.

After a detailed description of a full range of sexual behaviour and activity, which, it is implied, is fully open to children (passages which I do not quote for obvious reasons), there is a detailed statement of what is presumably intended to be regarded as the more conventional type of pornography. 'But,' says the book, 'there are other kinds' – and it goes on to describe, in concrete terms bestiality (in the specific sense of that term) and sado-masochism.

The book's general comment on what it has thus described is as follows: 'Porn is a harmless pleasure if it isn't taken seriously and believed to be real life. Anybody who mistakes it for reality will be greatly disappointed. But it's quite possible that you may get some good ideas from it and that you may find something which looks interesting and that you haven't tried before.' The invitation to child readers, who may well be under the age of consent, in this passage (as in the passages on contraception and sexual behaviour) is implicit and clear.

I quote these aspects of the book because it is essential that ordinary parents, doctors, teachers and other responsible people in public life should be aware of the paradox that is developing in this case. The book having been prohibited as obscene, they cannot see for themselves what it actually contains or therefore judge the real worth of the testimonials still coming from its active supporters. This paradox could enable the active advocates of the book to create by uncontradicted testimonials a climate of opinion in which the book seemed acceptable – and if they succeeded, parents might find out too late what precisely is the nature of the propaganda that is being directed to children of 11 years and upwards.

It is hard to believe that a parent in a thousand could really consider this book suitable reading for children. Both in providing many more 'facts' than would confront any ordinary child in this age-group, and in the approach to them, this book is an intensive conditioner. Since so many testimonials are still being given that it is harmless for publication, it seems to me right that someone should give a testimony against. I do so because I believe that the advocates of this book really want to establish that there is no such thing as childhood : no period in which a child should be in peace to find his feet and develop a sense of values and responsibility.

If the advocates of this book would band themselves into a Society for the Abolition of Childhood, we should know where we were. What is at stake is not a child's freedom, but the freedom to be a child.

MUST WE SHOW CHILDREN SEX?

Mary Miles

SOMEWHERE in the middle of Dr Martin Cole's film 'Growing Up', I began to be plagued by memories of the naughty little boy in Aldous Huxley's *Brave New World* who refused to indulge in directed sex play. The memory was, I think, provoked by Dr Cole's calm, explanatory voice accompanying the exhibiting of a nude girl and boy at various stages of development, in which the penis is handled, flaccid and then half-erect; the adolescents masturbating alone and with no sign of satisfaction; and the couple copulating apparently without zest, mutual enjoyment or affection.

Perhaps Dr Cole is trying to approach the subject of sexuality dispassionately in order to avoid seducing adolescents by displays of sexual excitement, but it is just this presentation that makes his film fundamentally suspect and open to criticism. Because of its low-toned approach, I can imagine some educationists thinking that this is a safe and effective way of teaching groups of adolescents about sexual development.

The fact remains, however, that the visual representation of sexual behaviour – as opposed to verbal information – has been found to carry much greater risk of exciting the young sexually, since it makes a more violent impact.

There is also something extremely disquieting in this deadpan presentation of situations which are in reality highly exciting sexually. Intercourse is not just the penis moving into the moist vagina, as the inexorable voice explains, and the young people obediently go through the actions. Where is the mutual excitement, the giving and receiving of pleasure? Where, oh, where is love, which the young sing about so much? The film shots of sexual activity are equally equivocal; carefully angled to reveal and yet not to reveal.

If my adolescent sons and daughters had to learn 'the facts of life' by watching a film – which heaven forbid – I think I would prefer it to be frankly erotic and about highly involved lovers who were not being supervised by an explanatory adult. Not by a film that uses young people in an exhibitionistic way, displaying them before an audience of the young which, if it were shown in school, would be captive.

Once again, as everywhere today, sex is presented as depersonalized, sex for the sake of sex, part of the drill of growing up, 'the done thing'.

Anyway, do children really need to have masturbation and sexual intercourse demonstrated? Do you *teach* a young child to walk by demonstration? You protect him from dangers, pick him up when he stumbles, help him when he becomes anxious, but he *learns* through his own drive to stand, to move, and through his own experience. Children and adolescents learn sexual behaviour from their bodily feelings, impulses, observations and experiments. Where they do need help is over anxieties, feelings of guilt, inadequacy or abnormality, and finally in harnessing their bodily sensations to eroticism (sexual love), and then to mature and lasting love. This kind of help, I think, is best given individually by someone reliable, though not in a very close relationship.

The whole question of group education about sex is open to doubt. My experience and that of many others, including the late Dr D. W. Winnicott, the well-known paediatrician and psychoanalyst, suggests that sex education given in a group is not only usually ineffectual but may very well increase anxieties, since these vary from person to person; what reassures one touches off anxiety in another. Dr Cole's film may well reassure adolescents that masturbation is not harmful physically, but it does not and cannot touch the deeper and more important point, that the fantasies contained in masturbation vary widely, and it is these that cause anxiety and guilt. In some people masturbation is compulsive and unsatisfying; in some girls and women it can be related to their unresolved conflict over not having a penis; other people never masturbate, possibly because of some experience during the more important and forgotten phase of infantile masturbation. It is no help, if guilt is very deep, to be told later in life it's all right to do this. There are, of course, other adolescents who use masturbation without much conflict on their way through to adult sexuality, satisfied in intercourse.

Various anxieties one meets in adolescents could be increased by seeing this film, which assumes that the mechanics of intercourse are straightforward and simple. Many boys suffer from great anxiety over the size of their genitals, over the late descent of their testicles, over involuntary emissions at the beginning of puberty, over difficulties in having an erection when faced with intercourse. Many girls suffer from deep anxieties because their body is not quite like those of other girls they see, in some small way. It is such anxieties as these that can interfere with happy intercourse.

I should be very interested to know the reactions to this film of adolescents who, because they have been wisely brought up, have no marked problems. I have known many of them show considerable indignation with teachers and other well meaning adults who intrude into their private world of sex with group education. They have their own ways of dealing with the situation – giggling, 'dirty' stories, helpless amusement at any word with a possible sexual connotation. I think these are the natural ways of dealing with their changing bodies and feelings in early adolescence. Children should be left to find their own way unless they show a clear need for help. One very sensible and natural girl told her mother of her embarrassment at hearing a grown-up speak of all the things she and her friends knew quite well and discussed in their own language.

A happy and natural attitude to sexuality is not formed by talks or films. It depends on all the child's experiences throughout his life: his bodily explorations, sensations, observations and the individual help he is given with his changing ideas and anxieties. When children express their passing fantasies about the bodily differences between girls and boys, their changing theories of the origins of babies, these ideas should all be corrected by constant repetition of the actual facts, but never by demonstrations from adults, which are over-exciting. It is important in early childhood to separate sexual feelings and affection. But it is equally important in late adolescence to weld them together again.

As an educationist and psychotherapist I would not show Dr Cole's film to adolescents, nor give them talks on the mechanics of sex, the normality of masturbation and pre-marital intercourse. I would encourage them to read – to read all the great love stories of the world, and the marvellous erotic poems there for the reading.

What growing children need from adults is feeling, imagination and understanding. Just as important are a respect for adolescents; honesty in answering questions; and statements of definite values. All these I find lacking in the film 'Growing Up'. At the psychological clinic where I work we regard it as an ominous sign when a boy or girl asks others to act out something sexual for them to watch; this suggests extreme passivity if not something more, and this the film might well stimulate.

Someone knowing I had been to see this film asked 'Did it shock you?' No, it depressed me. I went home and read the poems of

Catullus. These, as ever, warmed and lightened me and I felt better. He at least was honest in his enjoyment of all kinds of sexual experiences. He also knew love, and, as James Michie says in the introduction to his translation, 'he has a gift for finding the right word at the right moment.' This is one of the things that Dr Cole's film so lamentably lacks. I continued to be depressed about the film and its message of sex as the done thing, sex for the sake of sex, and depressed by its exhibitionism, which could make a dangerous impact on the young. It is, however, such a very pedestrian film that it might have the contrary effect and put adolescents off sex for quite a long time. This too would be a pity.

'WHERE DO BABIES COME FROM?'

Moira Keenan

(As Winnicott says, sex instruction should take place in the presence of trusted adults, 'with ordinary capacity for human friendship.' The following is an account of such work in such a context.)

'WHEN I asked Mum where babies came from, I was told a stork dropped me down the chimney. I kept looking up the chimney to see if any more babies were coming.'

'I was told Mum bought me in a shop and I cost 6d.; my brother cost one shilling. I've felt cheap ever since.'

'When I was six I asked Mum where babies came from. Mum said the mother had a little seed inside her which just grew into a baby. She told me I'd got a little seed inside me too, and for years I was terrified I was going to have a baby.'

'Today we are going to do the reproductive system of the rabbit,' said the biology mistress, eyeing the class defiantly. 'And I don't want any giggling.' That, and a totally unrelated earlier account of how my insides worked and how human babies grew in their mother's tummies, apparently through some sort of internal combustion, was the extent of my own formal sex education. And I think I was probably luckier than most of my generation because the classmate at my convent who eventually enlightened me (during a dull moment in an Easter retreat) was matter-of-fact and fairly accurate.

Even in today's permissive society things have not changed much. The quotes above all come from teenagers talking about sex, and a schoolgirl, says: 'Whenever you ask about sex they tell you about the rabbit, but we're not interested in the rabbit, and we know perfectly well they're getting out of it.' I am told that boys are lucky if they are even taught the love-life of the amoeba, and they do not link this with human relationships – why on earth should they?

Everyone agrees that the right people to explain the facts of life to children are their parents. But only a tiny percentage of parents are willing and able to do this properly, and many deliberately mislead their children in an effort to stem the flow of embarrassing questions. Most are up against their own background of inadequate sex education, and this being so, there seems to be a very strong case in favour of a great deal more sex education in schools, given by properly trained experts and starting as young as nine or ten years old. This is before they are old enough to be emotionally involved themselves and before they get sinister ideas or warped accounts of what it is all about. A number of primary schools have been experimenting on these lines.

Up on Merseyside, Mrs Jill Kenner, an Education Counsellor of the National Marriage Guidance Council has, for the past year, been giving talks on sex to small groups of primary school children, and they appear to have been an unqualified success. 'You can imagine how I felt about the responsibility of talking to other people's children about sex,' she says. 'But I think it is fair to say that it has been completely successful. Over something like sex parents would be up like a shot if there was anything wrong. Of course before you can give these kind of talks it is desperately important to have a meeting with the parents so that they know what your attitude to sex is and what you are going to do.'

Mrs Kenner's first talks were given just a year ago in St Peter's Primary School, Heswall. The idea was first suggested to Mr Cocker, the headmaster, by one of the parents and there were no objections from other parents. 'In fact,' says Mrs Kenner, 'I'm afraid that some are only too happy to hand it over to the schools.'

As both Mr Cocker and Mrs Kenner point out, you cannot just suddenly start holding this kind of class on its own, it has got to take its place in the curriculum. At St Peter's it happened to fit in very well with what they called the 'Growing Up' course, a combination of good health and family relationships, and the children saw sex education as a natural part of the life and growing up they were learning about.

Mrs Kenner's approach is friendly, natural and unselfconscious. This is very important, because as she says herself, sexual attitudes are caught, not taught. She manages to bring everything down to a level which the children can understand and accept without in any way talking down to them. She encourages a barrage of questions and answers them all easily and frankly, never showing any sign of shock or disapproval, but often turning a question neatly round so that it is the children themselves who answer it.

She insists that approachability and plenty of give-and-take in sex education, whether by parents or in school, is very important. The children's questions cover an astonishing range, reflecting the bits of gossip, out-of-context remarks and newspaper paragraphs which they must have picked up, mulled over and stored up in their young memories. Most start off: 'My Mum . . .'; 'Our neighbour . . .'; 'I saw in the paper . . .' and vary from something as obvious as 'Why do we have hair on our bodies?' to really deep and complicated inquiries about Siamese twins, illegitimacy, adoption and even abortion.

Mrs Kenner starts with what she calls the 'short story'. How a mother's egg is fertilized by the father's sperm, how it forms into a baby and how it is born. Then in greater detail, and with the help of her own very simple drawings she explains from the beginning how girls and boys grow up, mate and have children, and all the time the emphasis is on this being a warm, loving and happy process.

'Lots of parents can get as far as intercourse,' she says, 'but baulk at describing that, so they leave a gap and carry on from there. But that is the sixty-four thousand dollar question, the one children really want an answer to. Do you know it helps enormously to explain it if you stop yourself thinking of intercourse as a tremendously emotional and personal experience and think of it as a very clever method of getting the father's sperm as close as possible to the mother's egg to start a baby. That after all is the child's picture of it. It is a little difficult to explain why people want to do this rather extraordinary thing together. But I stress the fact that it is a loving thing.'

One of the simplest explanations I have ever come across was, strangely enough, in one of John Master's novels. An older woman explaining sex to a younger friend says that when you love someone very, very much you want to be part of that person, and how making love is the nearest one can get to being a part of someone else. A child should be able to understand that because it must feel something the same when it throws its arms round its mother and buries itself in her lap.

Mrs Kenner stresses the importance of a proper vocabulary. One mother said to her: 'I can't tackle the job because I don't even know the right words and names.' You have to use a vocabulary that is acceptable and common to doctors, children, teachers and parents. And there are two points she has found from experience that it is vital to clarify. The first is that the reproductive functions are absolutely separate from excremental functions. Children are enormously relieved to know this. More than one has said: 'I thought the baby came out of the back passage when the mother was on the toilet.' The other thing which sets their minds at rest is to know that the uterus and vagina are very elastic and designed to stretch as the baby grows. So many of them think the mother is going to split. 'You just can't stress that point enough.'

Not everyone believes in teaching sex so young. There are two main objections. One is that even in one age group there is a very wide range of maturity and you might be forcing information on a child which cannot take it in. Mrs Kenner doubts that this happens. 'I think the child absorbs what it can and forgets the rest.' The other is that talking about sex at this age puts ideas into their heads and arouses their sexual curiosity. But the great thing about early sex education is that it is impossible to arouse the 6–10 year-olds' emotions because at this age they have no sexual emotions of that sort. All they want is facts and information. Like anything else they are taught well the subject arouses their interest and they go home and talk about it. One mother commented : 'During the talks we had sex for breakfast, lunch and tea, but afterwards sex was put aside for more important things.'

Other parents have recounted how their children came home so fascinated and excited by what they had learnt that it completely broke the ice for the grownups who found they were able to talk about sex with their children quite spontaneously for the first time. Mrs Kenner says : 'This is how it should be; a joint thing between school and parents, with the school acting as a catalyst.'

Parents divide into two groups, says Mrs Kenner. There are those who worry because their children have started asking them questions and they do not quite know how to answer, and those who worry because their children have not started asking questions, and they do not know how to broach the subject. But if children have not asked questions by the age of 9 or 10 it does not mean they are not interested, and the parents should look for an opportunity to talk to them. 'Try to find some reason for bringing up the subject very naturally – it is easy if you know someone who is expecting a baby.'

And if your child asks you awkward questions at an awkward moment, like on top of a crowded bus, say : 'Oh yes, I want to talk to you about that, remind me when we are at home'; and make sure you are reminded.

For eight years now Mrs Kenner has been talking to older children about the facts of life. She has talked to teenagers in schools and youth clubs and over and over again she has been met initially with fear, embarrassment and worry from her young audiences. 'And it is not surprising,' she says, 'because the things they believe would make me afraid.'

For instance they believe that breasts must have holes punched in them before milk can come out for a baby. They have some pretty

253

funny ideas about intercourse too. One girl was told by a friend that a baby was started by a man 'cutting open a woman and spending a penny in her'. They do not know anything about sexual relationships, or the different reactions and emotions of girls and boys and they have no idea of sexual responsibility.

Mrs Kenner says she found much of her work was remedial. 'The damage was already done and I could only try to put it right. Teenagers would say to me: "If only we had been told all this properly earlier." And I realized that we ought to be doing this kind of thing with much younger children. I think it terribly important to tell children these things before they are old enough to be emotionally involved themselves and before they have picked up the wrong attitudes and ideas. Once they have become fixed they are very hard to unstick. I think of the factory girl who said to me: "Mrs Kenner, I wish I could think of sex as you do, as something clean and valuable, but to me it will always be cheap and dirty."

'We aren't being fair to the young today. We are giving them freedom and not the education to cope with it. But I believe that by giving every child a good sex education we can cut down the rate of illegitimacy. So much teenage sex is because of ignorance, loneliness, unhappiness and feeling not wanted. It all boils down to a question of personal relationships. I call my work education for personal relationships – then you see it in perspective."

Books

Mrs Kenner has written her own book on the facts of life for children based on her talks to primary schools and designed for children to read themselves. It is published by the National Marriage Guidance Council and called *Where do babies come from?* (price 17½ p). I think it is the best and most complete book of its kind available, and ideally would suggest parents read it for themselves and then go through it with their children.

Peter and Caroline, by Sten Hegeler (60 p) is another good conversational account of sex and childbirth for children. It is selling four times as well today as it did when first published about eight years ago when it was considered too advanced; parents did not like drawings which showed pubic hair!

The same sort of conversational approach, an expectant mother and two children talking, is used for a gramophone record produced by the Family Guidance Bureau of Ottawa. Called *Every child has a right to sex education* (£2·7½), it is simple and unembarrassed, but lacks essential diagrams, and if you are listening to it with children it is less easy to stop the record to answer questions than to stop reading.

The Ladybird Book, *Your Body* (12½ p) and the Puffin Picture Book, *The human body* (17½ p) both well illustrated, would make useful adjuncts to help parents talk about sex and reproduction.

(All available from the N.M.G.C., 58 Queen Anne Street, London, W.1. Another excellent book is *The Everyday Miracle*, Penguin Books.)

STEALERS OF DREAMS

Moira Keenan

JUST under three years ago I wrote a piece on this page about sex education in schools. It was called *Where do babies come from?* and described the work being done on Merseyside by Mrs Jill Kenner who was giving classes in personal relationships, which included the facts of life, to 9- and 10-year-olds in primary schools. I thought then, and still do, that Mrs Kenner was doing a marvellous job. Her approach was warm, sensitive and reassuring, and in a totally straightforward and unselfconscious way she managed to put sex in perspective as part of life and personal relationships. I said then that I thought there should be more of this kind of thing.

Re-reading that article this week I have absolutely no regrets about writing it, and I still believe that there should be more sex education given in the way Mrs Kenner does it. What I should hate, though, is to think that anything I might have said could have contributed to the rash of material that has been appearing under the cover of 'sex education' ever since, and which I am coming to think is an assault on the minds of children.

These are strong words, and of course there will be plenty of people ready to accuse one of taking part in the puritan backlash which may be why I have gone to such lengths to explain about my championing of Mrs Kenner's work.

And in trying to explain what is so deplorable about these books one is caught in a cleft stick because even if I could reproduce the illustrations, which are the chief offenders and which could not be shown in this or any other newspaper, I would just be perpetuating something I think is wrong. By the same token I am reluctant to identify them.

The main criticism of most of these books, and the same could be said for Dr Martin Cole's film *Growing Up* and *The Little Red School Book* (which says so itself), is that there is little or no mention of love or affection. They are cold and calculatedly impersonal when sex is not, or if it is, something is wrong.

256

The other major criticism is that even in some of the books where the text is real and warm and personal, the illustrations are horrifying and quite unnecessary. The worst one of all is the coloured picture of the blue-grey baby, emerging, with a good deal of blood, from between a pair of legs. As one man who has seen childbirth in real life and found no relationship between that experience and this picture, said: 'It looks like a dreadful kind of excretion, and to the child it would surely give the idea that birth is like the worst you can ever imagine about what happens to people when they go to the lavatory.'

Then there are the close-up photographs of the sex organs; the female genitalia, the erect penis, penis with condom being rolled on to it, and so on, all of which are rather repellent and very unattractive when pictured totally detached from the rest of the body.

The books are given a cover of respectability by the fact that each seems to have been written by a reputable scientist or have a foreword by a well-known sociologist. Even so, I, and all those people I have shown them to, have felt very dubious about their value. Could not this cold, detached approach to sex and these awful illustrations be just as harmful as the tight-lipped Victorian embarrassment about the subject.

To get a really authoritative view of the subject I gave a small collection of 'children's sex books' to two people who can speak with knowledge and experience. One is Mary Miles, educationist and psychotherapist, who works in a children's clinic, and the other Masud Khan, a distinguished psychotherapist presently writing a book about perversion.

Both of these intelligent and experienced people agreed that the current clinical approach to sex education was not a happy thing. Mr Khan, while acknowledging that the text was quite straightforward and factual, said of the books: 'Somehow or other this is visual-sensory data which tries to reduce the whole human dialogue to a sort of expertise of organs.' And both said, quite separately and in different ways, that they thought the ultimate effect would be, not to encourage a satisfactory sex life, but just the reverse.

Mrs Miles believes that the depersonalizing of sex coupled with the increased tendency to teach sex through films and pictures could lead to increased feelings of inadequacy in young men as well as voyeurism. She did not object to diagrams but to photographs. Mr Khan commented that 'what all this could lead to is boredom about sex, to more people watching and fewer doing' and with a neat turn

257

of phrase he suggested it could stimulate only a 'precocious promiscuity and premature jadedness'.

It has been suggested that by detaching love from sex we could be encouraging violence. Both Mr Khan and Mrs Miles acknowledged this possibility. Mr Khan explains, 'what controls violence is a sense of tenderness towards bodies, but if the barrier of tenderness and concern is not there how do you know at what point excitement will stop.'

The experience of love has become a pretty highly rated commodity in the mass media today. Is it not all the more curious, then, that we are trying to eliminate it from our teaching about sex. And it is not only love that has been eroded, what has happened to the warmth, the fun, even the naughtiness? As Mary Miles says: 'It is really rather dreadful that children have to be *taught* these things like masturbation.'

Looking at a picture in one of our books, Mr Khan commented that 'if somebody did not know how intercourse took place this picture would not tell them. It can only be there to help to sell the book.' Which to me rings rather sinisterly of pornography for children.

Mary Miles did, in fact, say she thought one of the books qualified as pornography, 'whatever that might be'. The definition of pornography is extremely elusive. Mr Khan says he believes: 'The essence of pornography is the pursuit of sensual sensation to the exclusion of emotion', which seems to be what a good deal of sex education has degenerated into. But not only does it leave little room for emotion, Mr Khan says, it allows no room for our fantasies either. 'Pornography,' he says, 'is the stealer of dreams.'

258

SEX EDUCATION IN SCHOOLS

D. W. Winnicott

CHILDREN cannot be classed together and described all in a bunch. Their needs vary according to their home influences, the kind of children they are, and their health. However, in a brief statement on this subject of sex education it is convenient to speak generally, and not to try to adapt the main thesis to individual requirements.

Children need three things at the same time:

(1) They need persons around them in whom they can confide simply by virtue of the fact that they are trustworthy human beings with ordinary capacity for human friendship.

(2) They need instruction in biology along with other school subjects – it is assumed that biology means the truth (in so far as it is known) about life, growth, propagation, and the relation of living organisms to environment.

(3) They need continued steady emotional surroundings in which they themselves can discover each in his or her own way the up-surging of sex in the self, and the way in which this alters, enriches, complicates, and initiates human relationships.

Quite another thing is the lecture on sex, given by a person who comes to a school, delivers a talk, and then goes away. It would seem that people with an urge to teach sex to children should be discouraged. Besides, what cannot be done by the school staff cannot be tolerated by the staff either. There is something better than knowledge about sex, and that is the discovery of it by the individual.

In boarding-schools the existence of married staff with growing families in the school surround provides a natural and favourable influence, more stimulating and instructive than many lectures. In day schools the children are able to be in touch with the growing families of relations and neighbours.

The trouble about lectures is that they bring something difficult and intimate into children's lives at moments that are chosen by chance rather than by the accumulation of need in the child.

A further disadvantage of sex talks is that they seldom give a true and complete picture. For instance, the lecturer will have some bias, such as feminism, the idea that the female is passive and the male active, a flight from sex play to mature genital sex, a false theory of mother-love that leaves out the hard features and leaves only sentimentality, and so on.

Even the best sex talks impoverish the subject, which when approached from within, by experiment and experience, has the potential of infinite wealth. But it is only in an atmosphere created by the maturity of the adults that healthy adolescents can discover in themselves the body-and-soul longing for union with body and soul. In spite of these important considerations it seems that there must be room for the real experts who make a special study of sexual function and of the presentation of this sort of knowledge. Would it not be a solution to invite the experts to talk to school staffs and to develop discussions of the subject in an organized way by the teachers? The staff would then be free to act according to their own personal way in their contacts with the children, yet with a firmer foundation of knowledge of facts.

Masturbation is a sexual by-product of great importance in all children. No talk on masturbation can cover the subject, which in any case is so personal and individual that only the private talk with a friend or confidant has value. It is no use telling children in groups that to masturbate is not harmful, because perhaps for one of the group it *is* harmful, compulsive, and a great nuisance, in fact, evidence of psychiatric illness. For the others it may be harmless, and even not any trouble at all, and it is then made complex by being referred to, with the suggestion that it might be harmful. Children do, however, value being able to talk to someone about all these things, and it should have been the mother who was free to discuss absolutely anything that the child can conceive of. If mother could not do this, then others must be available, perhaps even a psychiatric interview needs to be arranged; but the difficulties are not met by sex instruction in class. Moreover, sex instruction scares away the poetry and leaves the function and sex parts high and dry and banal.

It would be more logical to point out in the art class that ideas and imaginative flights have bodily accompaniments, and that these need to be revered, and attended to, as well as ideas.

There is one obvious difficulty for those who have adolescents in their care. It is no use whatever if those who talk about allowing children to discover themselves and each other sexually are blind to the existence of the liability of some of the girls to become pregnant. This problem certainly is a real one, and has to be faced, because the illegitimate child has an unhappy position, and has a much greater task than the ordinary child if he is to make the grade and eventually become a social being; indeed unless adopted at a very early stage, the illegitimate child is unlikely to come through without scars, and perhaps ugly ones. Everyone who manages adolescents must cope with this problem according to his or her own convictions, but public opinion ought to take into account the fact that in the best type of management risks are taken and accidents do occur. In free schools, where there is practically no ban on sex, the illegitimate child is surprisingly rare, and when pregnancies do occur it is usual to find that one at least of the partners is a psychiatric case. There is the child, for instance, who, unconsciously fearing and fleeing from sex play, jumps right over to spurious sexual maturity. Many children who have had no satisfactory infantile relation to their own mothers reach to inter-personal relationships for the first time in the sexual relationship, which is therefore extremely important to them, although from the onlookers' point of view insecurely mature, because not derived gradually from the immature. If there is a big proportion of such children in a group, sexual supervision must obviously be strict, because society cannot take more than a certain number of illegitimates. On the other hand, in most groups of adolescents the majority are more or less healthy, and in that case the question has to be asked, is their management to be based on what healthy children need or on society's fear of what may happen to a few anti-social or ill members?

Adults hate to think that children ordinarily have a very strong social sense. In the same way adults hate to think that little children have early guilt feelings, and quite regularly parents implant morality where a natural morality could have developed, and would have become a stable and pro-social force.

Ordinary adolescents do not want to produce illegitimate children, and they take steps to see that this does not happen. Given opportunity, they grow in their sex play and sex relationships to the point where they realize that the having of babies is what the whole thing is leading up to. This may take them years. But ordinarily this development comes, and then these new members of human society begin to think in terms of marriage, and of the setting up of the framework in which new babies and children can be.

Sex instruction has very little to do with this natural development which each adolescent must make for himself or herself. A mature and unanxious and unmoralistic environment helps so much that it can almost be said to be necessary. Also the parents and teachers need to be able to stand the surprising antagonism adolescents may develop towards adults, especially towards those who want to help at this critical time of growth.

When the parents are not able to give what is needed, the school staff or the school itself can often do a great deal to make up for this deficiency, but by example and by personal integrity and honesty and devotion and being on the spot to answer questions, and not by organized sex instruction.

For younger children the answer is biology, the objective presentation of nature, with no bowdlerization. At first most little children like to keep and to learn about pets and to collect and understand the ways of flowers and insects. Somewhere in the period before adolescence they can enjoy progressive instruction in the ways of animals, their adaptation to environment, and their ability to adapt environment to themselves. In among all this comes the propagation of the species, and the anatomy and physiology of copulation and pregnancy. The biological instructor that children value will not neglect the dynamic aspects of the relationship between the animal parents and the way family life develops in the evolutionary series. There will not be much need for conscious application of what is taught in this way to human affairs, because it will be so obvious. It is more likely that the children will by subjective elaboration see human feelings and fantasies into the affairs of animals than that they will blindly apply the so-called animal instinctual processes to the affairs of the human race. The teacher of biology, like the teacher of any other subject, will need to be able to direct the pupils towards objectivity and the scientific approach, expecting this discipline to be very painful to some of the children.

The teaching of biology can be one of the most pleasant and even the most exciting of tasks for the teacher, chiefly because so many children value this introduction to the study of what life is about. (Others, of course, come at the meaning of life better through history, or the classics, or in their religious experiences.) But the application of biology to the personal life and feelings of each child is altogether another matter. It is by the delicate answer to the delicate question that the linking up of the general to the particular is done. After all, human beings are not animals; they are animals plus a wealth of fantasy, psyche, soul, or inner world potential or whatever you will. And some children come at the soul through the body and some come to the body through the soul. Active adaptation is the watchword in all child care and education.

To sum up, full and frank information on sex should be available for children, but not as a thing so much as a part of the children's relationship to known and trusted people. Education is no substitute for individual exploration and realization. True inhibitions are resistant to education, and in the average case for which psychotherapy is not available, these inhibitions are best dealt with through the understanding of a friend.

POLITICAL QUESTIONS

In his *The Psychology of the Criminal Act and Punishment*, Dr Gregory Zilboorg says 'there seems to be as yet no satisfactory explanation of why certain individuals start *acting out* their fantasy life either in the form of annoying neurotic social behaviour, or in the form of criminal acts.' Recent events would seem to suggest that the predominance in our culture of schizoid modes, and of sexuality, sadism and violence, is having a deeply disruptive effect on the disturbed minority. As Zilboorg says, 'What we see in the courts and prisons are only a few examples of those specimens of humanity who feel victim or gave in to the pressure of their fantasies and impulses. There are innumerable similar instances in daily life.'

It has been one of the greatest treacheries of our time in England that the 'progressive' section of political thought has so largely given its support to the 'liberation' of pseudo-sexuality, and to holding the ring for the pouring out of sick and sadistic fantasies, into an already insecure society. Politicians fear that it might be thought 'reactionary' to 'put the clock back' even though powerful educational forces are teaching the public that the humiliation of woman, violence, and hate are respectable solutions to the problems of life. The political effects could well be a deep undermining of democracy, and even of values in the Humanities. Yet in the universities there seems to be little resistance, on the part of either students or senior members, to this destructive element in our cultural life. Yet the issues, as they affect political thought, would seem clear enough, and the dangers considerable, not least to rationality.

THE MISTAKES LIBERALS MAKE

Ronald Butt

THE language of politics is becoming desperately confused and in the prevailing state of the nation we could all do worse than analyze our political terminology, and the meanings which it is designed to reveal or conceal. What we say conditions, as well as reflects, what we think: language shapes our thoughts, as well as communicating them, and terminology goes a long way towards creating the basis of our political consent.

Language is also, however, a matter of fashion and in politics, as in everything else, it is only too easy to accept with little questioning the vogue words and the mode of thought-formulation which is dominant. We allow ourselves to see politics in terms of categories whose validity and assumptions we seldom challenge – and this process can distort our vision.

The dominant categorization of the moment is between 'liberals' (the small 'l' is important) and the rest. It is almost axiomatic that a 'liberal' is to be discovered by a series of litmus-type tests on specific issues: by his responses you will know him. The 'rest' may be amiable, decent, reactionary or intolerant but they share one characteristic. They are regarded as being deficient in true rationality and therefore not to be taken seriously. The 'liberal' language increasingly provides the terms of reference for political and social opinion.

The Liberal tradition is a great one and contemporary 'liberals' share the humane concern that traditional Liberals have always had with the rights and liberties of the individual, with political freedoms and social welfare. But none of these are, I think, the distinctive hall-mark of the contemporary liberal mode. The ideology which now provides the 'liberal' bond is loose but it is also pervasive and powerful, particularly in the most articulate sections of society. It is a profound belief in laissez-faire in a highly selected range of social rather than economic affairs.

Within this strictly limited range of subjects, the liberal lives by a sort of inverted Gresham's law which assumes that the good cannot possibly be driven out by the bad. He either refuses to believe in certain dangers or plays them down by setting them in a carefully contrived perspective. In other subjects, however, he is an environmentalist who is quick to perceive the danger of corruption and debasement: of conditioning and propaganda.

For example, almost any liberal would believe (rightly, I think) that people can be conditioned by language and by example to racial intolerance and he would therefore not be disturbed by legislation designed to restrain language or actions which provoked racial discrimination. Liberals also instinctively tend to blame crimes and social offences on society rather than on the individuals who commit them. To many liberals, the educational system seems almost as important as a means of social engineering as it does for strictly educational purposes.

In a different area of social affairs, however, and one which should be of increasing concern to the nation, liberals refuse to accept the reality of danger let alone the need for restraints. It is, for instance, almost axiomatic in contemporary liberal thinking that nobody can be conditioned by anything he reads, or sees in a theatre, cinema or television. (If by chance, conditioning is possible, then it is up to the individual to avoid it.) A liberal reflex action would be to fight for the rights of the television producer to have his say unimpeded rather than in the interests of the frequently young and largely captive audience at the other end. The motive is worthy: it is the defence of freedom. The effect is frequently to diminish or conceal some of the contemporary dangers.

The liberal language sometimes even seems quicker to stress that, in proportional figures, the drug menace is small than that so many more young people than ever before are hooked or vulnerable. Student violence and intolerance are similarly put blandly into a false perspective by comparing like with unlike. Student vandalism, the Proctor of Essex was reported as saying the other day, 'is not out of proportion with what goes on in the community at large' – as though this was a proper comparison for the selected students of a university. (Taking an even more bizarre basis for comparison, he found the slogans and obscenities on the walls 'no worse than you would find in any town or railway station toilet.')

'Liberal' attitudes too often provide a shelter under which people can operate who, for one purpose or another, are quite ruthless in their attack on the structure of society. The prevailing climate of humane scepticism has undermined the resistance of ordinary, sensible people who have become far too nervous of appearing to take an individual stand against some of the things that they know are wrong and dangerous in case they should appear to be ridiculously out of date.

It is the essence of the liberal position that there is no danger in all this and therefore no real case for resistance. The liberal language of non-resistance is exemplified by a chorus of teachers who are insisting that they are not to be shocked by obscenities in the classroom or bad manners. But, of course, if you aren't shocked by x, the natural thing for the would-be shocker is to try y and if that fails to move on to z. If you are not prepared to make a stand anywhere, it is you who have changed your standards. 'What's in a four-letter word anyway?' asked a teacher the other day. The answer, of course, is in the intention of the user which is not often amiable.

In much the same way, the liberal view can discern no more than a mild joke in the visitation of Mr Jerry Rubin, the American 'Yippie' leader and the free time which this apostle of violence was able to provide for himself on television and through the Press. Nor do I notice the same degree of concern among conventional liberals about the subversion of children to a drug and promiscuity culture in some half underground literature that is lavished on other causes.

Finally, of course, there is a disposition not to take too seriously the attempts to disrupt industry by politically-motivated destructive militancy. Apostles of disorder may flit through the factories – but they are a minority. And anyway, what common cause can be made by Communists, Trots, Maoists and the rest? How foolish to see in such sporadic and dispersed activities any real danger to society or to constitutional stability! For many liberals any such anxieties are a symptom of political neurosis: of a fear of grand conspiracies that do not exist.

Of course, no grand conspiracies exist, and there is no grand and sinister design. What one is seeing is the almost accidental inter-locking of political and social influences which, in one way or another, have as their object anihilistic destruction of the existing order – aided by the scepticism of more humane people who refuse to take them seriously. Revolutions are never pre-packaged by coherent conspiracy. The essential preparation for them is when a society exhibits symptoms of disintegration and a lack of self-confidence which leaves a vacuum to be filled by some purposeful minority. The road to most revolutions has been paved by the scepticism of liberals who are never so quick to see dangers on the Left as they are to respond to dangers on the Right.

The answer to all this is not, of course, legislation. Nor is it Government action except in so far as a Government can set example by firmness as the present Government is attempting to do. The answer is in the attitudes and reactions of ordinary people and their ability to see through and penetrate the double-speak of contemporary language. They have to decide what they believe and act on it. In the words of Burke: 'All that is needed for evil to triumph is for good men to do nothing.'

TELEVISION AND SEX EDUCATION

Ronald Butt

ONE question of rights which does not appear to induce much agitation among the most articulate and professed defenders of civil liberties is the right of parents to bring up their own children as they think best. Of course, it is possible to question fundamentally whether parents should have this right, and to argue that children might be better brought up communally. This, however, is not a proposition that has (yet) any relevance to the wishes and assumptions of the overwhelming majority of people in Britain.

We take it for granted that provided parents do not fall beneath certain minimum standards of responsibility, they should be held responsible as individuals for their children's physical and moral welfare – their main qualification for the job being their personal love for their child and their understanding of his needs. It seems only logical, therefore, that if parents have this responsibility, they should also be given the freedom and discretion to discharge it.

It now appears, however, that over one aspect of their children's education which most people would regard as being an important part of their moral upbringing, and as having a direct impact on the formulation of behavioural and psychological patterns, parents actually have no rights at all. Last week, the Secretary of State for Education, Mrs Margaret Thatcher, made it clear that parents have no legal right to withdraw their children from sex education in schools, whatever the quality or content of what is taught, and this it seems to me, raises a question of political and social significance.

The legal position is that sex education is just an academic subject like any other, over which the parent does not therefore have the same legal rights as he does over religious teaching. If this made some sense when sex-education teaching was little more than a biology lesson it certainly makes no sense in the context of the detailed and visualized sex instruction which is often produced today.

Mrs Thatcher has indicated that she hopes teachers will be reasonable in the matter and consult parents. Unfortunately, not all of

268

them will. In a television discussion in which teachers took part a year ago (following a late-night transmission for parents of the then newly produced B.B.C. sex education programmes) one headmaster made it quite clear that he for one would not consult parents to give them the opportunity to withdraw children, since he believed that those left out would feel deprived. Other teachers in the programme who were prepared to 'consult' parents also appeared to argue that the number of children withdrawn would be so few that, those who were withdrawn would feel left out so that in the end, parents would conform.

All this might not matter so much if children in schools were all being taught the simple facts of sex by teachers or qualified instructors approved by the ministry. But it is now quite clear that there is an increasing tendency to teach this subject by television or broadcasting, which is fundamentally responsible to nobody except itself. This saves teachers a job which many dislike: it has the merit, or de-merit, of being much more vivid. But it seems to me to raise an important matter of political principle.

The broadcast and televised sex education programmes (and, indeed, the general education broadcasts) that are beamed nationwide at the classrooms are not made by anyone with direct responsibility to the schools or to the Ministry of Education. Though the Department of Education, like other educational interests, nominates members (two) to the Schools Broadcasting Council, under whose aegis they are produced, there is no responsibility of the council to the ministry.

The results of this system are, to say the least, curious. Even the B.B.C. sex education programmes (and I saw them all) seemed to me to have an approach to the subject which many parents would question. There was, for example, an obsessional concern with pictorial detail and many people would think that there is a world of difference between what is shown and what is explained verbally.

But perhaps the most alarming feature is the attempt at 'blanket' sex instruction of the nation's children. Although we know very little about the consequences of different approaches to the subject, the B.B.C. is prepared to beam uniform programmes to every classroom in the land where teachers will take them. Where there are errors of judgment and taste, mistakes that a live teacher could correct next time against the responses of the class, these are perpetuated by being enshrined by modern broadcasting technology and repeated again and again.

The uniform and stereotyped nature of this instruction would surely be warranted only if we were far more certain than we are of the right techniques for teaching this difficult subject. But the producers and illustrators of these programmes feel no such doubts and the insouciance with which they and their advisers are prepared to tackle this subject is little short of arrogant.

Of course, these B.B.C. programmes are very different from the film which a Dr Martin Cole has recently produced for schoolchildren, showing an actual sex act performed by his friends. Mrs Thatcher has said that if Dr Cole's programme were to be offered to schools, she would think of writing to ask local authorities to take parents' wishes into account. But a different minister might not write – and, even if the request were made, there would be no legal obligation to heed it.

In fact, Dr Cole, who has also received a certain amount of attention for his reported advocacy of wife-swapping and the establishment of brothels as charitable trusts, appeared quite recently in a schools broadcast on 'sexual feelings'. Two points can be made about this. The first is that if B.B.C. schools broadcasts wish to put on Dr Cole to talk to children nobody can stop them and if teachers choose to take the programme, there is nothing to stop them either.

Secondly, Mr Kenneth Lamb, the Director of Public Affairs of the B.B.C., has publicly described those outside the school services (for example, parents) who happen to listen in on schools programmes as 'eavesdropping'. The attitude towards parents and their exclusion from the 'closed circuit', of this highly debatable form of 'education' could hardly be more explicit. It is none of the parents' business. If this curious quirk of our educational system is not a political matter, I do not know what is.

POLITICS AND MORALS

Ronald Butt

IT is a function of politicians to protect the right of the majority of citizens to live in the kind of society they want as well as the right of minorities to lead their private lives according to their tastes and beliefs, preserving a reasonable balance between the two. We have now, it seems to me, reached a point at which anything like a reasonable balance between the two rights is jeopardized by the insidious erosion of the standards to which the majority wants to adhere as a consequence of the public behaviour of some minorities. It is therefore time that the politicians began to take some notice of the problem as politicians.

To do so, however, they need more active support than they are yet getting from responsible private and quasi-public bodies, notably from the press and television, and from citizens of standing. At present, the majority of ordinary people, who are never publicly articulate, sit hypnotized, repelled and passive before the morally deathly gyrations of their new persuaders, waiting for a lead from those who could lead. But those who could effectively say something are also, for the most part, fearful to speak for fear of being devoured by ridicule.

The opening in London of Mr Kenneth Tynan's 'entertainment' *Oh! Calcutta!* should bring home to people what is happening. Its genre is basically the sort of exhibition of sexual voyeurism that used to be available to the frustrated and mentally warped in the side-turnings of a certain kind of sea-port. If Mr Tynan and his friends wished to satisfy themselves by this sort of thing in strict private, then, I suppose, the rest of us would have no cause for any reaction except pity. But, in fact, they seek to thrust it down the heaving throats of the majority; if they could, they would put it on in a major public theatre. As it is, they no doubt feel they have secured a certain triumph by staging it in a theatre which is in receipt of public money from the Arts Council.

Of course, nobody has to go and see it and comparatively few would have seen it even if it had secured a place in a larger theatre. Even so, this pathetic business could have a significant impact on public standards. In the first place, at least some people will see it who would not have done had Mr Tynan staged it privately for the gratification of himself and his circle. At least some other people will now see it as a response to what they may take as a cultural 'dare'.

Some of these may suffer some moral damage in their attitude to human relationships. It is usually assumed that the sights of younger people can be raised by reading and seeing the higher work of man's intellect, and I fail to understand the glib assumption that exposure to the lowest has no ill effect.

But more important is the ripple effect on people who do not actually see this debasing sort of entertainment whose conception of what is tolerable is conditioned by the liberal notice and the detailed description that the public communicators feel obliged to give to it. Even the reporters' descriptions of contents of *Oh! Calcutta!* must have some impact on the minds of older children and adolescents who read them.

Newspapers must report news but they do not have to play the game of the new persuaders in their manner of doing so. Detailed notoriety reports can provide a useful launching pad for degraded 'entertainment' which would otherwise not get off the ground. Newspapers should be careful about what they describe and how they describe it. With trusted critics, there is no reason at all why offerings should not be labelled simply 'pornographic: not reviewed'. What does harm is paying them the compliment of serious analysis and description which stamps them as in some way publicly acceptable.

Those responsible for the means of public communications have a duty to the majority who wish to lead decent lives; who try, however feebly, to prefer the higher to the lower and who are at the moment being forced at every turn to cower before culturally disguised assumptions which they reject.

For politicians, the task is more delicate. Their job is to be the protectors of freedom, not censors. But at the moment it is the freedom not of minorities but of the majority that is under attack — the freedom of ordinary citizens not to have their own and their children's environment forcibly conditioned by people with an interest in the destruction of a culture. The politicians should think about it.

BEYOND THE GARBAGE PALE, OR DEMOCRACY CENSORSHIP AND THE ARTS

Walter Berns

I

THE case against censorship is very old and very familiar. Almost anyone can formulate it without difficulty. One has merely to set venerable Milton's *Areopagitica* in modern prose, using modern spelling, punctuation, and examples. This is essentially what the civil libertarians did in their successful struggle, during the past century, with the censors. The unenlightened holder of the bishop's imprimatur, Milton's 'unleasur'd licencer' who has never known 'the labour of book-writing', became the ignorant policeman or the bigoted school board member who is offended by 'Mrs Warren's Profession', or the benighted librarian who refuses to shelf *The Scarlet Letter*, or the insensitive customs official who seizes *Ulysses* in the name of an outrageous law, or the Comstockian vigilante who glues together the pages of every copy of *A Farewell to Arms* she can find in the bookstore. The industrious learned Milton, insulted by being asked to 'appear in Print like a punie with his guardian and his censors hand on the back of his title to be his bayle and surety', was replaced by Shaw, Hawthorne, Joyce, or Hemingway, and those who followed in their wake, all victims of the mean-spirited and narrow-minded officials who were appointed, or in some cases took it upon themselves, to judge what others should read, or at least not read. The presumed advantage of truth when it grapples with falsehood became the inevitable victory of 'enduring ideas' in the free competition of the market. With these updated versions of old and familiar arguments, the civil libertarians have prevailed.

They prevailed partly because of the absurdity of some of their opposition, and also because of a difficulty inherent in the task their opponents set for themselves. The censors would proscribe the obscene, and even assuming, as our law did, that obscene speech is no part of the speech protected by the First Amendment to the Constitution, it is not easy to formulate a rule of law that distinguishes the non-obscene from the obscene. Is it the presence of four-letter words?

But many a literary masterpiece contains four-letter words. Detailed descriptions of sexual acts? James Joyce provides these. Words tending to corrupt those into whose hands they are likely to fall? But who is to say what corrupts or, for that matter, whether anything corrupts or, again, what is meant by corruption? Is it an appeal to a 'prurient interest' or is it a work that is 'patently offensive'? If that is what is meant by the obscene, many a 'socially important work', many a book, play, or film with 'redeeming social value', would be lost to us. The college professors said so, and if college professors do not know the socially important, who does? Be that as it may, they succeeded in convincing the Supreme Court, and the result was the complete rout of the 'forces of reaction'. To the college professors, therefore, as well as to the 'courageous' publishers and the 'public-spirited' attorneys who had selflessly fought the cases through the courts, a debt of gratitude is owed by the lovers of Shaw, Hawthorne, Joyce and Hemingway – and others too numerous to detail here. In the same spirit one might say that never has there been such a flourishing of the arts in this country.

Astonishingly, the editors of the *New York Times* disagree, and in an editorial printed on 1 April 1969, under the heading 'Beyond the (Garbage) Pale', they expressed their disagreement in language that we have been accustomed to read only in the journals of the 'reactionary right'.

The explicit portrayal on the stage of sexual intercourse is the final step in the erosion of taste and subtlety in the theater. It reduces actors to mere exhibitionists, turns audiences into voyeurs and debases sexual relationships almost to the level of prostitution.

It is difficult to see any great principle of civil liberties involved when persons indulging themselves on-stage in this kind of peep-show activity are arrested for 'public lewdness and obscenity' – as were the actors and staff of a recently opened New York production that, in displaying sodomy and other sexual aberrations, reached the *reductio ad obscenum* of the theatrical art. While there may be no difference in principle between pornography on the stage, on the screen and on the printed page, there is a difference in immediacy and in direct visual impact when it is carried out by live actors before a (presumably) live audience.

The fact that the legally enforceable standards of public decency have been interpreted away by the courts almost to the point of no return does not absolve artists, producers or publishers from all responsibility or restraint in pandering to the lowest possible public taste in quest of the largest possible monetary reward. Nor does the fact that a play, film, article or book attacks the so-called 'establishment', revels in gutter language or drools over every known or unknown form of erotica justify the suspension of sophisticated critical judgment.

Yet this does seem to be just what has been suspended in the case of many recent works, viz. one current best-seller hailed as a 'master-piece', which, wallowing in a self-indulgent public psychoanalysis, drowns its literary merits in revolting excesses of masturbation and copulation.

The utter degradation of taste in pursuit of the dollar is perhaps best observed in films, both domestic and foreign such as one of the more notorious Swedish imports, refreshingly described by one reviewer unafraid of being called a 'square' as 'pseudo-pornography at its ugliest and least titillating and pseudo-sociology at its lowest point of technical ineptitude'.

Far from providing a measure of cultural emancipation, such descents into degeneracy represent caricatures of art, deserving no exemption from the laws of common decency merely because they masquerade as drama or literature. It is preposterous to banish topless waitresses when there is no bottom to voyeurism on the stage or in the movie houses.

In the end, however, there may be an even more effective answer. The insensate pursuit of the urge to shock, carried from one excess to a more abysmal one, is bound to achieve its own antidote in total boredom. When there is no lower depth to descend to, ennui will erase the problem.

This must be reckoned an astonishing statement because in the liberal world for which the *Times* speaks it has not been customary – to put it mildly – to cast any doubt on the wisdom of an anti-censorship policy. Now suddenly, the *Times*, contrary to what its readers might expect of it and contrary even to the general tenor of its own drama and literary pages, registers its misgivings. This is not what they wanted to happen. In their struggle against the censor they did not mean to defend 'the explicit portrayal of sexual intercourse' on the stage or in films; they did not have in mind 'sodomy and other sexual aberrations'. They intended to protect the freedom of the arts from bigoted censors; they were defending *Ulysses* when the customs laws would have excluded it from the country, and sensitive foreign films, such as *Les Amants*, from Ohio's laws; but they certainly did not intend to establish a place for 'revolting excesses of masturbation and copulation'.

A Truly Invisible Hand

Nine months later one of the country's principal foes of censorship checked in with the same disclaimer. *Ulysses*, yes, said Morris Ernst, but 'sodomy on the stage or masturbation in the public area', no! Although it never appeared to figure with any prominence, or figure at all for that matter, in the arguments that had made him one of the foremost civil liberties lawyers in the country, Ernst now insists that he had always made it clear that he 'would hate to live in a world with utter freedom'. He deeply resents 'the idea that the lowest common denominator, the most tawdry magazine, pandering for profit ... should be able to compete in the marketplace with no restraints.' The free marketplace has become the dirty marketplace, and Ernst wants no part in it and no responsibility for it.[1]

But surely this was inevitable? Pornography and the taste for it are not new phenomena. What is new is the fact that it can display itself openly in the marketplace, so to speak, whereas in the past it had been confined by the laws to the back alleys, or to the underworld, where its sales were limited not by a weakness of the potential demand but rather by the comparative inaccessibility of the market. Prodded by the civil libertarians, the Supreme Court made pornography a growth industry by giving it a license to operate in the accessible and legitimate market, thereby bringing buyer and seller together. True, the Court did not directly license *Oh! Calcutta!* or *Che!*; but so long as the Court is consistent, these works are certain to benefit from the licences given *Les Amants* and *Fanny Hill* and the others. Consider the state of the law developed on their behalf. So long as a work is not '*utterly* without redeeming social value' (and the emphasis is the Supreme Court's), it cannot be proscribed even if it is 'patently offensive' and is found by a jury to appeal to a 'prurient interest'. All that is needed to save any work from the censor, or the police, is some college professor willing to testify as to its 'social value' or 'social importance', and there is no shortage of such professors with such testimony. Indeed, the work has not been written, staged, or filmed that cannot find its champions among the professors.[2]

It was not supposed to turn out this way. Some invisible and benign hand was supposed to operate in this market too, and guarantee the triumph of the true and the beautiful. People, said Justice

William O. Douglas in one of the obscenity cases only a couple of years ago, 'are mature enough to pick and choose, to recognize trash when they see it, to be attracted to the literature that satisfies their deepest need, and ... to move from plateau to plateau and finally reach the world of enduring ideas.' This is the liberal faith. The *Times* shared it, and it is worth noting that even in its distress it refuses to foresake it altogether. The editors express their disgust with what has happened, but they must know that this will be unavailing with those who are themselves disgusting. Certainly the 'artists, producers [and] publishers ... pandering to the lowest public taste in quest of the largest possible monetary reward' are not going to forego this reward simply because some fainthearted libertarians, even on the *Times*, look upon their work as disgusting. 'I paid to see filth and I want filth,' said the woman from Connecticut by way of protesting a showing of an expurgated 'I am Curious (Yellow)'. She paid to see filth and, no matter what the *Times* says, there will always be 'artists, producers [and] publishers' to see to it that she gets her money's worth. That is why there used to be laws against filth – because the legislators who wrote these laws knew full well the fruitlessness of relying on admonition or expressions of disgust. The *Times* does not call for the refurbishment of these laws, but appeals instead to the 'laws of common decency', as if these so-called laws had not passed into desuetude with the demise of the legislation that constituted their foundation. So it is that, in the end, it returns to the old liberal faith in an invisible hand that will provide our salvation : 'When there is no lower depth to descend to, ennui will erase the problem.'

Such a conclusion is pitifully inadequate, but it is an accurate reflection of the thinking that has been done on this issue during our time. Neither the *Times* nor Morris Ernst has a grasp of the principle with which – or even a suitable vocabulary in which – to challenge the powerful orthodoxy that has long governed the public discussion of censorship and the arts. To be a liberal is to be against censorship or it is to be nothing – or so it has been thought – and after a career spent arguing against censorship, it is not easy to formulate an argument in its favor. But the *Times* and Mr Ernst deserve our gratitude nevertheless, for, although they leave it undefined, their disclaimers do have the merit of acknowledging that there is something wrong with things as they are, that there *is* a problem. The respectability attached to their names makes it easier to reexamine this problem.

II

Just as it is no simple task to formulate a rule of law that distinguishes the non-obscene from the obscene, or is still more difficult to distinguish the obscene from the work of genuine literary merit. In fact, it is impossible – and our failure to understand this may be said to be a condition, if not a cause, of our present situation. Our laws proscribe obscenity as such and by name, and we are unwilling to admit that great literary and dramatic works can be, and frequently are, obscene. In combination these two facts explain how it came about that we now have, with the sanction of the law, what is probably the most vulgar theater and literature in history. The paradox is readily explained. The various statutes making up the law have made obscenity a criminal thing, and our judges assume that if a work of art is really a work of art, and not vulgar rubbish, it cannot be obscene. Thus, Judge Woolsey, in his celebrated opinion in the *Ulysses* case, recounts how he had asked two literary friends whether the book was obscene within the legal definition, which he had explained to them, and how they had both agreed with him that it was not. But of course *Ulysses* is obscene. Not so obscene as an undoubted masterpiece, Aristophane's *Assembly of Women*, for example, which would not be a masterpiece – which would not be anything – were its obscenity removed, but obscene nevertheless.

The trouble stems from the fact that the Tariff Act of 1930 would exclude 'obscene' books from the country, and Judge Woolsey, being a sensible man, did not want this to happen to *Ulysses*. So he fashioned a rule to protect it. But the same rule of law protects *The Tropic of Cancer*, because according to the rule's necessarily clumsy categories, the latter is no more obscene than the former, however it compares on another scale and whatever the aesthetic distances separating its author, Henry Miller, and James Joyce as writers. Eventually, and for the same reason, the protection of the law was extended to *Trim*, *MANual*, and *Grecian Guild Pictorial*, the homosexual magazines involved in a case before the Supreme Court in 1962, and then to *Fanny Hill*. At this point, if one ignores the Ginzburg aberration and the recent children's cases,[3] the censors seem to have given up, and we have – well, anything that anyone will pay to see or read. Thus, having begun by exempting the work of art from the censorship laws, we have effectively arrived at the civil libertarian's destination: the case where the Supreme Court throws in its hand and concludes that there is no such thing as obscenity.

Underlying this unfortunate development is the familiar liberal idea of progress. Rather than attempt to inhibit artists and scientists, the good polity will grant them complete freedom of expression and of inquiry, and will benefit collectively by so doing. What is good for the arts and sciences is good for the polity: this proposition has gone largely unquestioned among us for 200 years now. The case for censorship rests on its denial, and can be made only by separately examining its parts. What is good for the arts and sciences? What is good for the polity? The case for censorship arises initially out of a consideration of the second question.

The case for censorship is at least as old as the case against it, and, contrary to what is usually thought today, has been made under decent and even democratic auspices by intelligent men. To the extent to which it is known today, however, it is thought to be pernicious or, at best, irrelevant to the enlightened conditions of the 20th century. It begins from the premise that the laws cannot remain indifferent to the manner in which men amuse themselves, or to the kinds of amusement offered them. 'The object of art,' as Lessing put the case, 'is pleasure, and pleasure is not indispensable. What kind and what degree of pleasure shall be permitted may justly depend on the lawgiver.'[4] Such a view, especially in this uncompromising form, appears excessively Spartan and illiberal to us; yet Lessing was one of the greatest lovers of art who ever lived and wrote.

We turn to the arts – to literature, films, and the theatre, as well as to the graphic arts which were the special concern of Lessing – for the pleasure to be derived from them, and pleasure has the capacity to form our tastes and thereby to affect our lives. It helps determine the kind of men we become, and helps shape the lives of those with whom and among whom we live. So one can properly ask: Is it politically uninteresting whether men derive pleasure from performing their duties as citizens, fathers, and husbands or, on the other hand, from watching their laws and customs and institutions being ridiculed on the stage? Whether the passions are excited by, and the affections drawn to, what is noble or what is base? Whether the relations between men and women are depicted in terms of an eroticism wholly divorced from love and calculated to destroy the capacity for love and the institutions, such as the family, that depend on love? Whether a dramatist uses pleasure to attach men to what is beautiful or to what is ugly? We may not be accustomed to thinking of these things in this manner, but it is not strange that so much of the obscenity from which so many of us derive our pleasure today has an avowed political purpose.[5] It would seem that the pornographers know intuitively what liberals have forgotten, namely, that there is indeed a 'causal relationship . . . between word or pictures and human behavior'. At least they are not waiting for behavioral science to discover this fact.

The purpose is sometimes directly political and sometimes political in the sense that it will have political consequences intended or not. The latter purpose is to make us shameless, and it seems to be succeeding with astonishing speed. Activities that were once confined to the private scene – to the 'ob-scene', to make an etymological assumption – are now presented for our delectation and emulation in center stage. Nothing that is appropriate to one place is inappropriate to any other place. No act, we are to infer, no human possibility, no possible physical combination or connection, is shameful. Even our lawmakers now so declare. 'However plebian my tastes may be,' Justice Douglas asked somewhat disingenuously in the *Ginzburg* case, 'who am I to say that others' tastes must be so limited and that others' tastes have no "social importance"?' Nothing prevents a dog from enjoying sexual intercourse in the marketplace, and it is unnatural to deprive men of the same pleasure, either actively or as voyeurs in the theatre. Shame itself is unnatural, a convention devised by hypocrites to inhibit the pleasures of the body. We must get rid of our 'hangups'.

The Importance of Shame
But what if, contrary to what is now so generally assumed, shame is natural to man, in the sense of being an original feature of human existence? What if it is shamelessness that is unnatural, in the sense of having to be acquired? What if the beauty that men are capable of knowing and achieving in their living with each other derives from the fact that man is naturally a 'blushing creature', the only creature capable of blushing? Consider the case of voyeurism, a case that, under the circumstances, comes quickly to mind. Some of us – I have even known students to confess to it – experience discomfort watching others on the stage or screen performing sexual acts, or even the acts preparatory to sexual acts, such as disrobing of a woman by a man. This discomfort is caused by shame or is akin to shame. True, it could derive from the fear of being discovered enjoying what society still sees as a forbidden game. The voyeur who experiences shame in this sense is judging himself by the conventions of his society and, according to the usual modern account, the greater the distance separating him from his society in space or time, the less he will experience this kind of shame. This shame, which may be denoted concealing shame, is a function of the fear of discovery by one's own group. The group may have its reasons

for forbidding a particular act, and thereby leads those who engage in it to conceal – to be ashamed of it – but these reasons have nothing to do with the nature of man. Voyeurism, according to this account, is a perversion only because society says it is, and a man guided only by nature would not be ashamed of it.

According to another view, however, not to be ashamed – to be a shameless voyeur – is more likely to require explanation, for voyeurism is by nature a perversion.

Anyone who draws his sexual gratification from looking at another lives continuously at a distance. If it is normal to approach and unite with the partner, then it is precisely characteristic of the voyeur that he remains alone, without a partner, an outsider who acts in a stealthy and furtive manner. To keep his distance when it is essential to draw near is one of the paradoxes of his perversion. The looking of the voyeur is of course also a looking at and, as such, is as different from the looks exchanged by lovers as medical palpation from a gentle caress of the hand.[6]

From this point of view, voyeurism is perversion, not merely because it is contrary to convention, but because it is contrary to nature. Convention here follows nature. Whereas sexual attraction brings man and woman together seeking a unity that culminates in the living being they together create, the voyeur maintains a distance; and because he maintains a distance he looks at, he does not communicate; and because he looks at he objectifies, he makes an object of that with which it is natural to join; objectifying, he is incapable of uniting and is therefore incapable of love. The need to conceal voyeurism – the concealing shame – is corollary of the protective shame, the shame that impels lovers to search for privacy and for an experience protected from the profane and the eyes of the stranger. The stranger is 'at odds with the shared unity of the [erotic couple], and his mere presence tends to introduce some objectification into every immediate relationship.'[7] Shame, both concealing and protective, protects lovers and therefore love. And a polity without love – without the tenderness and the poetry and the beauty and, in a word, the uniquely human things that depend on it and derive from it – a polity without love would be an unnatural monstrosity.[8]

The Forgotten Argument

To speak in a manner that is more obviously political, there is a connection between self-restraint and shame, and therefore a connection between shame and self-government or democracy. There is, therefore, a political danger in promoting shamelessness and the fullest self-expression or indulgence. To live together requires rules and a governing of the passions, and those who are without shame will be unruly and unrulable; having lost the ability to restrain themselves by observing the rules they collectively give themselves, they will have to be ruled by others. Tyranny is the natural and inevitable mode of government for the shameless and self-indulgent who have carried liberty beyond any restraint, natural and conventional.

Such, indeed, was the argument made by political philosophers prior to the 20th century, when it was generally understood that democracy, more than any other form of government, required self-restraint, which it would inculcate through moral education and impose on itself through laws, including laws governing the manner of public amusements. It was the tyrant who could usually allow the people to indulge themselves. Indulgence of the sort we are now witnessing did not threaten his rule, because his rule did not depend on a citizenry of good character. Anyone can be ruled by a tyrant, and the more debased his subjects the safer his rule. A case can be made for complete freedom of the arts among such people, whose pleasures are derived from activities divorced from their labors and any duties associated with citizenshp. Among them a theatre, for example, can serve to divert the search for pleasure from what the tyrant regards as dangerous or pernicious pursuits.[9]

Such an argument was not unknown among thoughtful men at the time modern democracies were being constituted. It is to be found in Jean-Jacques Rousseau's Letter to M. d'Alembert on the Theatre. Its principles were known by Washington and Jefferson, to say nothing of the antifederalists, and later on by Lincoln, all of whom insisted that democracy would not work without citizens of good character. And, until recently, no justice of the Supreme Court and no man in public life doubted the necessity for the law to make at least a modest effort to promote that good character, if only by protecting the effort of other institutions, such as the church and the family, to nourish and maintain it. The case for censorship, at first glance, was made wholly with a view to the political good, and it had as its premise that what was good for the arts and sciences was not necessarily good for the polity.

There was no illusion among these thinkers that censorship laws would be easy to administer, and there was a reputation of the danger they represented. One obvious danger was that the lawmakers will demand too much, that the Anthony Comstocks who are always with us will become the agents of the law and demand not merely decency but sanctity. Macaulay stated the problem in his essay on Restoration Comedy (mild fare compared to that regularly exhibited in our day):

It must, indeed, be acknowledged, in justice to the writers of whom we have spoken thus severely, that they were to a great extent the creatures of their age. And if it be asked why that age encouraged immorality which no other age would have tolerated, we have no hesitation in answering that this great depravation of the national taste was the effect of the prevalence of Puritanism under the Commonwealth.

To punish public outrages on morals and religion is unquestionably within the competence of rulers. But when a government, not content with requiring decency, requires sanctity, it oversteps the bounds which mark its proper functions. And it may be laid down as a universal rule that a government which attempts more than it ought will perform less. . . . And so a government which, not content with repressing scandalous excesses, demands from its subjects fervent and austere piety, will soon discover that, while attempting to render an impossible service to the cause of virtue, it has in truth only promoted vice.

The truth of this was amply demonstrated in the United States in the Prohibition era, when the attempt was made to enforce abstemiousness and not, labels to the contrary, temperance. In a word, the principle. should be not to attempt to eradicate vice – the means by which that might conceivably be accomplished are incompatible with free government – but to make vice difficult, knowing that while it will continue to flourish covertly, it will not be openly exhibited. And that was thought to be important.

It ought to be clear that this old and largely forgotten case for censorship was made by men who were not insensitive to the beauty of the arts and the noble role they can play in the lives of men. Rousseau admitted that he never willingly missed a performance of any of Molière's plays, and did so in the very context of arguing that all theatrical productions should be banned in the decent and self-governing polity. Like Plato he would banish the poets, yet he was himself a poet – a musician, opera composer, and novelist – and demonstrated his love for and knowledge of poetry – or as we would say, the arts – in his works and in his life. But he was above all a thinker of the highest rank, and as such he knew that the basic premise of the later liberalism is false. A century later John Stuart

Mill could no longer conceive of a conflict between the intrinsic and therefore legitimate demands of the sciences and the intrinsic and therefore legitimate demands of the polity. Rousseau had argued that the 'restoration' of the arts and sciences did not tend to purify morals, but that, on the contrary, their restoration and popularization would be destructive of the possibility of a good civil society. His contemporaries were shocked and angered by this teaching and excluded Rousseau from their society; and taught by them and more directly by Mill and his followers – Justice Douglas, for example – we might tend to dismiss it as the teaching of a madman or fool. Are we, however, still prepared to stand with Mill and his predecessors against Rousseau, to argue that what is good for science is necessarily good for civil society? Or have certain terrible events and conditions prepared us to reconsider that issue? If so, and especially in the light of certain literary and theatrical events, we might be prepared to reconsider the issue of whether what is good for the arts is necessarily good for civil society.

III

In practice, censors have acted out of an unsophisticated concern for public morality, with no love for the arts, and with no appreciation of what would be sacrificed if their policy were to be adopted. Their opponents have resisted them out of a sophisticated concern for the freedom of expression, often with a true love for the arts, but with no concern for the effect of this freedom on public morality. It would appear that concern for public morality requires censorship and that concern for the arts requires the abolition of censorship.

The law developed by our courts is an attempt to avoid this dilemma by denying that it exists. But with what results? Rousseau predicted there would be, not only a corruption of public morality, but a degradation of the arts. His case for censorship appears only at first glance to be made wholly with a view to protecting the simple and decent political order from corruption at the hands of sophisticated literature and the theatre; it was in fact also a case made with a view to preventing the corruption of the arts themselves. Their popularization would be their degradation. To deny the tension between politics and the arts is to assume that the relation between them requires no governing, that what is produced by writers and dramatists may be ignored by the law in the same manner that the production of economic goods and services was once said to be of no legitimate concern of the law. The free market will be permitted

284

to operate, with the result that what appears in print and on the stage will be determined by the tastes operating in that market, which in a democracy will be a mass market. The law will no longer attempt to influence this market; having denied the distinction between the non-obscene and the obscene, it will in fact come to deny the distinction between art and trash. This is what has happened. Justice Douglas, who told us that the 'ideal of the Free Society written into our Constitution . . . is that people are mature enough . . . to recognize trash when they see it,' also denies that anyone, mature or immature, can define the difference between art and trash. 'Some like Chopin, others like "rock and roll". Some are "normal", some are masochistic, some deviant in other respects. . . . But why is freedom of the press and expression denied them? When the Court today speaks of "social value" does it mean a "value" to the majority? . . . If a publication caters to the idiosyncracies of a minority, why does it not have "social importance"?'[10] To him, whether a publication has 'social value' is answered by whether anyone wants to read it, which is to say that any publication may have 'social value'. It is all a question of idiosyncratic taste: some like Chopin, some like rock and roll; some are normal – or as he writes it, 'normal' – and some masochistic or deviant – or, as he ought to have written it, 'deviant'. These statements of course make nonsense of his business of ascending 'from plateau to plateau and finally reach[ing] the world of enduring ideas'; because if everything has value, and if there is no standard by which to judge among them, then there is no upward or downward, no 'plateau' higher than another 'plateau', no art or trash, and, of course, no problem. Art is now defined as the 'socially important', and this, in turn, is defined by Douglas as anything anyone has a taste for.

Distinguishing Art from Trash
It is true that Douglas is uniquely vulgar for a Supreme Court justice, but his colleagues have not been far behind him on the substantive issue. In principle they acknowledge the category of socially 'important' publications and productions, but they do not depend on an educated critical judgment to define it. They simply accept the judgment of any literary hack willing to testify, which amounts to transferring the mass market to the courtroom. It was solemnly said in testimony that *Fanny Hill* is a work of social importance, which was then elaborated as 'literary merit' and 'historical value', just the sort of thing to be taught in the classroom (and, as Douglas argued, in sermons from the pulpit). Another 'expert witness' described it as

a work of art that 'asks for and receives a literary response'. Its style was to be 'literary' and its central character, in addition to being a whore, an 'intellectual', which is probably understood to be the highest praise within the power of these experts to bestow. An intellectual, the court was then told, is one who is 'extremely curious about life and who seeks . . . to record with accuracy the details of the external world' – in Fanny's case, such 'external details' as her 'physical sensations'.

Censorship, undertaken in the name of the public necessity to maintain the distinction between the non-obscene and the obscene, has the secondary effect of lending some support to the distinction between art and trash. At a minimum it requires a judgment of what is proper and what is improper, which is to say a judgment of what is worthy of being enjoyed and what is unworthy, and this has the effect of at least supporting the idea that there is a distinction to be made and that the distinction is important. Our law as announced by the judges of our highest court now denies this, explicitly in the case of Douglas and implicitly in the case of his colleagues making up the rest of the Court's majority. The law has resigned in favor of the free mass market, and it has done so not because the free market is seen as a mechanism best calculated to bring about a particular result (for example, the material wealth desired by the *laissez-faire* economists) but because it attaches no significance to the decisions the market will make. The popularization of the arts will not lead to their degradation because there is no such thing as degradation.

The *New York Times* does not agree with this when it calls for 'sophisticated critical judgment' to save us from the pile of muck that now constitutionally passes for art. But the 'sophisticated critical judgment' of its own drama and book pages praised the very works condemned in the editorial; besides, much of the market is impervious to 'sophisticated critical judgment'. This is confirmed in the *Times* itself in a piece printed a few months later on the first page of the Sunday drama section: 'Nobody yet knows how to control the effect of nudity for a production's purposes, but producers encourage it anyhow. Why? The explanation, I should think, is obvious: sex, as always, is good box office.'[11] Exactly. It was the law, not the critics, that kept the strip tease and the 'skin flick' confined to the illegitimate theatre, and it is foolish to think, or to have thought, that the critics alone will be able to keep them there, or, in fact, from flourishing in the legitimate theatre. That game is caught, as Lincoln would have put it. What remains at large, unanswered, is whether 'sophisticated critical judgment' can preserve artistic tastes in another part of the same theatre, or whether there will be any 'sophisticated critical judgment'. To ask this is to wonder whether the public taste – or at least, a part of the public's taste – can be educated, and educated with no assistance from the law. This is an old question; to ask it is to return to Rousseau's quarrel with Voltaire and the Enlightenment, and to Tocqueville and John Stuart Mill – in short, to the beginnings of modern democracy where, in political philosophy, the question received thematic treatment.

A Role for the University

The principle of modern democracy is the natural equality of all men, and the problem was to find some way of preventing this principle from becoming all-pervasive, and especially from invading the arts and sciences themselves. Stated otherwise, the problem was to find a substitute for the aristocratic class which had formerly sustained the arts and sciences – some basis on which, or some citadel from which, the arts and sciences could resist public opinion. The constitutional principle of freedom of speech and press would, perhaps, protect them from hostile political passions, but this institutional device would not protect them from the much more subtle danger, corruption by public opinion, of coming to share the public's taste and of doing the public's work according to the public's standards. One solution, it was hoped by some, would be the modern university, which, as Allan Bloom has recently written, was to be 'a center for reflection and education independent of the regime and the pervasive influence of its principles, free of the overwhelming effect of public opinion in its crude and subtle forms, devoted to the dispassionate quest for the important and comprehensive truths.'[12] Tenure and academic freedom would protect the professors of the arts and sciences, and thereby protect the arts and sciences themselves, and the students would be educated in the principles of the arts and sciences and their tastes formed accordingly. The education of the public's taste in the arts, which will prevent the popularization of the arts from becoming the cause of their degradation, must take place in the universities if it is to take place at all.

But the so-called expert witnesses who testified in the obscenity cases came from these very universities. *Fanny Hill*'s champions were university professors, and not, by any means, minor institutions. To rely on the professors to provide the 'sophisticated critical judgment' or to educate the tastes of the mass market, or of any part of it, is to ignore what is going on in the universities. Several years

287

ago Cornell paid $800 to a man to conduct (lead? orchestrate? create?) a 'happening' on campus as part of a Festival of Contemporary Art. This happening consisted of the following: a group of students was led to the city dump where they selected the charred remains of an old automobile, spread it with several hundred pounds of strawberry jam, removing their shirts and blouses, and then danced around it, stopping occasionally to lick the jam. By 1970 standards this is not especially offensive; it is silly, as so many 'college boy' antics have been silly. What distinguishes it from goldfish swallowing and panty raids is that it was conducted under official university auspices and with the support and participation of professors.

The call for a 'sophisticated critical judgment' is merely a variety of the general call for education, which libertarians have customarily offered as an alternative to the policy of forbidding or punishing speech. It is an attractive alternative, attractive for its consistency with liberal principles as well as for its avoidance of the difficulties accompanying a policy of censorship; unfortunately, in the present intellectual climate, education in this area is almost impossible. Consider the case of the parent who wants to convince his children of the improprietry of the use of the four-letter verb meaning to copulate. At the present time the task confronting him is only slightly less formidable than that faced by the parent who would teach his children that the world is flat. Just as the latter will have to overcome a body of scientific evidence to the contrary, the former will have to overcome the power of common usage and the idea of propriety it implies. Until recently propriety required the use of the verb 'to make love',[13] and this delicacy was not without purpose. It was meant to remind us – to *teach* us, or at least to allow us to be taught – that whereas human copulation can be physically indistinguishable from animal copulation generally, it ought to be marked by the presence of a passion of which other animals are incapable. Now, to a quickly increasing extent, the four-letter verb – more 'honest' in the opinion of its devotees – is being used openly and therefore without impropriety. The parent will fail in his effort to educate because he will be on his own, trying to teach a lesson his society no longer wants taught – by the law, by the language, or by the schools. Especially by the schools. When in 1964 the University of California at Berkeley could not find a reason to censure the students for whom 'free speech' meant the brandishing of the four-letter verb on placards, it not only made legitimate what had been illegitimate, but announced that from that time forward it would

288

not attempt to teach its students anything contrary to their passions – sexual, political, or, with reference to drug use, physiological. What became true then at Berkeley is now true generally. The professors have nothing to teach their students. The younger ones have joined the students and have come to share their tastes and their political passions; the older ones are silent, and together they are in the process of abdicating to the students their authority to govern the universities, to enforce parietals, to prescribe the curriculum, and even their right to teach them. Critical judgment is being replaced by 'doing your own thing', which is what Justice Douglas was talking about; and this being so, it is doubtful, to say the least, whether the universities will be able to educate the tastes of anyone. And if this is not done in the universities, where can it be done?[14] Where in the midst of all the vulgarity and this incessant clamor for doing one's own thing can be found a refuge for the arts? Yet, there can be no 'sophisticated critical judgment' without it.

IV

One who undertakes to defend censorship in the name of the arts is obliged to acknowledge that he has not exhausted his subject when he has completed that defense. What is missing is a defense of obscenity. What is missing is a defense of the obscenity employed by the greatest of our poets – Aristophanes and Chaucer, Shakespeare and Swift – because it is impossible to believe, it is unreasonable to believe, that what they did is indefensible; and what they did, among other things, was to write a good deal of obscenity. Unfortunately, it would require a talent I do not possess to give a sufficient account of it.

They employed it mainly in comedy, but their purpose was not simply to make us laugh. Comedy, according to Aristotle,[15] makes us laugh at what is ludicrous in ugliness, and its purpose is to teach, just as tragedy teaches by making us cry before what is destructive in nobility. The latter imitates what is higher, the former what is lower, but they are equally serious; Aristotle discussed both, and Shakespeare, for example, was a comic as well as a tragic poet.

Those aspects of his soul that make man truly human and distinguish him from all other beings – higher or lower in the natural order of things – require political life. And no great poet ever denied this. Man's very virtues, as well as their counterparts, his vices, require him to be governed and to govern; they initiate demands that can be met only in political life – but the poet knows with Rousseau that the demands of human virtue cannot be fully met in political life because they transcend political life. The poet knows the beauty of that order beyond the polity; he reminds us that there is an order outside the conventional and that we are part of that natural order, as well as of the conventional. Shakespeare knows with Rousseau that there is a tension between this natural order and the conventional or legal order, and his purpose is to resolve it, at least for some men, at the highest possible level. These men must first be shown that this world of convention is not the only world, and here is where obscenity may play a part – that beyond Venice there is Portia's Belmont, the utopia where the problems that plague Venice do not exist.[16] Obscenity can be used to ridicule the conventional. But it is used in the name of the natural, that order outside the conventional according to which the conventional may be criticized and perhaps, if only to an extent, reformed. Obscenity in the hands of such a poet can serve to *elevate* men, elevate them, the few of them, above the conventional order in which all of us are forced to live our mundane lives. Its purpose is to teach what is truly beautiful – not what convention holds to be beautiful – and to do so by means of pleasure, for obscenity can be pleasurable.

Shakespeare expressed this conflict between nature and law in Edmund's soliloquy at the beginning of Act I, Scene 2, of *King Lear*:

> Thou, Nature, art my goddess; to the law
> My services are bound. Wherefore should I
> Stand in the plague of custom, and permit
> The curiosity of nations to deprive me
> For that I am some twelve or fourteen moonshines
> Lag of a brother? Why bastard? wherefore base?
> When my dimensions are as well compact,
> My mind as generous, and my shape as true,
> As honest madam's issue? Why brand they us
> With base? with baseness? bastardy? base, base?
> Who, in the lusty stealth of nature, take
> More composition and fierce quality
> Than doth, within a dull, stale, tired bed,
> Go to th' creating a whole tribe of fops,
> Got 'tween asleep and wake? – Well, then,
> Legitimate Edgar, I must have your land:
> Our father's love is to the bastard Edmund
> As to th' legitimate, fine word, – legitimate!

Well, my legitimate, if this letter speed,
And my invention thrive, Edmund the base
Shall top th' legitimate. I grow; I prosper : —
Now, gods, stand up for bastards!

This serves to illustrate the theme to which great poets address themselves – what is right by law and what is right by nature – and in the development of which the use of obscenity in comedy has a legitimate and perhaps even noble role. When it is so used it is fully justified, especially because great poetry, even when it is obscene, is of interest only to a few – those who read it primarily for what is beyond its obscenity, that towards which obscenity points. But when obscenity is employed as it is today, merely in an effort to capture an audience, or to shock without elevating, or in the effort to set loose idiosyncratic 'selfs' doing their own things, or to bring down the constitutional order, it is not justified, for it lacks the ground on which to claim exemption from the law. The modern advocates of obscenity do not seem to be aware of this consequence of their advocacy. They have obliterated the distinction between art and trash, and in so doing they have deprived themselves of the ground on which they might protest the law. What possible argument could have been used against the police had they decided to arrest the participants in the Cornell 'happening' for indecent exposure, or against a law forbidding these festivals of contemporary 'art'? In this generous world the police must be accorded a right to do their 'own thing' too, and they would probably be able to do it with the support of the majority and therefore of the law. In a world of everyone doing his own thing, the majority not only rules but can do no wrong, because there is no standard of right and wrong. Justice Douglas sees his job as protecting the right of these contemporary 'artists' to do their own thing, but a thoughtful judge is likely to ask how an artistic judgment that is wholly idiosyncratic can be capable of supporting an objection to the law. The objection, '*I* like it,' is sufficiently rebutted by, '*we* don't.'

How to express in a rule of law this distinction between the justified and the unjustified employment of obscenity is no simple task. That I have admitted and willingly concede. I have also argued that it cannot be done at all in the premise from which our law has proceeded. I have, finally, tried to indicate the consequences of a failure to maintain the distinction in the law; not only will we no longer be able to teach the distinction between the proper and the improper, but we will no longer be able to teach – and will therefore come to forget – the distinction between art and trash. Stated otherwise, censorship, because it inhibits self-indulgence and supports the idea of propriety and impropriety, protects political democracy; paradoxically, when it faces the problem of the justified and unjustified use of obscenity, censorship also serves to maintain the distinction between art and trash and, therefore, to protect art and, thereby, to enhance the quality of this democracy. We forgot this. We began with a proper distrust of the capacities of juries and judges to make sound judgments in an area that lies outside their professional competence; but led by the Supreme Court we went on improperly to conclude that the judgments should not be made because they cannot be made, that there is nothing for anyone to judge. No doubt the law used to err on occasion; but democracy can live without 'Mrs Warren's Profession', if it must, as well as without *Fanny Hill* – or to speak more precisely, it can live with the error that consigns 'Mrs Warren's Profession' to under-the-counter custom along with *Fanny Hill*. It remains to be seen whether the true friend of democracy will want to live in the world without under-the-counter custom, the world that does not know the difference between 'Mrs Warren's Profession' and *Fanny Hill*.

1 *New York Times*, January 5, 1970, p. 32. Whatever Ernst now says he used to say, or meant all along, what we remember from him is on the printed page, and there he said that 'censorship of the theater is truly an anomaly'; and there he scoffed at the idea that a book, any book, could be 'corrupting (whatever that may mean'; and there he insisted that censorship could be justified only if it could be demonstrated that a 'casual relationship' existed 'between word or picture and human behavior', and that such a relationship had never been demonstrated 'in the field of obscenity!' In fact, he added, 'the indications seem to be to the contrary'. Morris L. Ernst and Alan U. Schwartz, *Censorship: The Search for the Obscene* (New York: Macmillan, 1964), pp. 142, 200, 250–251.
2 'Long Beach, Calif. Jan. 13 [1970] (AP) – Four nude models – two male, two female – postured before the coeducational sociology class of 250 persons.
'On movie screens, lesbian and heterosexual couples went through acts of lovemaking.
'Sound systems blared recordings by the Beatles and from the rock musical "Hair".
'Two hours after the class ended yesterday, California State College suspended its teachers, Marion Steele, 31 years old, and Dr Donald Robertson, 29, for thirty days without pay. Further action was threatened.
'Mr Steele and Dr Robertson said they had staged the show to ridicule what they called America's prudishness about sex as contrasted with its toleration of what they considered such "glaring obscenities" as the Vietnam War, violence on television and pollution of air and water.
' "This produces hangups and keeps millions from enjoying genuine sexual pleasure and makes our entire world obscene," Dr Robertson told the class.' *New York Times*, January 14, 1970, p. 11.
3 In *Ginzburg* v. *United States*, 383 U.S. 463 (1966), the Supreme Court up-

held the conviction because Ginzburg had employed 'pandering' in the advertising of his obscene wares, a rule never applied in the past and inapplicable in the future. The next year it resumed its habit of reversing obscenity convictions, although the publications involved were at least as offensive as anything Ginzburg published. *Redrup v. New York*, 386 U.S. 767 (1967). States have been permitted to prohibit the sale of obscenity to minors, *Ginzburg v. New York*, 390 U.S. 629 (1968), but, on the other hand, not to classify films with a view to protecting minors—not, at least, with a 'vague' ordinance. *Interstate Circuit, Inc. v. Dallas*, 390 U.S. 676 (1968). Mr Justice Douglas would not prohibit the sale of obscenity even to children; he says, and he ought to know, that most juvenile delinquents are over fifty.

4 *Laocoön*, (New York: Noonday Press) ch. 1, p. 10.
5 'Che!' and 'Hair', for example, are political plays. See also note 2.
6 Erwin W. Straus, *Phenomenological Psychology* (New York: Basic Books, 1966), p. 219. I have no doubt that it is possible to want to observe sexual acts for reasons unrelated to voyeurism. Just as a physician has a clinical interest in the parts of the body, philosophers will have an interest in the parts of the soul, or in the varieties of human things which are manifestations of the body and the soul. Such a 'looking' would not be voyeurism and would be unaccompanied by shame; or, the desire to see and to understand would require the 'seer' to overcome shame. Plato, *Republic*, 439e. In any event, the case of the philosopher is politically irrelevant, and aesthetically irrelevant as well.
7 *Ibid.*, p. 221.
8 It is easy to prove that shamefulness is not the only principle governing the question of what may properly be presented on the stage; shamefulness would not, for example, govern the case of a scene showing the copulating of a married couple who love each other very much. That is not intrinsically shameful—on the contrary—yet it ought not to be shown. The principle here is, I think, an aesthetic one: such a scene is dramatically weak because the response of the audience would be characterized by prurience and not by a sympathy with what the scene is intended to portray, a beautiful love. This statement can be tested by joining a college-town movie audience; it is confirmed unintentionally by a defender of nudity on the stage; see note 11.
9 The modern tyrant does not encourage passivity among his subjects; on the contrary, they are expected by him to be public-spirited: to work for the State, to exceed production schedules, to be citizen soldiers in the huge armies, and to love Big Brother. Indeed, in Nazi Germany and the Soviet Union alike, the private life was and is discouraged, and with it erotic love and the private attachments it fosters. Censorship in a modern tyrannical state is designed to abolish the private life to the extent that this is possible. George Orwell understood this perfectly. This severe censorship that characterizes modern tyranny, and distinguishes it sharply from pre-modern tyranny, derives from the basis of modern tyrannical rule: both Nazism and Communism have roots in theory, and more precisely, a kind of utopian theory. The modern tyrant parades as a political philosopher, the heir of Nietzsche or Marx, with an historical mission to perform. He cannot leave his subjects alone.
10 *Ginzburg v. United States*, 383 U.S. 463, 489–490 (1966). Dissenting opinion.
11 *New York Times*, January 18, 1970. The author of this piece, Martin Gottfried, a man of 'sophisticated critical judgment' presumably—after all, the *Times* printed him—defends 'Che!' and others, and ends up with a very sophisticated defense of a homosexual rape scene from a production entitled 'Fortune and Men's Eyes', done, of course, in the nude and apparently

leaving nothing to the imagination. His principle is that 'no climactic scene, in any play, should happen offstage....'

12 'The Democratization of the University', to be published in Robert A. Goldwin (ed.), *How Democratic is America?* (Chicago: Rand McNally).

13 That this is not merely the product of English or American 'Puritanism' is proved by, for example, the French *faire l'amour* and the Italian *fare-all amore*, as well as the fastidious German *mit einem liebeln*.

14 In a number of universities, students are permitted to receive course credit for 'courses' taught by themselves to themselves. Not surprisingly, it was left to Cornell to carry this to its absurd extreme. In May, 1970, the Educational Policy Committee of the College of Arts and Sciences voted 5–2 to grant 'three credit hours to ten students who had "taught" themselves a course in children's literature' – including not only *Alice in Wonderland*, but *Pinocchio, Where the Wild Things Are,* and *Now We Are Six.* 'The students claimed that they had not read the books before taking their course.' This implies that it is one of the jobs of a university to remedy deficiencies in kindergarten education. In any case, as one of the two dissenters later reported to the full faculty, 'whether the books had ever been read to them remains unclear'. Cornell *Chronicle,* June 4, 1970.

15 *Poetics*, 1449a–35.

16 See the chapter on 'The Merchant of Venice' in Allan Bloom's (with Harry V. Jaffa) *Shakespeare's Politics* (New York: Basic Books, 1964).